THE
PERCEPTIVE
INVESTOR

For my family

TABLE OF CONTENTS

INTRODUCTION

I am a better investor because I am a businessman and a better businessman because I am no investor.

— Warren E. Buffett, chairman of Berkshire Hathaway

From the moment we are born, what is the fastest-reacting organ in our body? Think about it (there's a clue there). Still not sure? It's our brain. Our cognitive and behavioural functions are the subject of much of this book, so it makes sense that we start our journey together, quite literally, at our beginning. At birth, our brain is about a quarter of the size of the average adult brain. Incredibly, it doubles in size in the first year and keeps growing, to about 80 percent of adult size at age three and 90 percent at five. During this period of rapid growth, our brain 'goes wide'. Trillions of new neural pathways are formed, as we learn from our environment and develop many facets of our personality. From the age of five, until roughly the age of twenty our brain shifts gear and 'goes deep'. It is during this period that our brain specialises and discards the billions of neurons that we no longer need. Our early life experiences are the forge that will shape the rest of our life – our passions, our drive and, most importantly, how we think.

If you don't *think* like a businessperson, I don't believe it's possible for you to be a successful investor. We all know Warren Buffett to be the world's most successful investor, but I would say he is actually the world's most successful businessman. His business just happens to be investing in other businesses. It is his business acumen that has been instrumental for his investing success. This skill did not develop by chance; it began for Buffett at the age of six when he started buying bottles of Coca-Cola from his grandfather's grocery store for a nickel (5¢) and selling them to his friends at school for a dime (10¢). He then ventured into the coin-operated pinball machine business, newspaper delivery, selling tipsheets at the racetrack, and wedding car rentals, to name a few. Buffett was a practical business learning machine during the special-isation phase of his cognitive and behavioural development. By the age of twenty, Buffett's psychological make-up was essentially fully formed from his experiences as an entrepreneur and businessman. For those of you reading this who are older than twenty, there is still hope for you, but one of the lessons here is to 'go wide' early and then 'go deep' fast. If you do, you can gain an edge that no one can catch, such is the power of compounding that we will explore in the coming chapters.

Investing is, at its core, an entrepreneurial activity. You need to think like a business owner when it comes to investing your capital into other businesses. As Buffett's background shows, to be a successful investor, you must first have a passion for business. How else will you craft your own investment process to develop differentiated insights into how the businesses you research operate; how else will you be able to identify value? How else will you have the intellectual curiosity to read between the lines of the financial statements of a business to pinpoint the business models driving it? Or to fully embrace the 'ownership mentality' and understand just how unbelievable it is that, against all odds, the founder-operated business that you have identified is still flourishing?

Many investors believe businesses can be run from a spreadsheet, but I have never met a businessman or woman who agrees. Real business is messy. Nothing ever goes according to plan. The environment within which each business operates is in a constant state of flux. Nothing teaches this lesson better than founding and growing your own business. Especially one that fails. Only then will you come to truly understand the Darwinian nature of capitalism, the power of competition and the importance of a growing and defensible 'moat' around your business.

To be a great investor, you must first be a great businessman.

Today, I run an Investment Partnership which invests my capital and that of my partners in other businesses. Like Buffett, my entrepreneurial journey began much earlier, in my far-from-conventional childhood. My parents met at university in London. They had both left home at the age of sixteen – believing there was more to life than what was on offer where they had grown up. My mother is from a small steel-making town in North Wales, and my father is from an even smaller farming community in rural Denmark. They can best be described as 'citizens of the world' for their love of travel and adventure.

I believe that entrepreneurship is a trait that we are all born with but that its spark is either nurtured or extinguished by our early life experiences. At its core, it is a mindset, a contrarian streak that encourages us to go against the grain, to push the boundaries and believe that we can provide a product or service which no one else has yet provided or take something that already exists and make it better. My parents embody this mindset as outside-the-box thinkers. When I was a child, they always encouraged me to explore my interests, and their entrepreneurial spirit and love for business certainly rubbed off on me, something for which I will always be grateful.

The first business I can remember my parents starting was, during the infancy of the internet in the 1990s, an e-commerce business selling perfumes online via a website called Scent-Item.com – even today, I think it's a clever name. Their excitement for the business, taking me and my sister to visit trade fairs, finding suppliers and helping to design the packaging for the products were all formative experiences for me. At the dinner table they often talked of little else!

My parents helped me to 'go wide' from a very early age. I took my first flight when I was two months old. By the time I had graduated from high school, I had been to eight schools and lived in eleven different homes across six different countries. My parents even viewed the houses we lived in with an entrepreneurial mindset. They bought only houses that needed significant work. They renovated and then sold them (hopefully for a profit), then repeated the process. My childhood wasn't perfect – there were times when we had a lot, and times when we had very little – but those experiences, especially the painful ones, have shaped my current outlook on both life and business.

At the age of seven, I started my first business, The Console Club, to trade PlayStation and Nintendo 64 games amongst my friends in the school playground. This business taught me that your reputation with your customers is absolutely key, especially when you're trying to grow your business.

My next business was slightly more ambitious, as I graduated from local video game reseller to international gadget retailer. My family had moved to Australia when I was ten years old. On the way, we had made a stop in Hong Kong, where there were fantastic markets selling all sorts of toys and gadgets. I spent all the money I'd saved from my business ventures and from doing chores around the house (around $500) to buy a suitcase full of them. On arrival in Sydney, I began to sell them on eBay. This proved to be a real money spinner, so much so that I started ordering and receiving monthly shipments of merchandise direct from China. I learnt not only the power of 'buying wholesale and selling retail' but also the complexities of inventory management.

Next, I started a dog-walking business and learnt the importance of scalability. Although such a business was lucrative, I couldn't walk more than two dogs at once – and when your employees don't turn up, you really are left holding all the leads!

My first experience with the stock market didn't come until I was eleven years old (better late than never!). My father asked me to help him choose which funds to invest his Australian Superannuation Scheme (pension) into. Together we reviewed all the different fund options, and I remember being amazed at the range of choices and the variation of past returns. We reviewed his portfolio every quarter to see how it was doing. This was my first exposure to the core principles of investing and the importance of having a long-term mentality, as we were investing with a thirty-year horizon for my father's retirement.

My father also had a bookshelf of business books and biographies which he encouraged me to read. I remember being transfixed by the story of how Sir Richard Branson, with no money upfront, started Virgin Airlines and took on British Airways, the industry colossus at the time. This was my first lesson on business moats and also that supernormal profits will, whenever possible, attract competition that will eventually drain them away. I have loved reading books ever since. Learning about the successes and failures of others has always fascinated me – and it is also far cheaper to buy the book than experience the mistakes yourself!

When I was fifteen years old, we moved to Denmark. I took up a local newspaper round. It was a physically demanding job, through which I learnt the limitations of swapping time for money. There are only ever twenty-four hours in a day. I needed to work smarter. I became obsessed with trying to find the highest rate of interest for my savings, which amounted to around $40,000 thanks to my various business ventures and my obsession with saving. It was around this time that I discovered the power of compound interest, while doing sums during an English lesson. (Whoever said they never learnt anything useful studying Shakespeare?) This realisation led me to focus more of my attention on public markets.

As I began my investing journey in public markets, I made every mistake under the sun, from trying my hand at day trading foreign exchange (FX) and commodities and losing half my capital to trading derivatives on the Volatility Index – better known as the VIX or the 'Wall Street Fear Gauge' – and promptly making and then losing over $100,000 in a matter of weeks. In hindsight, this was incredibly naive; I was speculating, not investing. These experiences provided me with an invaluable but 'expensive' education, including learning that leverage is a double-edged sword that amplifies both gains and losses and should be approached with extreme caution. I tried charting, trend-following and even shorting, but nothing generated the same returns as those I made from buying great businesses when they had been beaten down by an exogenous factor, such as the 2007–9 Global Financial Crisis (GFC). Thankfully, once I realised that something didn't work for me or suit my temperament, I quickly left it alone and never touched it again. By the time I started university in the UK in 2009, I had about $150,000 of capital and was now solely focused on investing in the stock market.

My passion, I realised, was starting, operating and learning about different businesses. At university I studied accounting and finance as I wanted to better understand the language of business and the numbers behind it. To get more exposure to how real businesses worked, it made sense to me to apply for a job at the investment banks that provided them with capital to invest and grow. So, during my summer holidays, I completed internships with Goldman Sachs and Morgan Stanley. Competition for places was extremely fierce, as the internships were highly paid, so, in preparation for them, I wrote hundreds of pages of notes to formalise my knowledge of various businesses and investing strategies. It occurred to me that the notes I prepared could be useful to others, so I started a new business (InternAhead.com) selling them to other students trying to pass the internship tests. This business taught me about the value of intellectual property (IP) and the cost efficiencies available through online marketing and distribution.

Trying as many things as possible (going wide) to find your passion and then, having found it, following your passion (going deep) as early as possible has a real advantage: it gives you purpose and direction in life. My passion was business. To me, there was no better way of pursuing business than through the practice of investing. To be a successful investor, I knew I had to learn everything there was to know about both success and investing. And I knew that I wanted to start and run my own investing business. After graduating from university, I set myself the goal of launching my own fund in ten years' time with ten million dollars of my own capital. My objective for the interim was to gain as much practical investing experience as possible while learning everything I could about all aspects of investing, and to craft my own investment philosophy for success. The Gronager Partners – Global Fund was launched on 23 November 2022, right into the teeth of the post-Covid bear market (a value investor's dream!). With $8 million of capital (a few months late and $2 million short of my original goal, but who's counting?), I built up this capital by learning and focusing on the core principles of value investing that I will share with you throughout this book.

Investing is the very broadest of intellectual pursuits. For those who are curious and enjoy learning, there is no better calling. Of course, no investment journey (and no investment, for that matter) moves in a straight line. In the run-up to my fund's launch, we had perhaps the defining 'black swan' event of the twenty-first century: the Covid-19 pandemic. With the world in lockdown, I was unable to meet potential investors or do any of the preparatory work usually necessary for the launch of a fund. Instead, I spent much of my time reading in my library, which at the time numbered over 500 books on business, finance and investing, as well as psychology and behavioural economics. I never read a book without a pen; I like to highlight key passages and make notes in the margins as I read. I began reviewing all my notes in each book, arranging them by subject and adding to them my own experiences for context.

In *A Life in Leadership*, by John Whitehead (senior partner at Goldman Sachs 1976–84), I came across a passage I had previously highlighted: 'You don't really know anything until you try to help someone else to understand it.' That insight is the basis for this book. What started as a lockdown activity to help clarify my thoughts on investing resulted in a better understanding of successful value investing, and it fine-tuned my investment philosophy. I hope it helps you to do the same. In the investing game, we can learn so much from the greats. No one ever had a smooth ride to the top, and we can learn as much from their failures as their successes – if not more.

Throughout this book, you will meet hundreds of successful investors and businesspeople. Each new generation learns from the ones that went before. Sir Isaac Newton famously wrote, 'If I have seen further it is by standing on the shoulders of giants'. This book is your opportunity to see further by standing on the shoulders of business giants and to learn from the investing greats.

This is not a how-to book. There is no surefire recipe for investment success. No step-by-step instructions. Instead, this book explores what I have discovered to be the most important topics on my own journey. Each chapter pulls together the best thinking from the most successful investors and business leaders to offer a unique insight into the mindset and philosophy that is instrumental to their success.

Part One looks at the principles of economics and financial concepts that all successful value investors understand. This section also covers various approaches to investing, so you can get a better insight into what approach might work best for you.

Part Two delves into the art and science of building your own investment process. I encourage you to use this book as a starting point to discover where your investing interests lie. If you want to discover more detail on any topic, you can find in the bibliography (Appendix A) all the books you need to start your journey. For those in a hurry, there is a summary section at the end of each chapter.

Please feel free to add your own notes in the margins as you read. My hope is that these pages will reveal to you the core principles that will enable you to make good decisions in both life and investing and, perhaps more importantly, to avoid at least some of the potential failures.

That said, it is not my goal to simplify successful value investing. It is not simple. It is complex. It is an ever-evolving combination of art, science and temperament that I call Perceptive Investing.

Art, Science and Temperament

Successful investing is often more art than science, a concept that is beautifully captured by René Magritte's 1936 painting *La Clairvoyance*, and informally known as 'Perception'.

What do you see when you first look at the painting? What do you see if you look closer?

For many, at first glance the painting, much like the investing process, appears simple. However,

SOURCE: © DACS, 2024

Perception: [noun] from the Latin *perceptio*, meaning 'gathering' or 'receiving'.
1. The ability to see, hear or become aware through intuitive understanding or insight.
2. The ability to recognise subtle differences between similar objects or ideas. It takes the concept of wisdom deeper in the sense that it denotes a keenness of sense and intelligence applied to insight.
3. To indicate practical wisdom in the areas of politics and finance.

this simplicity is deceptive. The closer you look, the more complex the subject matter becomes. Investing is a zero-sum game. Success comes from 'seeing' things that others don't, whether that's correctly identifying an enduring moat around a business or recognising the growth opportunities open to a company which have not yet been discounted in the current share price.

The ability to correctly predict the future price of something while relying only on current and past information is the hallmark of the successful value investor. Most investors are first-level thinkers who, when presented with an 'egg', as in the painting, will treat it as an egg. Like the artist, it takes a particular focus and insight to be able to study the 'egg' and be able to 'see through' to the 'fully grown bird in flight'. This is second-level thinking.

Perceptive Investing is the ability to review incomplete data sets and, through intense focus and insight, project forward a different outcome from that priced in by the market. The art part of investing is the 'intangibles' or qualitative aspects of a business. How do we evaluate the soft factors such as business culture, competitive advantage (or 'moat') and business strategy?

The science part of investing is the straightforward part; it is the raw numbers, ratios and valuation metrics or quantitative factors that can be applied to determine if an investment is worthy of further analysis.

Take Amazon, which IPO'd at $18 on 15 May 1997. What evidence was there in the prospectus and the company's past behaviour that would have led you to invest? If you had invested, what evidence would have made you buy, sell or hold when the stock price peaked at $113 during the dot-com boom just two years later, having earned an approximately 5× return? Or if you hadn't invested at the IPO, what might have led you to invest after the dot-com crash in 2001 when the price had tanked about 95 percent to $5.51? By 2007, Amazon stock was back at $101.09, but just over a year later, it had fallen to \$34.68 as the full impact of the GFC was felt. What new investment decision, if any, would you have made based on the data available at the time?

The fact is that, at any point in time, if you understood the science of investing in Amazon or the numbers behind the business, there was always more than enough data to show what remarkable feats of financial performance Amazon had previously achieved. Mastery of the art of investing came from being able to see through the numbers to the incredible culture, management and 'scale economies shared' business model that Amazon was evolving. Amazon was clearly an exceptional business from both perspectives (art and science) regardless of the volatility of the stock price, which would have put off most investors.

For the long-term value investor who could correctly forecast Amazon's growth trajectory and its discount to intrinsic value, the purchase price was irrelevant at those two points in time. What was far more important was the decision to buy and hold. If you had invested \$10,000 at the IPO and held – that investment would be worth over \$12,000,000 in 2024. Even if you had invested \$10,000 at the dot-com peak, it would still be worth over \$500,000 in 2024 – a 50× return or 21 percent annualised! A valuable lesson here is that great businesses have very long runways and offer plenty of additional growth opportunities along the way.

Many investors have identified Amazon as an exceptional business over the years. Some even bought the stock, but arguably not even one of them had the foresight or the fortitude to hold the stock for any significant period. Had they held it, the *Forbes* World's Billionaires List would contain their names alongside that of Jeff Bezos. Why do I say that? In this book, I will make the

---

Intrinsic Value: First defined by John Burr Williams in his 1938 work *The Theory of Investment Value*, which was based on his PhD thesis. Williams defined the present value of an investment, or its 'intrinsic value', as the sum of all the future cash flows produced by it and discounted back to their present-day value. This value can be quantified using a Discounted Cash Flow (DCF) Analysis:

$$DCF = \frac{CF_1}{(1+r)^1} + \frac{CF_2}{(1+r)^2} + \frac{CF_n}{(1+r)^n}$$

CF_1 = The cash flow for year one
CF_2 = The cash flow for year two
CF_n = The cash flow for additional years
r = The discount rate

case that what separates exceptional investors from the rest is their *tempera-ment*. In the case of purchasing Amazon, the right temperament would have been essential to allow an investor to focus only on the underlying fundamentals of the business while treating the volatility of the share price as an opportunity and not a risk. Temperament would also have given an investor the necessary patience to allow the thesis behind their initial purchase decision to yield positive results.

It sounds so simple, and yet, like most things in both life and investing, the difficulty lies in the execution. As adults, with now-fully-formed brains, we like to think that we are entirely rational. But as we will see throughout this book, our unique cognitive and behavioural biases seek to undermine our decision-making processes at every turn. Investing, unlike almost all other activities, has no direct correlation between the time spent selecting the input (choosing investments) and the quality of the output (the investment results). Nor is there a positive correlation between intelligence and results. In fact, there can often be a negative correlation. As Buffett himself quipped, 'You don't need to be a rocket scientist. Investing is not a game where the guy with the 160 IQ beats the guy with the 130 IQ,' and 'If you have a 150 IQ as an investor, you should take the 20 points and sell them.'

The reason for this is that there are only two rules that matter in investing: Rule Number 1: Don't lose money; and Rule Number 2: Don't forget Rule Number 1. Absolutely everything else is subjective depending on your point of view and interpretation of the data based on your own investment philosophy. Of course, there are certain personal characteristics that can help an investor to achieve success. There are also certain investment characteristics, many of which we will explore in detail, that tend to work in an investor's favour over the long term to deliver outstanding results. At its core, this is a book about temperament.

The foundations of our temperament are present at birth. We begin building on them from that moment on, through our early life experiences as our brains grow rapidly and 'go wide'. The remainder of development occurs as our cognitive and behavioural functions reach maturity and our brains 'go deep'. Understanding and mastering our temperaments as both individuals and investors is the first step on the path to long-term investing success as Perceptive Investors.

CHAPTER 1: WHAT MAKES A SUCCESSFUL VALUE INVESTOR?

Why do smart people do things that interfere with getting the output they're entitled to? It gets into the habits, and character and temperament, and it really gets into behaving in a rational manner. Not getting in your own way.

— Charles T. Munger, vice-chairman of Berkshire Hathaway

One of the tricks I learnt early as a child with puzzle books was that if you started at the 'treasure' at the centre of the maze and worked backwards to trace the correct 'entrance', you solved the puzzle far faster than if you started the other way around. I did not know it at the time, but what this technique demonstrates is a well-known key problem-solving skill called 'inversion'. Take a problem and invert it, or look at it differently. With this concept in mind, we are going to start the journey to craft our investment philosophy at the conclusion, by answering this question: What makes a successful value investor?

To answer the question, we need to clarify what a value investor is and what success looks like. Value investing involves assessing businesses to identify value that is not currently represented in the share price. In other words, we are looking for businesses whose share prices are lower than they should be or are likely to be once the value we have identified is realised by the market and, therefore, their shares are trading at a discount to what we estimate the businesses' intrinsic or fair values to be.

Next, success. In the investment industry, success is cash earned, and it is relatively straightforward to measure. Your net worth (public or private) is your scorecard. It acknowledges the investment returns that you have generated over the course of your investing lifetime. Clearly, net worth is not the only measure of success, but it is the only useful one when it comes to investment. Perhaps you think reported investment returns are a better measure, but they are almost never like for like. From a returns perspective, the best definition of risk comes from billionaire debt investor Howard Marks, the chairman and co-founder of Oaktree Capital Management, a Los Angeles-based investment firm with approximately $80 billion under management: 'The highest incremental return for the lowest corresponding unit of risk.'

Of course, risk is also an incredibly subjective subject. Entire industries, including the hedge funds of funds business, have formed around the measurement of risk in relation to returns. Countless ratios have been devised to measure it, usually with fancy-sounding names including Sharp, Sortino and R^2, and a few with Greek letters. But I define risk the way Warren Buffett does, as 'the probability of a permanent capital loss.' This makes sense because the best way to protect ourselves from risk or a permanent loss of our own or our investors' capital is to only buy businesses for less than their intrinsic value – otherwise known as buying with a margin of safety.

The other aspect of success is *time*. Over what time frame do we measure success? I don't think anyone would argue that one year, regardless of how high the returns might be, is enough time to judge whether an investor is successful or not. And yet it's too late if we measure success only at the end of managers' careers when we can no longer invest with them. In the interim, there is always the risk that a method of investing that is working well today could have all its gains wiped out tomorrow. How do we square this circle? At Gronager Partners we measure the success of our own investments on a five-year rolling basis and ask that our investors measure their own performance along the same time frame. So, for our purposes in this book I am going to say that five years of investment returns is the minimum period over which success should be measured.

Therefore, by my definition, a successful value investor is one who increases their net worth during each five-year period by consistently identifying and buying into businesses when their intrinsic values are greater than their share price, and holding those stocks over the long term. The Investment Process at Gronager Partners centres around a dynamic checklist of about 250 questions that we use to assess potential investments and continuously reassess current investments. Two hundred and fifty questions might sound excessive, but we have found that they force us to look at all aspects of a business as objectively as possible, and in a particular order, so we can form an unbiased investment decision.

From these definitions, we can conclude that all successful investors are value investors. To be successful, they must have spent their careers uncovering underpriced securities, be they stocks, bonds, derivatives or any other type of investment. And they all succeed by buying 'value'.

The late Charlie Munger, Warren Buffett's long-time business partner, agreed: 'All investing is value investing, whereby we seek to buy an asset for less than its intrinsic value ... everything else is just speculation.'

Buffett and Munger are two of the most successful value investors of all time and are, therefore, central figures in this book. Other notable value investors include Benjamin Graham, widely regarded as the father of value investing, along with David Dodd and Philip Fisher, who emphasised the importance of quality and growth as factors in the calculation of a business's intrinsic value.

These investors, and the many others you will meet in this book, are never swayed by fashion or fad, and they believe that the markets often overreact to good or bad news. Although such news may impact the share price, the movement in the price rarely corresponds to a company's long-term fundamentals. This discrepancy between the business's intrinsic value and its share price can provide an opportunity to buy shares at a discount or sell at a premium.

Let's take a closer look at Buffett's track record to see just how potent a value-investing approach can be. From 1957 to 1968, before his takeover of Berkshire Hathaway, Buffett ran his own early incarnation of a hedge fund called the Buffett Partnerships. [**FIG. 1**]

1 Buffett Partnerships vs. The Dow

YEAR	Annual Percentage Change	
	Partnership Results	Overall Results From Dow
1957	10.4%	-8.4%
1958	40.9%	38.5%
1959	25.9%	20.0%
1960	22.8%	-6.2%
1961	45.9%	22.4%
1962	13.9%	-7.6%
1963	38.7%	20.6%
1964	27.8%	18.7%
1965	47.2%	14.2%
1966	20.4%	-15.6%
1967	35.9%	19.0%
1968	58.8%	7.7%
Compounded annual gain 1957–1968	31.6%	9.1%
Overall gain 1957–1968	2,598%	184%

SOURCE: https://novelinvestor.com/notes/buffett-partnership-letters-by-warren-buffett

During its twelve years of operation, the Buffett Partnerships earned an average annual return of 31.6 percent (25.3 percent after fees). This was an astonishing result compared to an average return of 9.1 percent per year for the Dow Jones Index, the most widely followed index of the period. The Buffett Partnerships didn't have a single losing year, whereas the Dow Jones had four losing years over the same period. To put this into perspective, a $10,000 investment in the Buffett Partnerships at inception would have been worth $149,765 (after fees) when the partnerships were dissolved – versus just $28,437 for an equivalent investment in the Dow Jones Index!

Next, let's look at Buffett's track record as the steward of Berkshire Hathaway from 1965 to 2023. [FIG. 2]

During this almost sixty-year period, Berkshire compounded its share price by almost 20 percent per year; the S&P 500 Index returned 10.2 percent. To put this into perspective, a $10,000 investment in Berkshire Hathaway shares in 1965 would be worth approximately $438 million today – versus just over $3 million for an equivalent investment in the S&P 500. For any original Buffett Partnerships investor who had invested $10,000 at inception and rolled it (net of fees) into Berkshire Hathaway at the end of 1968, their investment would have been worth over $3 billion by the end of 2023!

This raises the question: Why has no subsequent investor come even close to replicating or beating Buffett's sixty-five-year-plus track record? Through his annual investor letters (a must-read for any investor), Buffett himself suggests that it comes down to three reasons:

1. Group think
2. Playing it safe
3. Illogical diversification

Buffett believes that too many investment managers take the easy route and follow the crowd. As a result of group-think investment policies and actions, all the funds start to look the same and, therefore, get roughly the same results. This in turn plays into the second reason: playing it safe. No one is going to be fired for doing what everyone else did. Being a contrarian investor is therefore seen as a 'career risk' by most investment managers, who are more interested in their job security and a steady pay cheque. The idea of buying out-of-favour assets, even at attractive prices, involves too much risk to them personally so that they stick with group think. Or as the early

2 Berkshire's Perfomance vs. the S&P 500

YEAR	Annual Percentage Change	
	in Per-Share Market Value of Berkshire	in S&P 500 with Dividends Included
1965	49.0	10.0
1966	(3.4)	(11.7)
1967	13.3	30.9
1968	77.8	11.0
1969	19.4	(8.4)
1970	(4.6)	3.9
1971	80.5	14.6
1972	8.1	18.9
1973	(2.5)	(14.8)
1974	(48.7)	(26.4)
1975	2.5	37.2
1976	129.3	23.6
1977	46.8	(7.4)
1978	14.5	6.4
1979	102.5	18.2
1980	32.8	32.3
1981	31.8	(5.0)
1982	38.4	21.4
1983	69.0	22.4
1984	(2.7)	6.1
1985	93.7	31.6
1986	14.2	18.6
1987	4.6	5.1
1988	59.3	16.6
1989	84.6	31.7
1990	(23.1)	(3.1)
1991	35.6	30.5
1992	29.8	7.6
1993	38.9	10.1
1994	25.0	1.3
1995	57.4	37.6
1996	6.2	23.0
1997	34.9	33.4
1998	52.2	28.6
1999	(19.9)	21.0
2000	26.6	(9.1)
2001	6.5	(11.9)
2002	(3.8)	(22.1)
2003	15.8	28.7
2004	4.3	10.9
2005	0.8	4.9
2006	24.1	15.8
2007	28.7	5.5
2008	(31.8)	(37.0)
2009	2.7	26.5
2010	21.4	15.1
2011	(4.7)	2.1
2012	16.8	16.0
2013	32.7	32.4
2014	27.0	13.7
2015	(12.5)	1.4
2016	23.4	12.0
2017	21.9	21.8
2018	2.8	(4.4)
2019	11.0	31.5
2020	2.4	18.4
2021	29.6	28.7
2022	4.0	(18.1)
2023	15.8	26.3
Compounded Annual Gain – 1965–2023	19.8%	10.2%
Overall Gain – 1964–2023	4,384,748%	31,223%

NOTE: Data are for calender years with these exceptions: 1965 and 1966, year ended 9/30; 1967, 15 months ended 12/31.

SOURCE: https://www.berkshirehathaway.com/letters

twentieth-century economist, fund manager and father of modern macroeconomics John Maynard Keynes put it, 'Worldly wisdom teaches that it is better for a reputation to fail conventionally than to succeed unconventionally.'

The final reason for investor underperformance is illogical diversification, or, to use Buffett's aphorism, 'Deworsification'. According to Buffett, 'Diversification is a protection against ignorance. It makes little sense if you know what you are doing.' In other words, if you are a speculator or are not assessing businesses to identify value and are instead buying based on rumour or news reports, then diversification makes sense, because when one share price drops (and it will), the others in your portfolio will help balance out the loss. But if you are a value investor conducting a rigorous investment process up front, unnecessary diversification is exactly that: unnecessary. Concentration, not diversification, will lead to higher investment returns. As Andrew Carnegie said, 'The secret to getting rich is to put all of your eggs into one basket and then watch that basket very, very carefully.'

I believe that the secret to Buffett's success is that he invests only in things that he understands, known as his 'circle of competence'. He thinks like an owner of a business rather than just a shareholder. He has the right temperament; he is comfortable being lonely or a contrarian in his views; and he is focused, passionate and intellectually honest as well as curious and patient when it comes to his investment process. But when the time is right, he is decisive. To conclude, he does all the above while acting with humility. In this chapter, we are going to explore the aspects identified in more detail, along with thoughts on the subject from many other exceptional investors and business leaders.

Circle of Competence

It ain't so much the things that people don't know that makes trouble in this world, as it is the things that people know that just ain't so.

— Mark Twain, American writer and humorist

Buffett's concept of investing only in businesses that you understand – that is, those within your circle of competence – is seemingly straightforward. It certainly makes intuitive sense. The complexity comes when seeking to define your circle of competence. What does it encompass? Where are its boundaries? How can you prove that you really understand a sector or business? Perhaps most importantly, how do you maintain your conviction that you are right and the market is wrong when the share price falls by 50 percent after you buy?

An investor's circle of competence is the sum of all the knowledge they have accumulated over the course of their lifetime. As we like to remind ourselves at Gronager Partners, 'In the investment business all knowledge is cumulative.' The boundaries of an investor's circle of competence are therefore constantly changing as they learn and experience more. In the investing business, experience counts.

However, one competence that is non-negotiable is the language of business, namely accounting. Financial and accounting literacy is an essential element in any investor's toolbox because it allows them to read and analyse a company's financial statements. From these documents and other sources, investors use fundamental analysis to forecast the company's economic prospects. They then discount those prospects back to their present value, which gives them an assessment of the intrinsic value of that business.

Clearly, to do this well, we need to have a thorough understanding of the company: how it makes money; how it will grow in the future; and any competitive advantages (or 'moat' around the business) that will ensure its enduring success. But as Ian E. Wilson, a former chairman of GE, once said, 'No amount of sophistication is going to allay the fact that all your knowledge is about the past and all your decisions are about the future.'

Predicting the future is not enough. We must also ensure a business sits within our circle of competence and buy it at the right price. The most successful investors have a strong intellectual curiosity about business and why things work the way they do. They have a thirst for knowledge and can't help but ask questions. The information gleaned from reading newspapers, trade and industry journals, investor forums, books and annual reports passes through their investment filters and helps their investment process, not only in relation to idea generation but also building 'muscle memory' for analysing and evaluating new businesses.

When it comes to risking your capital, you must invest only in things that you truly understand. This is what builds your margin of safety, meaning that, even if you are wrong, you will not lose all your capital. When the market crashed in 1973, Buffett bought a major stake in the Washington Post Company, which he held for over forty years. A decade later, in his article 'The Superinvestors of Graham and Doddsville', he wrote that when he invested, the company was valued at $80 million, and yet 'you could have sold the assets to any one of ten buyers for not less than $400 million' – now that's a margin of safety! Remember: Rule Number 1: Don't lose money; Rule Number 2: Don't forget Rule Number 1.

Every investor's circle of competence is likely to start off small, but its breadth and depth will expand over time through constant learning and evaluating potential investment opportunities. However, it's also important to remember that you don't need to know or have an opinion on everything. It's perfectly acceptable to pass on a stock or sector on which you don't have an opinion or with which you're not comfortable. This is an essential part of your investment process that will allow you to narrow down your investable universe. There are over 45,000 equities listed globally, so it is more than okay to say, 'I don't know.' Buffett famously has a tray on his desk marked 'Too Hard'. More than half of the businesses that I look at almost immediately end up in my own 'Too Hard' pile.

Succeeding as an investor never depends on how much you know; it depends on whether what you know is right or wrong. As Buffett said at the 1998 Berkshire Hathaway AGM, 'We don't get paid for activity, just for being right.' Operating within your circle of competence means you increase the likelihood of being right, more often than being wrong.

Every day there are companies in the news. Some are IPOing; some are hitting new all-time highs; others are entering bankruptcy. The action and noise are relentless and can easily overwhelm your senses as an investor if you let them. Being clear about your circle of competence helps to minimise the noise and reduce any potential FOMO (fear of missing out). Too many investors are sucked in by the noise and try to widen their circles of competence too quickly. When it comes to successful investing, you are better off having knowledge an inch wide and a mile deep than a mile wide and an inch deep. Every investor has a subset or type of company or sector that they find the most interesting. That, in my experience, is always the best place to start building your circle of competence.

It is this curiosity about the sector or business that will encourage you to ask the right questions and motivate you to keep digging until you find satisfactory answers. Once you have some experience investing within your circle of competence, you can purposefully start to expand it. If your instincts are telling you that you've found an opportunity worth pursuing, use that curiosity to become an expert in that business or sector through thorough, independent research.

Thinking Like an Owner

Investing is most intelligent when it is most businesslike.

— Benjamin Graham, father of Value Investing and author of *The Intelligent Investor and Securities Analysis*

Many investors point to this quote as referring to the fundamental corner-stone of value investing. A stock should not be looked at as a piece of paper or numbers on a screen. It should be treated as a fractional ownership interest in the underlying business.

For me, however, this interpretation is too simple. I believe Graham was also alluding to the way in which each investor conducts their own affairs. The very act of buying a fractional ownership interest in an underlying business is not simply a transaction but also an act of entrepreneurship, and the purchase should be treated with the same respect as any business venture. Just think about this for a moment. If the share price of a company drops but it buys back its own shares, who is more likely to be right? The market or the company's executive team? Obviously, it's the executive team, because they know what is going on inside the business.

When most investors want to know how a business is doing, they will look at the share price. Graham is saying this is a mistake. Ignore the share price and, instead, think like a business owner. Focus your attention on the fundamentals of the business. Are they getting

What are the Fundamentals?

The fundamentals of a business include:

- Products and services
- Management team
- Inventories
- Working capital needs
- Capital reinvestment needs (e.g. property, plant & equipment)
- Raw materials
- Expenses
- Labour relations

better or worse? There is a clear distinction between knowing a business and investing based on its fundamentals and buying or selling pieces of paper that change in price second by second.

You are either an investor or a speculator. If you are the latter, Mark Twain has some useful advice: 'There are two times in a man's life when he should not speculate: when he can't afford it, and when he can.'

Buffett, who is the most well recognised of Ben Graham's disciples, fully embodies this concept. He considers it extremely foolish to view constantly changing share prices as being closely related to changes in a company's intrinsic value. Adding or removing positions based solely on stock price movements, rather than actual changes in the underlying business, he regards as equally foolish. For Buffett, there is no difference between owning one share of a business and owning the entire business. The mentality of operating like a business owner or entrepreneur applies equally to both.

In June 1996, Buffett issued a booklet to Berkshire Hathaway's shareholders titled *An Owner's Manual*. Its purpose was to explain Berkshire's broad economic principles of operation. In it, he explained Berkshire's partial ownership of both Coca-Cola and Gillette (publicly tradeable businesses) and why they were not interested in their short-term share price movements:

> We think of Berkshire as being a non-managing partner in two extraordinary businesses, in which we measure our success by the long-term progress of the companies rather than by the month-to-month movements of their stocks. In fact, we would not care in the least if several years went by in which there was no trading, or quotation of prices, in the stocks of those companies. If we have good long-term expectations, short-term price changes are meaningless for us except to the extent they offer us an opportunity to increase our ownership at an attractive price.

Many investors, including me, believe that you never really understand a business until you own it – until there is real money on the line. To see yourself as an owner of a business is a psychological process. Once you have capital at risk, you will be twice as motivated to learn everything you possibly can about the business and track its progress to ensure that it remains a sound investment. If you monitor potential investments on a 'paper' watchlist, you don't have any skin in the game. Instead, I suggest buying even one share to help put you into the right psychological space that fosters the ownership mentality. Once purchased, that business will suddenly be on your mental radar, as you now have money at risk. From my experience, you will pay far closer attention to the business and be more motivated to find out if it is worthy of a larger position in your portfolio.

The endowment effect posits that it is human nature to care more for things that are ours than those that are not (more on this and other biases in Chapter 8). This is why when we are an owner of the business and see ourselves in that light, we can commit the time required to understand all aspects of the business and to constantly evaluate new information to ensure it remains a good investment.

When I analyse a business, I look at it as if I were going to buy the entire business, not just a small portion of it. To encourage this perspective, I like to ask myself two related questions:

1. If I were to inherit the business today, would I keep it or sell it?
2. If I had the money to buy the whole business, would I buy this one or a different one?

Owning your own business is the surest path to wealth. Research in the US and Europe suggests that over 90 percent of individuals with a net worth over $5 million would be classified as entrepreneurs or SME (small and medium enterprise) business owners. There would have been countless times during their respective journeys when the owners would have been approached by prospective buyers or would have received offers to cash out, but they refused. Usually because they knew they were onto a good thing and had 100 percent confidence that their business would only become more successful and valuable over time. This is what it means to properly understand a business, to think like a business owner, and to be willing to have all your eggs in one basket and watch that basket very carefully.

Successful value investors don't believe in overdiversification. We aim to understand the businesses that we invest in as well as the founders or executive management teams that lead them. Only by achieving this degree of comfort with our investments can we have the confidence to add to our positions when the share price falls and the discount to intrinsic value increases. Thus we can ride the subsequent stock price rally to higher highs as the business outperforms over the long term. This is how the real money is made in markets, and in life – by seeing and recognising intrinsic value where others don't.

Temperament

One of the key elements to successful investing is having the right temperament – most people are too fretful; they worry too much. Success means being very patient, but aggressive when it's time. And the more hard lessons you can learn vicariously rather than through your own hard experience, the better.

– Charles T. Munger, vice-chairman of Berkshire Hathaway

Bill Miller is one of the most successful investors of any generation. When he was the lead portfolio manager of the Legg Mason Capital Management Value Trust from 1991 to 2005, he outperformed the S&P 500 Index for fifteen consecutive years, compounding at 9.4 percent per annum (versus 9 percent for the S&P 500). When asked what separated exceptional investors from the rest, he said, 'Broadly speaking, there are only three competitive advantages to be had in investing: informational (I know a meaningful fact that nobody else does); analytical (I have used the publicly available information to arrive at a superior conclusion); and psychological (behavioural). It is the third that distinguishes the exceptional from the rest.'

Buffett and Munger have also long argued that what distinguishes the successful from the unsuccessful in investing is not IQ or experience – it's temperament. Although, to a certain extent, the right temperament can be taught through repetition and reward, the bulk of temperament is innate. It forms a key part of who the greatest value investors *are*, both as individuals and investors. Let's look at the key characteristics in turn.

The first is to operate with what Buffett calls an 'inner scorecard', that is, not caring what others think, versus living by an 'outer scorecard' whereby we live our lives based on how we think others will perceive us. This concept was made famous when Buffett posed the question, 'Would you rather be the best lover in the world but known as the worst or the worst lover in the world but known as the best?' Buffett argued that when you have an 'inner scorecard', no one can define success but you. And your knowledge of the truth is what matters. But this is not necessarily easy, and, just because of the way they are wired, it's harder for some people than others. Human beings are naturally sociable animals; it is, therefore, unusual for an individual to go against the herd and not be influenced by group think. However, this is a necessary trait to be a contrarian investor and see value where others do not.

Investors who have this innate ability to be independent can look at a potential investment in an industry or business and not care what the person next to them thinks. Nor what the television pundits say about it or the column inches devoted to it in the newspaper. As Peter Lynch, investor, fund manager and philanthropist, puts it, 'Stop listening to professionals! Dumb money is only dumb when it listens to the smart money.'

As the manager of the Magellan Fund at Fidelity Investments between 1977 and 1990, Lynch averaged a 29.2 percent annual return, making it the best-performing mutual fund in the world at the time. During his thirteen-year tenure, assets under management increased from $18 million to $14 billion!

Successful value investors like Lynch prefer to form their own conclusions using all the available information, regardless of the multitude of sources telling them that something is or isn't going to happen. If there isn't sufficient information available to arrive at an unbiased decision to invest, or their analysis leaves too many unanswered questions, or it's found to be an unsuitable investment, it's discarded. Walking away from an investment after reaching your own conclusion, despite everyone around you claiming it to be a 'no-brainer', is a unique ability. The key here is to let the information, and your analysis, do the talking, and never allow yourself to be swayed by the opinions of others, however well-intentioned they may be. Clearly there is money to be made by 'pump and dump' tactics in this arena, but that is the domain of the speculator, not the successful value investor. Independence is an incredibly important attribute for successful investors. You will constantly face the temptation to act, and you need to be able to say 'No!', firmly and confidently.

The ability to remain objective and unemotional when conducting the investment process is also essential. Bill Miller argues that value investing is the search for truth – the separation of what is right from what is wrong. By objectively and rationally evaluating the facts, you can purposefully step out of the herd mentality that pollutes the market. As evidenced by the dot-com bubble or, more recently, the ICO bubble or GameStop mania, human beings are emotional. Expecting emotions to stay out of your investment process is unrealistic. However, if you are aware of them and how they can impact your investment process, you've already won half the battle.

Whenever I am completing our 250-question Investment Checklist for a current or potential holding, I write down how I am feeling before I start the work. If I feel angry or stressed or tired, I know it's not the best time to be doing investment research, because my mood will almost certainly colour my analysis. It's just human nature. Dr Kenneth Shubin Stein has shown through studies and scientific literature that hunger, anger, loneliness, tiredness, pain and stress are common preconditions for poor decision-making. Once we recognise the creeping influence of any one of these emotions or conditions, we should take a break, and only after recalibrating our emotional state should we make decisions. We should continue with the investment process only after our emotional balance has been fully restored. The ability to make mindful decisions is a key component of the correct temperament for successful value investing.

Dr Shubin Stein also found four actions that can improve brain health and function: meditation, exercise, sleep and nutrition. By focusing on these aspects of our lives, we should be able to sustain superior performance for longer periods of time. The key takeaways from these studies are that everybody, including investors, needs to be more aware of their emotional state. We need to be honest in acknowledging when our emotions are compromising our best judgement and proactive in finding ways to rebalance them. How we respond emotionally to the ups and downs of the market is a key factor in our ultimate success or failure.

The complementary ability to remain optimistic despite the adversity that value investors will face is equally important. For example, there is currently a widespread opinion that artificial intelligence will render investment professionals obsolete (along with many other occupations). AI is all about statistics and data, and in our industry there has always been more data and statistics than anyone could sensibly use. Whilst AI may be able to predict trends based on massive data sets and spot patterns faster, it is likely to leave value investing relatively untouched. AI will not be able to answer questions such as what moats a business enjoys or how defensible those moats are. For day trading and quant trading, AI may be helpful, but for a concentrated value investor, outsourcing aspects of the investment process is unlikely to yield positive results.

Besides, for a successful investor, the investment process is the best part. Why would you want to outsource any of it?

Optimism about the future is always preferable – in any endeavour. As Peter Lynch said, 'When you invest in stocks, you have to have a basic faith in human nature, in capitalism, in the country at large, and in future prosperity in general.' If you spend too long thinking of all the potential bad outcomes and coming up with any number of the countless reasons not to invest, you doom yourself to failure. As the German philosopher Friedrich Nietzsche said, 'Stare too long into the abyss and you become the abyss.'

Success in investing comes down to temperament. As Lynch suggests, 'Ultimately, it is not the stock market nor even the companies themselves that determine an investor's fate. It is the investor.' No successful investor credits their IQ for their success. They love what they do and are happy to spend their lives constantly refining their competitive edge in markets by thinking about business and investing. They embody the adage that 'if you love what you do, you will never work a day in your life' – something that we can all aspire to.

The Willingness to be Lonely

The stock market is the only market in the world where everyone runs away when things go on sale.

– François Rochon, founder and president of Giverny Capital

Simply put, to beat the market, you must do something different to the rest of the investors in the market. You must be a contrarian. As David Swensen, former CIO of the $35 billion Yale University Endowment Fund, said, 'Investment success requires sticking with positions made uncomfortable by their variance with popular opinion.' Or as American-born British investor, fund manager and philanthropist Sir John Templeton suggested, 'Buy when others are despondently selling and sell when others are euphorically buying ... It takes the greatest courage but provides the greatest profit.'

Templeton returned an average of 15 percent a year for thirty-eight years to the investors in his Templeton Growth Fund, so he clearly knows what he's talking about. But it's not just courage that's needed. Implicit in his comment is his willingness to be lonely.

As mentioned earlier, human beings are conditioned to be social. We are herd animals. The biological imperative means we are driven to survive and one lesson we've learnt is it's much easier to survive when we belong to a tribe. Little wonder that when stocks plummet, the average investor instinctively follows the tribe by selling stocks and fleeing to the 'safe haven' of cash. What the members of the tribe fail to recognise is that if they are willing to be lonely, this might be the perfect time to buy those stocks, because as the opening quote from François Rochon suggests, they are 'on sale.' The influence of the crowd clearly has a strong hold on most inexperienced investors. Buffett, on the other hand, is entirely unemotional when it comes to stock selection and decision-making.

The efficient market hypothesis (EMH) states that current share prices reflect all available information. One of the main criticisms of EMH is that 'all available information' does not include human emotion. Human beings are rarely objective, something that has been proven time and time again. Rising prices induce greed, overconfidence and euphoria, while falling prices induce fear, panic and depression. Speculators buy when the price rises and sell when it falls, regardless of the fundamentals of the underlying business. Buffett, however, is entirely immune to the vicissitudes of the markets and the emotions caused by rising or falling prices. In fact, he advises to 'be greedy when others are fearful and fearful when others are greedy … The less prudence with which others conduct their affairs, the greater the prudence with which we should conduct our own.'

The willingness to be lonely and get comfortable with it stems from a core sense of identity that all the great investors possess. They have the courage to take a position. They know from experience and a robust investment process that the worst of times in the markets in terms of price performance is the best of times for opportunities to hoover up underpriced stocks. It is this contrarian mindset which sets apart the investors from the speculators.

The greatest investors are truly able to separate themselves from the herd, whether that be physically, like Buffett, who works in Omaha, Nebraska – far away from the hustle and bustle of Wall Street. Or emotionally, by creating distance between themselves and the opinions and judgements of others. It is in this relative isolation that they are most comfortable. Where most investors crave the warmth of the centre of the herd, the successful investor is content to be lonely.

Focus

Dedication of an unusual degree is required to achieve mastery, and in the simplest definition, one could say that genius is the capacity for an extraordinary degree of mastery in one's calling. A formula followed by geniuses, prominent or not, is: Do what you like to do best, and do it to the very best of your ability.

— David R. Hawkins, MD, PhD, and author of *Power vs. Force*

When Bill Gates (the founder of Microsoft) first met Warren Buffett, he did not believe he would have anything in common with someone who 'just picks stocks'. After rearranging several times, they finally met. The evening began with an icebreaker – they were each asked the question, 'What is the single most important factor in your success?' They both gave the same answer: 'Focus.' And so began a decades-long friendship.

The market is always full of distractions, whether they be other people's opinions, filling your diary with analyst calls and company meetings, or various administrative tasks. We marvel today at the speed and convenience of email, the internet and Zoom calls as great time-saving inventions, but they can also be huge distractions. Personally, I prefer to look at my emails only once in the morning and once in the evening. Unless you are an on-call brain surgeon, no one is that important that they need to be reachable every second of every day. We must be the master of our own environment, carefully cultivating our intellectual intake and avoiding costly distractions. No matter who you are, there are only twenty-four hours in a day, and outside of sleeping, eating and exercising, there are a limited number of high-functioning, productive hours left. Ultimately, we are each in charge of how accessible we are and how open we are to distractions. As the old adage goes, time is money.

Jason Zweig, the editor of the 2009 edition of Ben Graham's *The Intelligent Investor*, wrote:

> Think of Munger and Miller and Buffett: guys who just won't spend a minute of time or an iota of mental energy doing or thinking about anything that doesn't make them better … Their skill is a focus on self-honesty. They don't lie to themselves about what they are and aren't good at. Being honest with yourself like that has to be part of the secret. It's so hard and so painful to do, but so important.

Adopting small, incremental and positive changes into your routine and persevering with them will ensure they become habits. Whether that's writing in a daily journal and noting where significant portions of time are wasted or switching your phone to silent for set periods of intense concentration and focused productivity, these changes will add materially to your mental firepower when conducting your investment process. The point is not perfection but to always be moving in the right direction.

Passion

> When asked what his favourite day of the year was to train, Daley Thompson, who won gold for decathlon at two Olympics, answered, 'Christmas Day, as I know this is the only day that my competitors won't be training.' That is true commitment, and it is a key part of why he won.
>
> – Skip Rosen, author of *Daley Thompson: The Subject is Winning*

I am yet to meet a single person who is happy in life who is not passionate about how they spend their time. In fact, I would say that the single biggest differentiator between people who are highly successful at investing – or anything else for that matter – and those who are just good at it is passion. The correlation between passion and success is unmistakable. Passionate people work harder and invest more physical and mental energy into achieving their goals. Passionate people tend to read more, study harder, and think more critically to further develop mastery over their subject. It is this drive to go further that forms the clear distinction between the 'good' and the 'great'.

As fund manager Howard Marks wrote, 'Luck is not enough, but equally intelligence is not enough, hard work is not enough, and even perseverance is not necessarily enough. You need some combination of all four.' It is passion that binds those things together. Luck will last only so long without passion. Intelligence might get you so far, but your edge will come from hard work. But hard work is next to impossible to sustain if you are not passionate about what you are doing. In *Outliers*, journalist and bestselling author Malcolm Gladwell suggests that the mastery of any subject requires a minimum of

10,000 hours of activity and practice. There is no way anyone could achieve 10,000 hours without passion.

Long term, you will not be able to outperform if you do not have a passion bordering on an obsession for your subject area. How else can you motivate yourself to do the work necessary for value-investing mastery? In *The Investor's Manifesto*, William Bernstein, a successful investor in his own right, stated his belief that 'Successful investors … must possess an interest in the process. It's no different from carpentry, gardening or parenting. If money management is not enjoyable, then a lousy job inevitably results.'

Many an investor's best returns have been generated by allowing their passions to guide their circle of competence and investment research. If something piques your interest, that is the first sign that you may be onto a winner. If you want to be a successful investor, investing must be your passion. Each of us has our own calling. You know in your core when something connects with you or not. Allow your passions to guide you in life, and use those passions to accumulate and compound knowledge, to be the very best that you can be. As Nelson Mandela famously said, 'There is no passion to be found playing small – in settling for a life that is less than the one you are capable of living.'

Intellectual Honesty and Curiosity

It is not the strongest of the species that survive, nor the most intelligent, but those most adaptable to change.

— Charles Darwin, English naturalist and father of evolutionary biology

Curiosity is one of the most important traits that all successful investors share. I define it as the desire for truth through the constant acquisition of knowledge. This is attained by questioning, seeking answers or explanations, and never taking anything at face value. Especially when other investors will settle for less-than-satisfactory answers. Continuous learning is at the core of all great investors' processes. Buffett has been described as a 'learning machine'. He has never stopped learning and looking for opportunities to improve himself and his investment process. On the importance of reading, Munger once said,

In my whole life, I have known no wise person over a broad subject matter area who didn't read all the time – none, zero. Now, I know all kinds of shrewd people who by staying within a narrow area can do very well without reading. But investment is a broad area. So, if you think you're going to be good at it and not read all the time, you have a very different idea than I do. ... You'd be amazed at how much Warren reads. You'd be amazed at how much I read.

This thirst for knowledge explains how Munger read hundreds of books per year. Remember his quote at the start of the section on temperament: 'The more hard lessons you can learn vicariously rather than through your own hard experience, the better.' Learning through the successes and failures of others is the fastest way to become wiser and smarter. And it also comes with a lot less pain. In many aspects of life, experience counts; however, in investing, the effects of experience compound over time. Experience enables greater pattern recognition, which can result in better investment ideas and an improved ability to spot and avoid costly mistakes.

The mental skill of critical analysis is also fundamental to successful investing. Perfecting that skill – developing the mindset of thoughtful, careful analysis – is intimately connected to the skill of thoughtful, careful reading. Each reinforces the other in a kind of positive feedback loop. Good readers are good thinkers; good thinkers tend to be great readers and, in the process, learn to be even better thinkers. So, the very act of reading critically improves your analytical skills. At the same time, the content of what you read adds to your accumulated knowledge, which is enormously valuable. Learning to be a careful reader has two enormous benefits for investors. First, it makes them smarter, in an overall sense. Secondly, it makes them see the value of developing a critical mindset and not taking information at face value. This critical mindset, in turn, has two requirements that relate to the reading process: (1) evaluate the facts; and (2) separate the facts from opinions.

If you adopt the right mindset when it comes to your reading, any type of reading can be used to build your repository of knowledge. Obviously, a fundamental interest in business and finance is essential for successful investing – along with an understanding of accounting, which is the language of business. However, as our knowledge increases cumulatively, whatever the subject, expanding our minds by reading any material can make us more 'worldly wise'. Much of our world is made up of the business of human affairs, and anything that can help us to understand how that world works, at any level, will be accretive to our investment process. The more you learn about human behaviour, the more you will develop your own ability to spot investment opportunities to evaluate.

My favourite aspect of investing is the fact that it is a never-ending game. You can never truly 'win', as the game is constantly changing and evolving. As an investor, no matter what the scoreboard says today, there is always room for improvement. You can only improve by embracing your mistakes in a spirit of intellectual honesty and continuous learning. In terms of performance, the rewards for doing so are significant. (This is the opposite to what is done in most other careers, where people seek to bury their mistakes. As the old saying goes, 'Success has many fathers, but failure is an orphan.') This degree of intellectual honesty is only really found in academia and is demonstrated by peer-reviewed literature, where previously accepted scientific understanding can be questioned, tested and, sometimes, disproved − and such breakthroughs are celebrated as progress. This is intellectual honesty at its purest and a refreshing approach to error correction that we should all embrace.

Intellectual honesty also includes personal integrity in how you conduct yourself and how you deal with others. Take, for example, Buffett's 'newspaper test'. How would you feel if the details of what you are thinking of doing were published on the front page of a national newspaper for all to see. If that makes you even slightly uneasy, don't do it. As the saying goes, 'It takes a lifetime to build a reputation and a single second to demolish it.' Make sure to surround yourself with people you admire and who seek to make you a better person. If there is ever any doubt, cut them loose. Life is too short to be dragged down by people who lack integrity.

In a VUCA world (volatile, uncertain, complex and ambiguous), embracing lifelong learning through intellectual curiosity may be the single most important factor in achieving success in life and in financial markets. Lifelong learning is closely associated with humility, having an open mind, a willingness to take risks, a capacity to listen, and honest self-reflection. If you can go to bed each evening a little wiser than when you woke up, the effects of compounding over many years will be even more spectacular, and not just for your financial returns. For the maths fans out there, a 1 percent improvement each day for a year yields about a 38× increase (1.01^{365}) − the awesome power of compounding in action. Imagine the results over the course of a lifetime!

Patience

The number one skill in investing is patience – extreme patience.

– Mohnish Pabrai, Indian-American fund manager and
philanthropist

The ability to delay gratification today for the possibility of a larger gain tomorrow requires time to pass; it requires patience. Patience in investing encompasses the concept of 'beneficial inactivity', which is at odds with what we would usually expect. We often associate activity with success and importance. By nature, we are impatient. This inherent impatience is at the root of gambling, speculation and the pursuit of get-rich-quick schemes, and even the lottery. Gambling is clearly a 'present moment' consumption activity as opposed to the 'delayed consumption' activity that is investing. We often confuse activity with ability. This leads many money managers to constantly churn their portfolios, looking for the next hot thing. But that is not investing; it is, in fact, speculating. As Buffett wrote in *Outstanding Investor Digest* in 1997, 'If you're an investor, you're looking on what the asset is going to do; if you're a speculator, you're commonly focusing on what the price of the object is going to do, and that's not our game.'

As value investors, we look for net present value positive bets. The best of these come around very infrequently and are realised over a long period of time. Munger expressed Berkshire's approach at their 1998 AGM: 'Around here, I would say that if our predictions have been a little better than other people's, it's because we've tried to make fewer of them.'

This long-term investment strategy requires patience – extreme patience. Wall Street actively encourages short-term behaviour, as they are paid through commissions on activity. Investors also tend to reward short-term behaviour; they wonder why they should pay a fund manager if he or she is not doing anything. Ironically, it is for precisely this reason that an investor should focus on the long term rather than the short term. By lengthening their investment time horizon, they vastly expand their prospective investment opportunity set. The competition for these opportunities disappears as the rest of the market focuses on the next quarterly earnings release rather than the next five-to-ten-year trajectory of the business. With less competition, excess returns are more readily available. Always remember, *not* doing something can also be an important decision when it comes to your own portfolio management.

Stanley Druckenmiller, while manager of George Soros's $40 billion Quantum Fund, wrote, 'The key to being a successful investor and to building superior long-term returns is to preserve capital and wait patiently for the right opportunity to make extraordinary gains. The waiting is the hard part!' Druckenmiller, along with Soros, famously made over $1 billion by 'breaking the pound' when the UK crashed out of the European Exchange Rate Mechanism (ERM) on Black Wednesday (16 September 1992).

As a value investor, your interests are directly opposed to those of Wall Street and the crowd. Your job is to meticulously select and cultivate a small number of exceptional businesses and hold them. Be patient, and you will be rewarded for your inactivity. Beware the saying, 'You'll never go broke taking a profit.' You may not go broke, but you won't get rich, either. Great fortunes are made by buying and holding; just look at any rich list. A child at a Berkshire AGM once asked the question '*How can I become rich?*', to which Buffett replied, 'Charlie and I always knew we would become very wealthy … but we weren't in a hurry … after all if you're even a slightly above average investor who spends less than you earn, over a lifetime you cannot help but get very wealthy – if you're patient.'

Patience is so important to successful investing that we will return to it in Chapter 15.

Decisiveness

Your goal as an investor should be simply to purchase, at a rational price, a part interest in an easily understood business whose earnings are virtually certain to be materially higher, five, ten, and twenty years from now. Over time, you will find only a few companies that meet those standards – so when you see one that qualifies, you should buy a meaningful amount.

– Warren E. Buffett, chairman of Berkshire Hathaway

Because we discussed in the last section the importance of patience in the investment process, it may now seem counterintuitive to be discussing the importance of decisiveness or quick decision-making. When you first come across a great business, you may find that it is too expensive. As the saying goes, 'a rising tide lifts all boats' – as the market rises, it lifts all prices with it. This presents a significant obstacle to any serious investor who wishes to deploy their capital. This is where patience is required to continue identifying other great businesses for potential investment but holding fire until the price of the first one corrects and drops below its intrinsic value. A rising tide may indeed lift all boats, but a receding tide affects boats in the opposite direction. Great businesses can often stumble, or the market can fall precipitously, and it is at exactly these moments that value investors need to be decisive and spring into action.

As Buffett has demonstrated on multiple occasions during times of market panic, he doesn't take weeks, nor even days, to reach conclusions on investment decisions; he knows intuitively, through all his experience and previous work, what is a bargain and what is not. He ignores all the news, unless it influences the intrinsic value of a business, focusing instead on remaining rational when all around him are losing their heads. He doesn't need to know everything about the business, just the things that he has previously identified as key to its success. He has a knack for knowing what these are and acting with impressive speed. As he says, 'The best thing that happens to us is when a great company gets into temporary trouble. … We want to buy them when they're on the operating table … in the meantime we sit on our hands.'

When it comes to decisiveness, Seth Klarman, the billionaire founder of the hedge fund Baupost Group, says that most successful investors tend to allow the 'fear and greed of others to play into their hands.' By having confidence in their own analysis and judgement, they respond to market forces not with blind emotion but calculated reason. Successful investors, for example, demonstrate extreme caution in frothy markets and steadfast conviction in panicky ones. When opportunity arrives, they act decisively, without hesitation. Or, as Buffett puts it, 'When it's raining gold, reach for a bucket, not a thimble.'

Decisiveness is an essential component of any investor's toolkit – the ability to react quickly when favourable prices appear unexpectedly. Experienced investors are far less likely to panic, and therefore they view a falling share price as an opportunity to buy. These investors succeed in the long run, at the expense of everyone else. Many attribute market timing to luck, but, as the first-century Roman philosopher Seneca wrote, and as all four successful investors mentioned here (Buffett, Druckenmiller, Soros and Klarman) have demonstrated, 'Luck is what happens when preparation meets opportunity.'

Humility

Those whom the gods would destroy, they first make proud.

– Ancient Greek proverb

Humility in life and humility in markets are two sides of the same coin when it comes to success. There is a fine line between confidence in one's convictions and hubris or arrogance. Knowing where you are on the scale is vitally important. In life, the most successful people are those who fail well. Ray Dalio, the billionaire founder of the world's largest hedge fund, Bridgewater, defines failing well as 'being able to experience painful failures that provide big learnings without failing badly enough to get knocked out of the game.'

I mentioned in the Introduction that my parents were both entrepreneurs. As such, they certainly experienced their fair share of setbacks. When we were in Australia, my father discovered that his business partner back in the UK had absconded with all the money from their joint property development. He had to rebuild the family finances from scratch. Although it was tough on all of us, I was amazed and inspired by his pragmatic assessment of reality and his grit and determination to get back up and try again. My parents are my role models when it comes to conducting myself with humility, optimism, and a drive towards ultimate success.

Everyone makes mistakes; everyone experiences setbacks and failures; but successful people learn from them. In investing, we recognise our humility through the concept of 'margin of safety'.

Investing with a margin of safety was first described by Ben Graham in the core text for any value investor, *Securities Analysis*, first published in 1934, and still in print today. To summarise, a margin of safety is achieved when securities are purchased at prices sufficiently below their underlying value to allow for: human error, bad luck, or extreme volatility in a complex, unpredictable, and rapidly changing world. This final point is the most important. Rapid change in the world around us makes errors in our forecasting inevitable, so the purchase price must act as compensation and provide protection. When we invest with a sufficient margin of safety, we know that if we have made a mistake, we will have at least preserved our capital. If we were conservative enough, we will come out ahead, and if we were even slightly correct, our returns should be significant.

As investors we must acknowledge that, despite our best efforts, we will often be wrong. Dan Loeb, the billionaire investor who runs the hedge fund Third Point, said to a graduating MBA class at Columbia University (coincidentally also where Ben Graham taught), 'Investing in public equities is a dangerous pursuit that requires risking real money based on limited information. Even when you are diligent about buying at a margin of safety, you will still make money-losing mistakes. Aspiring investors who require perfection have gotten into the wrong business.'

On average we can expect to 'fail' in our investment selection about 40 percent of the time. This does not mean that we will lose money 40 percent of the time but that our investments will not live up to our original investment thesis about 40 percent of the time. It is therefore inevitable that successful investors will go through periods of poor performance, even extended periods of poor performance. Howard Marks once observed,

> It matters enormously how the fund manager reacts to these poor periods. The combination of client pressure and peer pressure can be intense. You need deep reserves of resilience. Confidence in your convictions. Confidence in yourself to come through the valley. A strong character will use the period of underperformance to lay the foundation for the next period of good performance, be re-examining every assumption, every thesis, discarding some and doubling down on others. A weak character will freeze, their decision-making impaired. Or they might take flight, mentally at least, and avoid the difficult thinking. … You need to keep your feet on the ground at all times and always remember that you are never as good or as bad as you (or others) think you are. … Ultimately, of course, it is all about character. If you do not begin your fund management career with a sense of your fallibility, you are likely to learn it. If you do not learn it, you are likely to fail.

Humility is the fallibility that Marks is talking about. Once we are intellectually honest enough to accept that we will make mistakes, we can begin the process of insuring against them. At a minimum, the purchase price must reflect the risk inherent in the business; otherwise, your decisiveness should kick in with a firm 'No!' Patience (our old friend again) is also key, as the temptation to ride the new market fad will never be far from your mind. Most market participants fixate on their potential short-term return, paying little attention to the risks involved, that is, how much they can lose. Your job as a value investor is to do the opposite: to be long-term orientated and risk-averse.

Remaining grounded when you experience success, especially repeated success, can be exceedingly difficult. Success can imbue us with a false sense of security in our abilities and thus alter our perception of risk.

One of the most spectacular examples of the devastating impact of hubris is given in Roger Lowenstein's book *When Genius Failed*: the rise and fall of the hedge fund Long Term Capital Management (LTCM). Following several years of spectacular returns, the Nobel Laureates who founded it believed that they had cracked the financial markets. They came to believe that they could do no wrong. The result? They lost 98 percent of their investors' money.

It's useful to remember Munger's quip about LTCM: 'It's remarkable how much long-term advantage people like us have gotten by trying to be consistently not stupid, instead of trying to be very intelligent.' Munger followed up on this topic by adding,

> The biggest problem with intelligence is complicating things more than they need to be. Occam's Razor. A successful investment usually hinges on only one or at most several critical factors; if you cannot boil it down to these and isolate them out of the myriad of things that could affect the business, then you cannot make a balanced investment decision. This is the art of investing. An eight-hour presentation on a stock is the polar opposite of this ability and, thankfully, where most people in the industry think the gold lies. … Intelligent people are easily seduced by complexity while underestimating the importance of simple ideas that carry tremendous weight.

To be successful in markets, your investment style must evolve as you learn from your mistakes. The original value investors of the Graham school were educated during the Great Depression when companies were trading below their net asset (or liquidation) values. If there was a mathematical probability of making money because the share price represented a value lower than the assets of the company, Graham would purchase the shares. And to increase his probability of success, he would purchase as many as he could find.

Out of this school – and as the markets changed, with companies now trading less frequently below their liquidation values – evolved the investment approach of Phil Fisher, a pioneer in the field of growth investing. In addition to performing Graham's quantitative analysis of a business, Fisher also included a rigorous qualitative analysis. He was looking not just for 'cheap' stocks like Graham but also stocks that had the potential to significantly increase their intrinsic value over the long term. The humility to acknowledge that what works today may not work in the future and to constantly improve your investment process to incorporate new information is key to long-term success.

We investors must always question our beliefs and be willing to change our minds when the facts change. Being wrong is an inevitable part of investing. Sticking with a failing strategy because we don't want to lose face, or we believe we are too clever to fail, is just foolish. Nothing 'always works' in investing because the environment is in a constant state of flux, and efforts by investors in response to the changes will cause the environment to change further (second-order systems again).

If you are currently in short supply, the first step in developing humility is to admit that you *will* be wrong. Even great investors are wrong – and wrong often. But when their focus is to protect their capital first and seek gains second, they will only buy with a significant margin of safety, thus minimising the impact of any potential mistake. You are going to be painfully wrong *a lot*, so knowing how to do that 'well' is critical to your long-term success. The difference between average investors and the most successful ones is that the most successful ones learn and grow from their mistakes, whereas average investors are set back by their mistakes or keep repeating them. Through recognition of our fallibility, we will begin to incorporate a margin of safety into our investment process, thus ensuring our long-term success. Stay hungry. Stay humble.

Summary

Investing is hard. That's why having a disciplined, methodical, long-term investment strategy that makes sense is essential to making it through and being successful in almost any market environment.

– Joel Greenblatt, founder, managing principal and co-CEO of Gotham Asset Management

There must be a reason why there is only one Warren Buffett and why no other investor has come even close to his long-term performance. In the end, investors' emotions will almost always get the better of them, which is why they make mistakes or fail. As discussed, Buffett seems immune to emotion. He seems to be entirely rational. That rationality is facilitated by a robust and continuously evolving investment process combined with decades of experience operating within his circle of competence. This rationality applied over the long term and all the other traits mentioned in this chapter constitute the temperament that produced Buffett's exceptional results.

Successful investing is hard, and that is why having a disciplined, repeatable, adaptable, and long-term investment strategy makes sense. Ben Graham laid out the fundamental principles of value investing three generations ago. Despite the enormous changes in markets and in the world that have occurred since then, these principles have stood the test of time:

1. Treat a share of stock as a proportional ownership of the business.
2. Buy at a significant discount to intrinsic value to create a margin of safety.
3. Make a bipolar 'Mr Market' your servant rather than your master.
4. Be rational, objective and dispassionate.

Under the guidance of Phil Fisher and the encouragement of Charlie Munger, Buffett added another point:

5. It is better to buy a wonderful business at a good price than a good business at a wonderful price.

Of course, patience is required to wait for that wonderful business to be available to buy at a good price and to hold it long enough until it gets to a wonderful price and beyond. In this chapter, we also explored the qualities of humility, passion, focus and decisiveness. To me, Charlie Munger captured a near perfect balance of them all when he said, 'It was obvious to me that if I worked at it, I would find a few things in which I had an unusual degree of competence. This is where I could make significant returns.'

To be a successful investor, you must be wise, unemotional, rational and objective. When you find a business whose discounted future cash flows are worth significantly more than the present value of the business, you must act decisively to buy a meaningful amount, and then wait patiently for the rest of the market to arrive at the same conclusion. Everyone feels emotions, but the great investors balance risk aversion with opportunity to reach rational conclusions. This is the exact opposite of most people, who tend to swing wildly between delight when the market is rising and they are making money and fear when the market is falling and wiping out all their returns, and then some. They become greedier as prices move higher and more depressed as prices fall, the exact opposite of successful value investors. As Buffett says, 'The stock market is designed to transfer money from the active to the patient.'

Value investing is a lot like a sea voyage. Your objective is to travel through stormy seas to the safe haven of your destination, where you can float peacefully on calm water. Eventually you will learn to be at peace with the market no matter how it behaves. Through your passion for finance and business, you will build your own circle of competence to find potential investments. Through your search for truth, you will discover things about yourself and your investments. Some you'll like; others, not so much. But all this self-knowledge and awareness needs to be incorporated into your investment process. Being humble in your successes and embracing your failures will make you a better person and a better investor. Finally, make investment decisions *rarely*, and only when the investment sits well within your circle of competence – when it has a significant margin of safety. When you find a suitable investment, think like an owner, and commit a significant amount of capital for the long term.

Do all that and you, too, will be a successful value investor.

PART ONE

CHAPTER 2: ECONOMICS, BUSINESS AND FINANCIAL HISTORY

The natural effort of every individual to better his own condition ...
is so powerful a principle, that it is alone, and without assistance,
not only capable of carrying on the society to wealth and prosperity,
but of surmounting a hundred impertinent obstructions with which
the folly of human laws too often incumbers its operations.

— Adam Smith, Scottish economist and author of *An Inquiry into*
the Nature and Causes of the Wealth of Nations

Although a comprehensive run-through of the subject of economics is beyond the scope of this book, there is a basic level of economic theory and history that will apply to every investment decision.

In his book *The Living Company*, Dutch businessman and theorist Arie de Geus provided a good summary of basic economic theory, which states that there are three key sources of wealth: land (including all natural resources); labour (people); and capital (the accumulation and reinvestment of possessions). The combination of those three creates all the products and services that society needs for its material well-being. During most of human history, the critical factor of economic success was land. Those who could dominate and possess land were guaranteed the controlling role in creating wealth. Therefore, owners of land – in Western society, at least – were rich, and the people who had no land were poor.

Then, as historians such as Fernand Braudel and Henri Pirenne have described, a dramatic shift in importance from land to capital took place between the late Middle Ages and the beginning of the twentieth century. The addition of more capital into the wealth-creating process led to considerable increases in the effectiveness and efficiency of technological and commercial activity. Ships became bigger, longer voyages were attempted, and machines became faster. These business savings and efficiencies were converted into assets of the growing commercial ventures, which evolved into mining companies, shipping associations, trade enterprises, textile manufacturers, and eventually modern corporations. The modern company, in short, developed when capital became available for the wealth-creating processes of the medieval tradesperson.

In the age of capital, wealth expanded from those who owned and controlled the land to those who controlled access to capital. The rich were no longer just the landowners; they were also the owners of capital. The ability to finance endeavours became the scarcest commodity of production. Moreover, with the loss of influence of the old craft guilds (think, for example, formal groups of tanners and blacksmiths) and their evolution into companies, the owners of capital were able to control the human or labour factor of production. In the language of economic theory, capital was worth far more, and was far scarcer, than labour. Labour moved from being an integral aspect of the human community to being a commodity offered for sale on the market.

Over the centuries, a new element emerged in management thinking. If a company fell into trouble, jobs were cut first, because the capital assets and the investors' goodwill were considered far scarcer and more valuable. Thus, managers saw the optimisation of capital as their priority. For example, during the Great Depression of the 1930s it was considered good banking practice to liquidate and destroy client businesses that fell behind on their loans, along with all the jobs associated with them, if this would help the lenders to recover even a scrap of invested capital. This may seem harsh, but at the time it was necessary. Capital-supplying institutions (banks, mostly) were a lot less robust than they are today, and they were fighting for survival. In their attitude towards capital, companies were very different from the church or the military. Even in the grim evacuation at Dunkirk during the Second World War, the British forces scuttled their war machines and focused on saving their soldiers. In wartime, when people's lives are at risk, capital assets are of lesser importance.

However, over the course of the twentieth century, Western nations moved out of the age of capital and into the age of knowledge. Few managers recognised it at the time, but capital was losing its scarcity. The end of the Second World War marked the beginning of a period of enormous capital accumulation. Individuals, banks and companies became much more resilient. Technology also began to change, thanks to telecommunications, television, computers and commercial air travel. These innovations made capital far more fungible and resilient, easier to move around, and, consequently, less scarce.

With capital more easily available, the critical production factor shifted to the third source of wealth, labour. But it did not shift to simple labour. Instead, knowledge displaced capital as the scarce production factor and the key to corporate success. Those who had knowledge and knew how to apply it became the wealthiest members of society: technological specialists, investment bankers, creative artists, and facilitators of new understanding. This was not merely a function of the need for people to supply technical skills; the growing complexity of work also created a need for people to be inventive, to become distributors and evaluators of inventions and knowledge, through the now-global economy. Decisions made on behalf of the company could no longer remain the exclusive prerogative of just a few people at the very top.

Economists like to treat supply and demand as independent variables, but almost every variable in the investment and business world can be affected by the participants. Markets are congregations of buyers and sellers that represent supply and demand, and expectations of future supply and demand dynamics can affect both in the present. As George Soros points out, 'Anyone who trades in markets where prices are continuously changing knows that participants are very much influenced by market developments. How could self-reinforcing trends persist if supply and demand curves were independent of market prices?' Even a cursory look at commodity, stock and currency markets will confirm that such trends are the rule rather than the exception.

The theory of rational expectations suggests that market participants, in pursuing their own self-interest, base their decisions on the assumption that the other participants would do the same thing. This sounds reasonable, but it isn't. Participants act *on their own perception* of their own best interests. Therefore, they act on imperfect understanding, and their actions have unintended consequences. The realisation of this fact has led to the emergence of the field of behavioural economics, which we will explore in depth in Chapter 8.

Companies produce goods and services by trying to find the optimum combination of the three production factors: land, labour and capital. And the optimum combination in economic theory is the one where the company is producing goods and services at the lowest cost and selling them at the highest price that will realise maximum profits. In practice, however, as we will come to see, for the best businesses which are continuously growing their moats, this simplistic equation does not always hold true.

Macro vs. Microeconomics

Where there is scarcity, price is no object. This basic tenet of supply and demand would later become a governing principle of my investment philosophy.

– Sam Zell, American businessman and philanthropist

In investing, broadly speaking, there are two camps: those investors who focus on macroeconomics and those who focus on microeconomics. Macroeconomic investors consider the broader economy first, and how it affects the firms and people involved second (a top-down view). Microeconomic or 'theory of the firm' investors focus on individual businesses first and how they operate within the broader economy second (a bottom-up view). Where you as an investor sit on the spectrum between the two is a personal choice. But it's worth exploring the arguments for each, as many of the successful investors and businessmen quoted in this book disagree on what matters.

On the one hand, value investing is about buying companies in which you have confidence due to previous research when they are cheap, which is often after a significant downturn in the market. Most downturns are brought on by changes in macroeconomic variables. Rarely does an individual firm pose a systemic risk that could precipitate a broader market downturn – although there have been exceptions, for example, LTCM in 1998 and Lehman Brothers in 2008. One thing that all investors agree on is that consistently making correct macroeconomic predictions is not just hard but it is also impossible. Perhaps my favourite quote on this topic comes from Phil Fisher:

> The amount of mental effort the financial community puts into this constant attempt to guess the economic future from a random and probably incomplete series of facts makes one wonder what might have been accomplished if only a fraction of such mental effort has been applied to something with a better chance of proving useful. I have already compared economic forecasting with chemistry in the days of alchemy. Perhaps this preoccupation with trying to do something which apparently cannot yet be done properly permits another comparison with the Middle Ages.

Although the inherent inaccuracy of forecasting is also relevant when forecasting future cash flows for an individual business, the number of variables that go into this type of forecasting is nowhere near as difficult or complex as macroeconomic forecasting, which needs to account for a myriad of interrelated variables.

Because of the complexity of macroeconomic forecasting, Buffett's advice to investors is to ignore entirely the political and macroeconomic environments when constructing a portfolio or performing individual securities analyses. He elaborated on his view in his 1994 letter to Berkshire shareholders:

> We will continue to ignore political and economic forecasts, which are an expensive distraction for many investors and businessmen. Thirty years ago, no one could have foreseen the huge expansion of the Vietnam War, wage and price controls, two oil shocks, the resignation of a president, the dissolution of the Soviet Union, a one-day drop in the Dow of 508 points, or treasury bill yields fluctuating between 2.8% and 17.4%.
>
> But, surprise – none of these blockbuster events made the slightest dent in Ben Graham's investment principles. Nor did they render unsound the negotiated purchases of fine businesses at sensible prices. Imagine the cost to us, then, if we had let a fear of unknowns cause us to defer or alter the deployment of capital. Indeed, we have usually made our best purchases when apprehensions about some macro event were at a peak. Fear is the foe of the faddist, but the friend of the fundamentalist.

On the other hand, Howard Marks argues that investors must be mindful of the macroeconomic situation to the extent they can assess where they think a company is in the business and market cycles. We will explore both views in depth in Chapter 5. For a value investor to say they ignore the macro and always buy stocks when they are trading below half their intrinsic value isn't sensible outside the context of a market panic. Instead, a value investor may want to purchase an initial position but keep some of their powder dry in case the discount to intrinsic value widens even more. In Marks's own words,

> I think it is unrealistic and maybe hubristic to say 'I don't care about what is going on in the world. I know a cheap stock when I see one.'

If you don't follow the pendulum and understand the cycle, then that implies that you always invest as much money as aggressively [*sic*]. That doesn't make any sense to me. I have been around too long to think that a good investment is always equally good all the time regardless of the climate.

Personally, I think the best position is closer to Marks than Buffett. Ultimately, to invest in a business we need to forecast its future cash flows. If those projections are entirely 'blue skies' and compound 20 percent growth rates for the next thirty years, everything will look cheap today. The current interest rate environment also matters, as this and the forecasted future interest rates will affect our discount rate for our company's future cash flows. For a microeconomic-focused investor, somewhat of a macro view is still required. Like Marks, I use a macro perspective to identify potential major themes and trends, which may also help to scope out potential investment opportunities amongst businesses affected by those changes. After this, my mindset changes to being all about the micro and assessing whether the businesses identified are undervalued and whether they have a great compounding engine or two. As Charlie Munger writes, 'Factors that drive sustained improvement of returns on capital are not always obvious even to the management of the company, but once you identify a long-term compounding engine you should buy as much as you can and then wait.'

Summary

There are three takeaways from the 'macro vs. micro' debate that are worth keeping in mind for investment purposes. The first is that the saying 'They lie like a finance minister on the eve of devaluation' is based on truth. It would be a good policy to assume this of all politicians and public servants whose motives are to appease the people and especially if they hold elected office. Always take everything they say with a pinch of salt. As Ray Dalio said, 'The more strongly they make the assurance that everything is fine, the more desperate the situation probably is.'

The second takeaway is to remember the market truism that 'It is better to be approximately right than precisely wrong.' The new focus of economics, known as econometrics, is a mathematical approach that attempts to add a degree of precision to otherwise broad economic theories. But beware of its appearance of exactitude. As Paul Volcker, the former US Federal Reserve Chairman, wrote in his memoir, 'I came to sense that, in contrast to the later fashion for econometrics and its dependence on mathematical "regressions", market prices and trading activity hinged on inherently volatile human expectations about what might or might not happen – the next day, next month, or next year.'

The third and final takeaway is that the long-term growth rates of businesses and those of the economies in which they operate are linked in a similar way to the stock price of a company and the business that underlies it. As Charlie Munger elucidates,

> It's hard for a stock to earn a much better return than the business which underlies it earns. If the business earns 6% on capital over 40 years and you hold it for that 40 years, you're not going to make much different than a 6% return – even if you originally buy it at a huge discount. Conversely, if a business earns 18% on capital over 20 to 30 years, even if you pay an expensive-looking price, you'll end up with one hell of a result.

From both the macro and microeconomic perspectives, a good place to look for potential investments is where the growth is.

CHAPTER 3: UNDERSTANDING RISK AS A VALUE INVESTOR

In markets, the tails are always fat.

— Nassim Nicholas Taleb, Lebanese-American risk analyst,
trader and author of *The Black Swan*

Countless pages have been devoted in both investing and business literature to the subjects of risk and risk management. This chapter will walk you through the salient points for both individual businesses and portfolio management.

Understanding risk is essential for value investors to protect capital, identify opportunities, maintain a long-term perspective and effectively manage their portfolios. It allows investors to make informed decisions that align with their own investment objectives and individual risk tolerance. Understanding risk, what creates it and how to mitigate it is, therefore, crucial for success.

The modern word 'risk' derives from the early Italian 'risicare', which means 'to dare'. This makes intuitive sense, as everything in life could have odds attached to it. Every action you take or don't take has an associated risk. Do we cross the road immediately because it's faster, or do we take the safer option and walk to the pedestrian crossing? Do we purchase travel insurance in case the airline loses our luggage, or do we trust them to deliver it safely? Do we choose to buy an electric car despite there being less resale data on which to base our decision than exists for combustion-engine cars? As these examples show, risk, and how much of it we are willing to accept, is an innately personal choice, which explains why there are so many diverging views on the subject.

As mentioned in Chapter 1, value investors can define risk simply as the probability of a permanent loss of capital.

Aspects of Risk

To understand risk, we need a greater appreciation of its component parts. Some parts, such as volatility and uncertainty, may be recognised as investment risk factors, but the nature of their risk is different for value investors compared to all other investors. Other factors such as probability and the impact of human behaviour are frequently ignored or vastly underestimated.

Volatility

Using [a stock's] volatility as a measure of risk is nuts. Risk to us is 1) the risk of a permanent loss of capital, or 2) the risk of inadequate return. Some great businesses have very volatile returns – for example, See's Candies [an immensely profitable business] usually loses money in two quarters of each year – and some terrible businesses can have steady [hopeless] results.

– Charles T. Munger, vice-chairman of Berkshire Hathaway

Most investors are terrified of volatility. They interpret increased volatility as increased risk. But as Munger points out, this may not be the case.

If you were to look at the current price of just about any stock, I'd be willing to bet that, on average, the fifty-two-week range will have been about 50 percent above and 50 percent below the current price. And yet is it even remotely plausible that the underlying business value of Apple, Alibaba or any other stock you choose actually varied in that manner over the last year? Absolutely not! (At least, not as dramatically.)

Instead, volatility can often provide an opportunity to be 'paid' for assuming the risk of volatility that someone else does not wish to bear. A good example is commodity markets, where there are often more farmers or producers who wish to protect themselves against falling prices than people wishing to buy and assume the price volatility risk. This leads to a price hedge for long-term investors willing to assume the risk. Because of the oversupply of sellers, the price is less than it should be. Therefore, in the commodities markets, the producer's loss aversion gives the commodities buyer a spectacular built-in advantage. This phenomenon goes by the name of 'backwardation'.

Backwardation: When the current price of an underlying asset is higher than prices trading in the futures market.

For the unleveraged long-term value investor (we will come back to leverage in Chapter 10), volatility is your friend. It allows you to buy when asset prices are depressed and sell when they are euphoric. Without volatility, neither of these situations would occur with enough frequency. Value investors are the opposite of closet indexers; they are variance-seekers. They know that only by doing something different from the rest of the market can they seek to outperform it. As Graham said, we should ignore 'Mr Market' most of the time. If the price of a stock we own goes down for no apparent reason, this is only a 'paper loss' – not a 'realised loss' or a 'permanent capital loss'. There is only one reason for a permanent loss of capital: you sold. Whether that sale was made because you realised you were wrong and had invested with an insufficient margin of safety or you panicked when the price dropped, the decision to sell is the single decision that separates the successful investor from the rest.

Volatility is something to be taken advantage of. This is completely counter to how most investors behave in real life: they focus on reducing volatility at all costs. Economist and academic Robert Shiller contends that financial markets exhibit excess volatility and that security prices fluctuate far more than is required to represent changes in their fundamental value. He adds, 'If price movements were rescaled down … so as to be less variable, then price would do a better job of forecasting fundamentals.'

The inverse can also be true: financial markets can exhibit very little volatility for extended periods. For example, from 1950 to the end of 1965, the Dow Index was within 5 percent of its all-time high 66 percent of the time and within 10 percent of its all-time high 87 percent of the time. Although there were clearly certain days when the market was significantly more volatile than others, even 'Mr Market' can have extended periods of relative calm – which are often followed by shorter periods of intense volatility. Bull markets tend to grind higher over extended periods of time, whereas bear markets tend to be fast and short.

Uncertainty

Truth is stranger than fiction as truth has to make sense.

– Mark Twain, American writer and humorist

Financial markets hate uncertainty. We have already explained that stock prices represent the value of all the future cash flows of a business discounted at an appropriate rate to their present value, today. The stock price is based on the average of all the market participants' expectations of earnings. Therefore, anything that is not captured during the development of expectations of future cash flows and earnings can create a significant discrepancy between a stock's price and the price that would reflect the state of the underlying business. This explains why stock prices are particularly volatile during the earnings season, when a slight 'beat' or 'miss' in results versus expectations can cause significant moves in the stock price. Markets demand certainty and will punish any business that fails to meet expectations.

But to the long-term investor, this makes absolutely no sense. What does one quarter's earnings tell us about the long-term value of a business? Unless there has been a radical strategic or material change in the business over the previous three months, it tells us very little. The real world is messy. Everything exists in a constant state of flux. Why should our analysis be based on the extrapolation of the recent past indefinitely into the future? The range of outcomes from any business decision is wide, something that markets often fail to recognise. As a result, the market often reacts extremely when something occurs outside the very narrow path of expected outcomes.

Fund manager Seth Klarman points out that '[h]igh uncertainty is frequently accompanied by low prices.' We value investors look for high-uncertainty, low-risk businesses. The high uncertainty surrounding a business with volatile earnings may lead to a depressed share price. This may present a good investment opportunity to the long-term investor who can ride out the volatility and capture the upside. As in the previous commodities example, there are times when stock market investors will sell at a low price, therefore paying a significant premium to offload potential risk and investment uncertainty. This usually happens when a company goes through some sort of crisis, for example, the oil spill in the Gulf of Mexico caused by BP's Deepwater Horizon drilling rig. The surrounding uncertainty associated with the business caused investors to flee BP's stock, which fell 50 percent in a matter of days. Such a crisis can present the value investor with an opportunity to buy a great business at a reasonable price.

Whilst it is true that, over time, stock prices and markets will tend towards their intrinsic value, in the interim, prices can diverge wildly, and for extended periods of time. This leaves a significant opportunity for focused value investors who recognise the difference between uncertainty and risk to purchase a stock at its lows – when its uncertainty is at its highest but, conversely, its risk is at its lowest – and hold it for the long term. For value investors, uncertainty is not a risk factor; it is a source of opportunity that arises largely because of human behaviour.

Time

The stock market's been the best place to be over the last 10 years, 30 years, 100 years. But if you need the money in 1 or 2 years, you shouldn't be buying stocks.

– Peter Lynch, American investor and manager of the
Fidelity Magellan Fund

The length of your investment horizon also has a significant impact on risk. Over time, we can confidently assume that the stock price and intrinsic value of a company's underlying business will converge. We also know that over long periods of time, stock markets (in the U.S., for example) tend to rise around 8 percent per year. Clearly, if you are a long-term investor, you are far less concerned with short-term fluctuations in market value because you know that over longer time frames there is far less volatility or uncertainty in the rates of return. This is a very different risk proposition to the investor who is trying to work out what the market will do tomorrow, next week or next month – which is entirely unpredictable and, therefore, an impossible task.

Burton Malkiel, author of the investment classic *A Random Walk Down Wall Street*, demonstrated this through a series of studies of portfolio returns over various time periods. Using historical data in the US and a 100 percent equity allocation, he showed that for a one-year holding period, there would have been a 5 percent chance that investors would lose at least 25 percent of their money, and a 5 percent chance that they would make more than 40 percent. Over thirty years, though, the worst '5 percent outcome' would have been a 5 percent chance that a 100 percent stock portfolio would grow by less than 20 percent and a 5 percent chance that owners of this portfolio would end up over fifty times richer than they were when they had started.

Over time, the difference between returns on 'risky' securities and 'conservative' investments widens dramatically. Over twenty years, there would have been a 5 percent chance that a portfolio consisting of only long-term corporate bonds would quadruple while there would have been a 50 percent chance that a 100 percent stock portfolio would grow at least eightfold. Malkiel concluded that even small differences in annual returns over many years produced big differences in an investor's wealth in the long run. As value investors, we are only interested in returns over the long term; therefore, the impact of time as a risk factor decreases significantly.

Probability

There's a big difference between probability and outcome. Probable things fail to happen – and improbable things happen – all the time. That's one of the most important things you can know about investment risk.

— Howard Marks, co-founder and chairman of Oaktree Capital Management

Outlier events in the normalised probability distribution occur frequently in financial markets, and just because something hasn't happened in the past or not for a very long time, that does not mean it cannot happen in the future. Or as world-renowned risk expert and fund manager Nassim Taleb puts it, 'All we can learn from history is that the unpredictable will happen – and does – time and again. The most dangerous error that an investor can make is to mistake probability for certainty.'

Taleb discusses probability in his books *Anti-fragile*, *The Black Swan* and *Fooled by Randomness*, pointing out that there are 'known knowns', such as the risk of holding positions over a weekend when the market is closed, and 'known unknowns', such as the fact that San Francisco sits on a fault line, and another significant and potentially devastating earthquake will inevitably hit that city but we just don't know when. Furthermore, there are 'unknown unknowns', which are possibilities that we cannot yet understand and are only knowable in hindsight. Looking back, we could say the risk of a global Covid-19 pandemic was, for most of us, an unknown unknown.

Whereas humans resist randomness, markets resist prophesy. The fact that something has happened many times previously does not mean that it will happen again in the future. Equally, the fact that something has *never* happened in the past does not mean that it cannot happen in the future in what is known as a black swan event.

Much like life, investing is not based on absolutes or exact mathematics. As Howard Marks says, one sign of a healthy market is risk aversion (not irrational exuberance). However, when risk avoidance is taken too far, it condemns you to return avoidance.

The key is finding balance around probability. Economist John Maynard Keynes pointed out that 'Some of the things which I vaguely apprehend are, like the end of the world, uninsurable risks and it is useless to worry about them.' Mohnish Pabrai referred to these 'end of world' risks as 'the Yellowstone factor', after Yellowstone National Park, home to the largest active supervolcano on earth. It has a history of erupting about every 600,000 years – and the last one was about 630,000 years ago! Probability alone should make us decide not to visit Yellowstone this summer!

But as investors, if we paid too much attention to the probabilities of black swans, volcanic eruptions, or some other six-sigma event or one-in-a-billion long shot, we wouldn't invest in anything. Besides, as Keynes reminds us, if such a thing happened, we would all be dead anyway, so what was happening in the market really wouldn't matter!

There is not a single business or investment whose future is 100 percent assured. Seeking that sort of assurance in the face of uncertainty, volatility and probability is futile and would lead to too much risk aversion. Although Phil Fisher has had a big impact on the field of value investing, his son Ken Fisher, also an investor and a billionaire in his own right, is highly critical of his father's approach to risk:

> He worried everything over until he had worried it to death. Maybe he had reduced risk that way. But that also may well have contributed to why he wasn't richer than he was. He wasn't willing to take risks on things for which he hadn't worried the mistakes down to marginality. In that way, he was never a big risk taker, and those who get really rich take bigger calculated risks than he was ever willing to take.

Sam Zell, one of the greatest investors and entrepreneurs of his generation, recognised well this flawed approach to risk recognition and risk avoidance. He saw early on that the basics of business were straightforward:

> It's largely about risk. If you've got a big downside and a small upside, run the other way. If you've got a big upside and a small downside, do

the deal. Always make sure you're getting paid for the risk you take, and never risk what you can't afford to lose. Keep it simple. A scenario that takes four steps instead of one means there are three additional opportunities to fail.

He goes on to say, 'Nothing refines your understanding and assessment of risk better than experience. But at any time, it's about being aware and simplifying the worst downside scenario – seeing over the abyss. It's about discipline and avoiding emotional response. And then you decide whether to play or walk.' Also, 'Experience builds discipline and insight that sometimes allows you to see over the abyss before you step into thin air. It's about being risk aware not being risk averse.'

Financial markets are inherently volatile, with 'fat tails'. As Paul Tudor Jones, one of the most successful macro investors of the last forty years, says, 'You should expect the unexpected in this business; expect the extreme. Don't think in terms of boundaries that limit what the market might do. If there is any lesson I have learnt from the years that I've been in this business, it is that the unexpected and the impossible happen every now and then.'

To allow for the possibility of the unexpected, a value investor must always look for investments that have an adequate margin of safety to compensate for the risk of investing. We believe that the greater the margin of safety there is in a business, the lower will be the risk and the higher the expected return. This

Fat Tail

In investing, a 'fat tail' refers to the occurrence of extreme events, or outliers, that happen more frequently than would be expected under a normal distribution. In a normal distribution, extreme events are very rare, as most data points cluster around the mean (average) with a predictable frequency of distribution. However, in financial markets and many other complex systems, extreme events occur much more frequently than would be predicted by a normal distribution.

When a distribution has fat tails, this means that there is a higher probability of extreme events happening. These events can have significant impacts on investment portfolios, as they often involve large losses or gains. Fat tails are a characteristic of financial markets due to their complex and interconnected nature, underscoring the importance of risk management strategies for investors.

is not in line with how academics frequently view the world, proclaiming that any increase in return must be matched by a commensurate increase in risk.

Human Behaviour

The fault, dear Brutus, is not in our stars, but in ourselves.

– Julius Caesar, Act I, Scene III

According to the Austrian philosopher Ludwig Wittgenstein, 'When we think about the future of the world, we always have in mind its being at the place where it would be if it continued to move as we see it moving now. We do not realize that it moves not in a straight line … and that its direction changes constantly.' This is because people typically don't really grasp the nature of volatility, uncertainty or probability. And most certainly don't understand regression to the mean.

Regression to the Mean

Before we delve more deeply into the human aspects of risk, it's important to understand a potent force in both life and markets – regression to the mean. Investors like to presume that whatever conditions are present today will continue indefinitely into the future. This is known as recency bias (more on that in Chapter 8). Times of significant optimism are followed inevitably by times of excess pessimism. The peaks and troughs of the business or economic cycles are based around the mean. Most investors, as we have seen, are incapable of emotionally escaping this cycle, which leads them to make poor investment decisions such as selling at the bottom and buying at the top. If someone they know is making money in the market with their stock picks and they are not, fear of missing out (FOMO) motivates them to take bigger risks. You might think that fear and anxiety would make people more risk-averse, but they don't. Studies have shown that people only become more risk-averse when they have more to protect. It's actually very easy to be overcome by fear or greed, which causes people to run with the crowd rather than remembering that running in the opposite direction is their safest course of action … because almost everything in markets is mean reverting.

Howard Marks suggests that when people believe something is risky, their unwillingness to buy it usually pushes its price down to the point where it's not risky at all. Thus, broadly speaking, negative opinions can reduce risk by driving all the optimism out of a price. This can only happen if most investors think that quality, as opposed to price, is the key determinant of whether something is risky or not. But high-quality assets can be risky, and low-quality assets can be safe. Marks says, 'It's just a matter of the price paid for them. Elevated popular opinion, then, isn't just the source of low return potential, it's also almost always higher risk.'

Since we never know exactly what will come tomorrow, it is easier to assume that the future will resemble the present than to accept that it may bring some unknown change. Thus, there is a bias towards ease and intellectual laziness. A stock that has been going up for a while somehow seems a better buy than a stock that has been heading back down to earth. We assume that a rising price signifies that the company is flourishing and that a falling stock price signifies that the company is in trouble. But as we've discussed, this is often not the case, especially in the short term.

Professional investors are just as likely as novice speculators to try to play it safe. For example, in December 1994, analysts at the brokerage firm Sanford C. Bernstein & Co. found that professional investors who tended to forecast a higher-than-average growth rate for a company consistently overestimated the actual results, while pessimists consistently underestimated them. On average, neither the expectations of the optimists nor those of the pessimists were met.

The consequences of expectations not being met are easy to see in markets, where stocks with optimistic, blue-sky forecasts climb to new highs, while stocks with disappointing forecasts drop to new lows. This is the exact moment when regression to the mean comes into play, with value investors buying the undervalued securities that others are selling and pushing their prices back up. Unlike the market itself, this outcome is entirely predictable because of human behaviour. The inevitable earnings disappointments that eventuate as the hot stocks can no longer meet the euphoric expectations of Wall Street cause uneducated investors to all rush to sell at once, thus depressing the price.

Remember, financial markets are auction-driven; investors constantly outbid each other for the quantity of a security available for sale, and the highest bidder always receives the allocation. You need only look at every speculative market bubble in history to see that auction-driven markets tend to fluctuate erratically, which, in turn, makes people behave even more irrationally.

This type of thinking is endemic in auction-driven markets. As Graham said, 'Mr. Market is your servant not your master; in general, it pays to ignore the random prices that he shouts, and only buy when he is depressed and prices are very low or sell when he is elated and they are very high.'

Of course, Eugene Fama's efficient markets hypothesis (EMH) is supposed to account for this human bias. EMH posits that current market prices account for all available information. Therefore, it is impossible to beat the market on a risk-adjusted basis, as the only thing that makes stock prices move is new information, which no one can consistently forecast correctly. If you believe this, then there is no point in even trying to beat the market, and you should simply index. (As we shall see in Chapter 6, the rewards for passive investing can still be pretty good.) The irrationality of the EMH approach is captured in an old joke: Two finance professors are walking along a sidewalk. When one spots a hundred-dollar bill and bends over to pick it up, the other grabs his arm and says, 'Don't bother. If it was a real hundred-dollar bill, someone would have taken it already.'

Such is the absurdity of human behaviour.

Behavioural Economics

Contrary to popular opinion, humans are not rational decision-makers. Thankfully, the field of behavioural economics was developed to explore the emotional and behavioural biases that people have and need to be aware of to improve their lives as well as their investment decision-making.

Daniel Kahneman and Amos Tversky were two of the most prominent experts in this field. Some of their most important work involved exploring how people react when confronted with risk or the possibility of loss – a constant in the world of investing, where results are often anything but rational.

For example, given a choice between a definite gain of $1,000 or a 50/50 chance of winning $2,000, most people tend to take the sure thing. A bird in the hand is worth two in the bush. However, if given the choice between a definite loss of $1,000 and a 50/50 chance of losing $2,000, the same people prefer to take their chances. This seems entirely counterintuitive, until you understand Daniel Bernoulli's theory of utility, which suggests that a guaranteed loss causes more 'displeasure' than the levels of 'displeasure' or 'pleasure/relief' associated with the possibility of a larger loss, or no loss at all.

Another example is 'Samuelson's bet', named after a scenario first posed by economist Paul Samuelson. People offered a single bet in which they have a 50/50 chance to win $200 or lose $100 will usually decline the bet. However, if they are offered the chance to make the same bet a hundred times over, most will accept the bet. For some reason, they determine that a hundred bets will put the odds in their favour, as opposed to a single bet. Clearly, the more times you play a game with the odds in your favour, the less likely you are to lose. But the more times you play Samuelson's game, the *more* you stand to lose in total. As Tversky says, 'The difference between being very smart and very foolish is often very small.'

Bernoulli stated that people do not seek to maximise value; they seek to maximise 'utility' (i.e. the value that they assign to money). This is known as expected utility theory. The value assigned to money clearly varies from person to person depending on how much money they have to begin with. This goes some way to explaining common human behaviour that is at odds with rationality, for example, why gamblers accept bets that have well-known negative expected values (e.g. casino games) and why people buy insurance, regularly paying premiums that are lower in value than the potential losses against which they are insuring.

Tversky took Bernoulli's theory one step further and defined risk aversion in this manner: 'The more money one has, the less he values each additional increment, or, equivalently, the utility of any additional dollar diminishes with an increase in capital.' In other words, the value of your first thousand dollars is perceived as being greater than the value of your second thousand dollars, and the third thousand after that. The marginal value of the dollars you give up to buy fire insurance on your house is less than the marginal value of the dollars you would lose if your house burned down – which is why even though insurance is, strictly speaking, a stupid bet, you buy it.

Kahneman suggested that it is the anticipation of regret that affects decisions, along with the anticipation of other consequences. He thought that people anticipated and adjusted for regret in a way that they didn't with other emotions. 'What might have been is an essential component of misery,' he wrote. 'There is an asymmetry here, because considerations of how much worse things could have been is not a salient factor in human joy and happiness.' Happy people do not dwell on some imagined unhappiness the way unhappy people dwell on what they could have done differently to be happier. People do not seek to avoid other emotions with the same energy they expend to avoid regret. Kahneman's conclusion was that when people make decisions, they do not seek to maximise utility; they seek to minimise regret.

When choosing between a sure thing and a gamble, people's desire to avoid losses usually far exceeds their desire to secure gains. For most people, the happiness involved in receiving a desirable object is smaller than the unhappiness involved in losing that object. It isn't hard to imagine why this might be – a heightened sensitivity to pain is what has allowed us to survive, individually and as a species. As Kahneman wrote, 'Happy species endowed with infinite appreciation for pleasures and low sensitivity to pain would probably not survive the evolutionary battle.'

Whatever the emotion, it becomes stronger as the odds become more remote. If you tell people there is a one-in-a-billion chance that they'll win or lose $10 million, they'll behave as if the odds were one in ten thousand. They will fear a one-in-a-billion chance of loss more than they should and attach more hope to a one-in-a-billion chance of gain than they should. People's emotional responses to extremely long odds lead them to reverse their usual taste for risk. They become 'risk seekers' when pursuing a long-shot gain and 'risk avoiders' when faced with the extremely remote possibility of loss – which is why so many people buy lottery tickets and insurance. 'If you think of the possibilities at all, you think of them too much,' wrote Kahneman. 'When your daughter is late and you worry, it fills your mind even when you know there is very little to fear. You'd pay more than you should to get rid of that worry.'

Finally, the renowned economist and essayist on risk Dr Kenneth Arrow explained why people take money-losing propositions such as gambling or buying insurance *despite* the probability they will lose money on both. We gamble because we are willing to accept the large probability of a small loss in the hope that the small probability of a large gain will work in our favour. We buy insurance because we cannot afford to take the risk of losing our home to a fire. That is, we prefer a gamble that has 100 percent odds of a small loss (the premium we must pay) versus a small chance of a large loss if catastrophe strikes.

Humans are a mass of contradictions – never mind their biases and misplaced optimism or pessimism. It is impossible to reach adulthood, even if we grow up in a stable and loving home, without accumulating a bunch of conditioned responses, known as heuristics, that help us to shortcut our decision-making. Heuristics save time (think the 'fight or flight' response), which is crucial in dicey situations, but they essentially perform risk assessment by rule of thumb. This problem-solving approach leads to many of the psychological biases we will explore in Chapter 8, all of which are potentially harmful to investors.

Having a robust investment process can help to mitigate human misjudgement. Being aware that our decision-making processes can become clouded and deeply flawed without a robust investment process also helps us to stay on track. It helps us to remember to resist our evolutionary tendency to panic as a first response when the markets inevitably fall from time to time.

Portfolio Management Theory

No amount of observations of white swans can allow the inference that all swans are white, but the observation of a single black swan is sufficient to refute that conclusion.

– John Stuart Mill, English philosopher and political economist

There is a common market parable in risk management about the six-foot-tall man who drowned crossing a stream that was five feet deep... on average. The implication of the parable is that 'average' is a useless measure if the stream happens to be seven feet deep in places and the man cannot swim. As evidenced by probability, outlier events occur far more frequently in financial markets than might be expected. Taking the average of past market movements to project forward can be very dangerous. Like the man crossing the stream, you cannot survive 'on average'. Your portfolio needs to be resilient so it can survive the worst of days. Our objective is to be the 'last man' standing. It is partly for these reasons why significant leverage of any sort, either directly by yourself as the portfolio manager or in the companies in which you invest, is always a bad idea. Leverage introduces fragility into your portfolio and your portfolio businesses – when the objective is to be anti-fragile.

Portfolio management theory provides a framework for investors to make informed decisions about asset allocation, risk management and portfolio construction for the ultimate aim of achieving their investment goals in a systematic and disciplined manner. It helps investors to be anti-fragile. And that means building a portfolio with resilience.

Investors always need to carefully balance risk versus reward when it comes to portfolio construction and individual security selection. Howard Marks suggests that we focus on building 'un-fragile portfolios and un-fragile lives' that are unlikely to collapse, even in dire circumstances. To do so, he suggests that we avoid a lot of debt and leverage and, importantly, not let our dreams of success lead us to take decisions that would also expose us to the possibility of catastrophe. As Ray Dalio wrote after almost having to declare bankruptcy due to significantly mis-sizing a position in his fund, 'It enhanced my fear of being wrong and taught me to make sure that no single bet, or even multiple bets, could cause me to lose more than an acceptable amount.' Dalio's mistake was an example of gambler's ruin: the size of his bet was too large for his bank account, and it almost sent him broke.

An important key to investing, and life, is to be conservative and make bets only when the odds are firmly in our favour. Financial independence is a key aspiration for many people, and many will take enormous risks to get it. However, financial *security* is not something you need to take significant risks to get; that comes from living within your current means. In other words, spending less than you earn and saving/investing the rest. Your personal level of 'anti-fragility' comes from the gap between your savings/investments and your expenses. The larger the gap, the less fragile you are. I have found that in both investing and life, it is always best to have a significant margin of safety. The difficulty comes when we see others doing 'better' than us or when things are going well for us and we can only see blue skies ahead. It is the human tendency to alter course during these periods that often results in disaster.

Many investors and academics conflate volatility with risk, but there is no single model that encompasses how markets behave all the time. Academic models provide, at best, guiding principles for how markets and portfolios *may* behave *some* of the time. From a portfolio management perspective, what you are searching for is a series of uncorrelated bets to enhance your risk/ return profile. Relying too much on past correlations, however, is a mistake. As the saying goes, 'Just because you put your eggs in separate baskets does not mean they cannot break at the same time.' The blow-up of the hedge fund LTCM was a clear demonstration of that. In times of market stress or bear markets, all risk assets tend to become correlated.

As mentioned earlier, Taleb explores in his books the evaluation of probabilities and risk in terms of portfolio management. He points out that bear markets tend to teach investors to learn to manage risk in a different way, focusing not on the odds but the *size* of the risk. Just how large is my downside?

Let's say you are offered a wager where you're told you have 999 chances out of 1,000 to make $1,000, but a 1 in 1,000 chance that you'll lose $10 million. Would you take the wager? Of course not. Although the probability of loss is only 1 in 1,000, the risk of losing $10,000,000 makes the bet untenable.

Yet when investing their life savings, especially if they have been 'trained' by a long bull market, investors are too quick to focus on the *probability* rather than the size of the risk. Investors pay too much attention to what happens 'on average'. Leveraged investments in equities can be a successful strategy, but it does not matter how frequently a strategy succeeds if failure is catastrophic. In other words, an investor must always ask, 'What is the worst thing that can happen, and can I withstand it?'

This is why a seventy-year-old investor with a nest egg of $250,000 would be foolish to put 100 percent of their money into the stock market. Even if the odds are high that they will make money over the next five years, if they are wrong, their retirement will be immeasurably impaired. There is always the possibility, however slim, that markets will fall precipitously and not recover within their expected time horizon.

The most dangerous error investors can make is to mistake probability for certainty. By focusing on what is probable, or what happens on average, investors often ignore worst-case scenarios. For precisely this reason, Taleb says that investing can be much more treacherous than a game of Russian roulette: 'Reality is far more vicious ... First, it delivers the fatal bullet rather infrequently, like a revolver that would have hundreds, even thousands of bullets, instead of six. After a few dozen tries, one forgets about the existence of the bullet, under a numbing false sense of security.'

Secondly, unlike a well-defined game of Russian roulette where the risks are visible to anyone capable of simple maths, we do not observe the 'barrel' of reality. We are, therefore, capable of unwittingly playing Russian roulette – and calling it some alternative 'low-risk' name. We see the survivors and never the losers… The game seems terribly easy, and we play along mindlessly. For example, in the late eighties, investors buying stocks at 100 times earnings in the so-called 'Nifty Fifty' did not recognise the size of the risks they were taking. They called their high-risk game of picking stocks 'investing in an efficient market'.

The truth is that Taleb's black swan could appear tomorrow. The stock that everyone says is safe could blow up. Following a bear market rally, the S&P 500 could drop a thousand points. People tend to think of low-probability events as being somewhere in the distant past or future. In other words, we say, 'Well, yes, gold went to $800 an ounce, but that was more than twenty years ago.' Or 'Well, yes, in 1980 we had double-digit inflation – that couldn't happen now.' And yet, in October 2022, we got *very* close to double-digit inflation again (9 percent annualised) in the US.

Taleb is emphatic on this point. Probability has *nothing* to do with time. The surprise that could upset the best-laid plans and forecasts could be waiting just around the corner. As he sees it, the risk inherent in different asset classes has meaning only when it is related to the investor's liabilities. That is, the real risk of holding a portfolio is that it might not provide its owner – either during the interim or at some terminal date, or both – with the cash required to make essential outlays. For example, an owner like our seventy-year-old investor with their $250,000 nest egg.

Summary

The real trouble with this world of ours ... is that it is nearly reasonable but not quite. Life is not an illogicality; yet it is a trap for logicians. It looks just a little more mathematical and regular than it is; its exactitude is obvious, but its in-exactitude is hidden; its wildness lies in wait.

– G.K. Chesterton, English philosopher and author

In this chapter we have explored the key components of risk as they relate to both life and our investment process. For an investor to be successful, they are required to not just assess a business's value and decide the right time to buy it; they must also have a solid understanding of the risk of doing so. This understanding must go beyond the treatment of risk as a historical measure of volatility. That definition is analogous to driving a car by looking in the rear-view mirror, when all the risk lies ahead of you. Value investors define risk as the probability of a permanent loss of capital – and every effort must be made to reduce that probability.

We must also recognise and mitigate against our innate human irrationalities and biases when it comes to assessing risk in our investment process. Although we may believe we are rational, behavioural economics has proven we are not – especially when emotions, or markets, are running high or low!

If investments are riskier, that simply means they have a wider scope of possible outcomes for which we need to be compensated. We must have a sense of the probability of permanent loss for each prospective investment. And be willing to invest only when the reward more than compensates for the risk, with an acceptable margin of safety. Always beware both personal and business leverage; leverage is often the fastest path to ruin.

A solid grounding in the concepts of risk, uncertainty, probability and behavioural economics will always help a value investor on their path to success.

CHAPTER 4: MARKET EFFICIENCY

People get smarter but they don't get wiser. They don't get more emotionally stable. All the conditions for extreme overvaluation or undervaluation absolutely exist, the way they did 50 years ago. You can teach all you want to people, you can tell them to read Ben Graham's book, you can send them to graduate school, but when they're scared, they're scared.

— Warren E. Buffett, chairman of Berkshire Hathaway

Are markets efficient? The consensus seems to be 'Yes, most of the time.' However, how efficient they are depends on whom you ask. Graham's personification of the stock market as the manic-depressive 'Mr Market' is still an apt description of auction-driven markets today. We've established that the correct way to think about a share of a business is not as a rapidly fluctuating number on a screen but as a proportional share in the underlying business. This means we need to adopt the mindset of the long-term owner of an unlisted business – an owner who does not require a share price to tell him what his business is worth. Of course, this is hard for a public markets investor to do, because, unlike the private business owner, they have access to the temptation of instant market liquidity.

Because of their slow-moving nature, you could argue that businesses are fundamentally unsuited for public markets. The fickle nature of a constantly changing share price is easier to understand when we compare it to another asset: property.

Say you own your own home. If you call an estate agent today and ask for a valuation, they will be able to advise you very quickly based on the current market sentiment, comparable sales in your area, and the features of your property. Let's say they value your home at $500,000. If you were to call the agent every day for a month to ask if the value had changed, they would think you were, at best, slightly crazy. In normal circumstances, the value of your property just does not change that quickly. The same is true with businesses. The value of a business doesn't fluctuate a great deal on a daily, weekly, monthly, or even a yearly basis.

Now imagine you had a friend who came to your home every day and made you an offer to buy it. Some days, he was in a good mood and offered a bit more than the estate agent's valuation, but on other days, when he was in a bad mood, he would offer a bit less. Now it would be your turn to think your friend was slightly crazy. However, if he was feeling incredibly flush and offered you twice the 'fair' or 'intrinsic' value, you might agree to sell. If he was feeling blue, and offered you much less, you would (hopefully politely) tell him to go away. These are logical and intelligent reactions to strange situations. So why, when the share price of their carefully researched company halves, do most investors think it's a good idea to sell instead of buying more?

As mentioned in Chapter 3, most individual stocks, when examined, have a very wide fifty-two-week range. It is very unlikely that the value of the underlying business of each stock has genuinely fluctuated so much. The same goes for the market in general. Just look at the change in the S&P 500, one of the largest and most liquid capitalisation indexes in the world. Decide for yourself whether you believe that the combined fundamental values of all the underlying businesses fluctuated by as much as the index did. [FIG. 3]

How then, with this evidence, can anyone possibly conclude that the financial markets are efficient?

The performance of IPOs is another area of intrigue for most market participants. Everyone likes to look at the 'shiny new thing' and Wall Street loves to promise exclusive access to IPOs. But the entire IPO process is nothing

3 The Difference Between Price and Value

Period	Change in Index
1996 – 2000	Doubled
2000 – 2002	Halved
2002 – 2007	Doubled
2007 – 2009	Halved
2009 – 2019	Tripled

SOURCE: Bloomberg

more than a marketing exercise designed to convince non-investors that they should buy shares from IPO insiders who have decided to sell all or a portion of their holdings. Remember, these insiders know everything there is to know about the company. If its future prospects are so great, then why are they selling? This information asymmetry alone should raise an immediate red flag for investors to approach IPOs with extreme caution. 'Caveat emptor' (Latin for 'buyer beware') should be written all over every IPO prospectus!

J.P. Morgan once undertook a study analysing the performances of IPOs versus the broader market. Using data from 7,000 IPOs since 1980, they evaluated each post-IPO performance (i.e. after the close of the first day) for the following three years and compared it to the performance of the broader market, and also to a group of stocks with similar market caps and price-to-book ratios. The charts below show the results based on the year of the IPO. There are, obviously, large differences between individual stocks, but overall they concluded that post-IPO performances were not significantly better than diversified equity market alternatives. [FIGS. 4 & 5]

A closer look at the data shows that IPOs of smaller firms (~$50 million of sales in 2011) tended to perform worse than larger ones. This was particularly true of technology and biotechnology IPOs. Caveat emptor!

4 Post-IPO Returns vs. The Market
Average 3-year buy-and-hold IPO returns vs. the market

SOURCE: 'Initial Public Offerings: Updated Statistics on Long-run Perfomance' Ritter (Univ. of Florida) April 2014
NOTE: Returns for stock within 3 years of IPO are through 12/31/2013. Ritter defines the broad market using an index from the Chicago Booth School (Center for Research in Security Prices) which incorporates all stocks on the Amex, Nasdaq and NYSE exchanges.

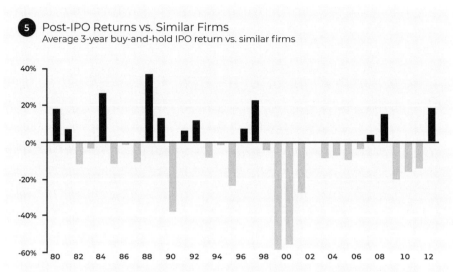

5 Post-IPO Returns vs. Similar Firms
Average 3-year buy-and-hold IPO return vs. similar firms

SOURCE: 'Initial Public Offerings: Updated Statistics on Long-run Perfomance' Ritter (Univ. of Florida) April 2014
NOTE: Returns for stock within 3 years of IPO are through 12/31/2013. Ritter defines the broad market using an
index from the Chicago Booth School (Center for Research in Security Prices) which incorporates all stocks on
the Amex, Nasdaq and NYSE exchanges.

Not So Efficient After All

In his latter years, George Soros has become somewhat of a financial markets philosopher. He contends, through his theory of reflexivity, that not only do prices influence other prices, but they in turn influence business fundamentals in a feedback loop. Thus, markets don't just anticipate economic developments; they also drive them and are, in turn, driven by them, because 'human beings are not merely scientific observers but also active participants in the system.' Soros uses his theory to demonstrate the limits to both understanding and predictability in a self-referential system – a system where observers are part of what they are observing. In other words, going back to the irrationalities of human behaviour, the market is not efficient because the people in the market prevent it from being efficient.

On 17 May 1984, an event was held at the Columbia University School of Business in honour of the fiftieth anniversary of the publication of Benjamin Graham's and David Dodd's value-investing bible, *Security Analysis*. During the event, Warren Buffett took to the stage to refute the accuracy of the efficient market hypothesis, stating that his success was down to more than just luck, as EMH followers had suggested. Remember, according to the proponents of EMH, stock prices reflect all available information about companies, and investors can't beat the market indexes by picking stocks. They say investors trying to find a secret formula are wasting their time because stock prices follow a random path or 'walk'. Interestingly, this theory also implies that a monkey selecting stocks by throwing darts at a newspaper's financial pages should perform as well as any 'star fund manager' who may or may not use inside information.

Of course, EMH was a huge relief for millions of stock market investors. Suddenly they didn't need to worry about market timing or stock-picking skills. Since all the information was incorporated into stock prices, there was no need to do any research about the companies or the macroeconomic or regulatory environment. Want to invest in an internet start-up that sells pet toys, with $30 million in revenue, $50 million in losses and $6 billion in market cap (Pets.com in 1999)? Don't worry. Markets are efficient. The share price is accurate; just buy it. Simple as that! Epilogue: Pets.com filed for bankruptcy in 2000.

Buffett proceeded to show the significantly market-beating track records that he and eight other 'super investors of Graham and Doddsville' enjoyed. All had apprenticed under the teachings of Ben Graham. Each had trounced the market averages over time by looking for value with a significant margin of safety relative to the price paid. Buffett gave the analogy of a coin-flipping contest in which all nine investors participated against everyone else in the market and, as a group, they all came out ahead, thus showcasing the superiority of their method. [FIG. 6] Buffett added,

> So these are nine records of 'coin-flippers' from Graham-and-Doddsville. I haven't selected them with hindsight from among thousands. It's not like I am reciting to you the names of a bunch of lottery winners – people I had never heard of before they won the lottery. I selected these men years ago based upon their framework for investment decision-making. I knew what they had been taught and additionally I had some personal knowledge of their intellect, character, and temperament. It's very important to understand that this group has assumed far less risk than average; note their record in years when the general market was weak. While they differ greatly

6 Returns of the Super Investors of Graham and Doddsville

Fund	Manager	Investment approach and constraints	Fund Period	Fund Return	Market return
WJS Limited Partners	Walter J. Schloss	Diversified small portfolio (over 100 stocks, US$45M), second-tier stock	1956 – 1984	21.3% / 16.1%	8.4% (S&P)
TBK Limited Partners	Tom Knapp	Mix of passive investments and strategic control in small public companies	1968 – 1983	20.0% / 16.0%	7.0% (DJIA)
Buffett Partnership, Ltd	Warren Buffett	Various undervalued assets, including American Express, Dempsters, Sun Newspapers, and prominently Berkshire Hathaway	1957 – 1969	29.5% / 23.8%	7.4% (DJIA)
Sequoia Fund, Inc.	William J. Ruane	Preference for blue chip stock	1970 – 1984	18.2%	10.0%
Charles Munger, Ltd.	Charles Munger	Concentration on a small amount of undervalued stock	1962 – 1975	19.8% / 13.7%	5.0% (DJIA)
Pacific Partners, Ltd.	Rick Guerin		1965 – 1983	32.9% / 23.6%	7.8% (S&P)
Perlmeter Investments, Ltd	Stan Perlmeter		1965 – 1983	23.0% / 19.0%	7.0% (DJIA)
Washington Post Master Trust	3 different managers	Must keep 25% in fixed interest instruments	1978 – 1983	21.8%	7.0% (DJIA)
FMC Corporation Pension Fund	8 different managers		1975 – 1983	17.1%	12.6% (Becker Avg.)

SOURCE: https://www8.gsb.columbia.edu/sites/valueinvesting/files/files/Buffett1984.pdf

in style, these investors are, mentally, always buying the business, not buying the stock. A few of them sometimes buy whole businesses. Far more often they simply buy small pieces of businesses. Their attitude, whether buying all or a tiny piece of a business, is the same. Some of them hold portfolios with dozens of stocks; others concentrate on a handful. But all exploit the difference between the market price of a business and its intrinsic value.

I'm convinced that there is much inefficiency in the market. These Graham-and-Doddsville investors have successfully exploited gaps between price and value. When the price of a stock can be influenced by a 'herd' on Wall Street with prices set at the margin by the most emotional person, or the greediest person, or the most depressed person, it is hard to argue that the market always prices rationally. In fact, market prices are frequently nonsensical.

To conclude he said, 'Ships will sail around the world, but the Flat Earth Society will flourish. There will continue to be wide discrepancies between price and value in the marketplace, and those who read their Graham & Dodd will continue to prosper.'

Buffett's central point is irrefutable. When investment managers are viewed merely as sets of performance numbers, the handful of success stories can be dismissed as products of chance – the equivalent of the rarity of a ten-heads-in-a-row coin toss. But if investment managers are understood as belonging to distinct intellectual 'villages' or 'styles', their successes may be concentrated in a way that is not random. I belong to the village of value investing, Graham and Doddsville, and I invite you to join us.

Summary

Investors should take the view that markets, although mostly efficient, are inherently bad at estimating and then discounting the long-term growth and earnings streams of the businesses that comprise them. Therefore, the optimum strategy is to buy and hold quality companies.

There are other ways an investor can have an edge. Clearly, the more widely followed the market, sector or stock, the more efficiently priced it would be or the more rapidly it would correct a mispricing. As more and more investors find the investment, their buying and selling activity would cause the mispricing to disappear. For a value investor looking for anomalies, a good place to start searching would be with the least-followed or least-popular markets, sectors and stocks.

CHAPTER 5: MARKET CYCLES

Study the past if you wish to divine the future.

— Confucius, Chinese philosopher, fifth century BC

In my office, I keep a framed copy of the chart below. It shows the performance of the Dow Jones Industrial Average (DJIA) from its inception in 1896 to 2020. [FIG. 7]

As you can see, it shows a relentless upward trajectory punctuated by market corrections and recoveries spanning more than one hundred years. Every time I look at it, I'm amazed at how much history can fit into a single image and how cyclical that history is.

Cycles are an inherent part of life – from birth to growth and, ultimately, death. This is as true for us as it is for the sun, the planets and stars, and maybe even the universe itself. Everything around us is cyclical in one way or another. Nothing is constant. As Howard Marks likes to say, 'Trees do not grow to the sky.' No company can grow forever, even at the smallest of growth

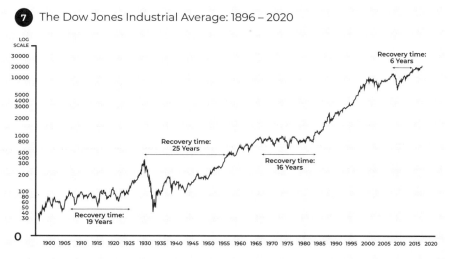

7 The Dow Jones Industrial Average: 1896 – 2020

SOURCE: Bloomberg

rates. Very few things go to zero and nothing moves in the same direction forever. This final point is very important for an investor. Most financial projections involve extrapolating today's conditions into the future. But as we discussed in Chapter 3, this is inherently dangerous. We already know from probability theory and life experience that the past does not always predict the future. If there is one guarantee in life and investing, it's that the future will remain unpredictable.

That said, by studying the events of the past and understanding the underlying cycles that are at play, we can get a better understanding of what markets are capable of and what range of behaviour might be expected in the future – *if* conditions in the future are similar to those in the past. Understanding market cycles is, therefore, a critical skill for the value investor.

Business Cycle and Longevity

As equity markets are made up of their constituent businesses, it makes sense to begin with examining the life cycle of business or industry. [FIG. 8]

The life cycle of an individual business will often follow that of the industry within which it operates. There is an initial period of growth, followed by a period of plateauing growth, or maturity, then, ultimately, decline. This is

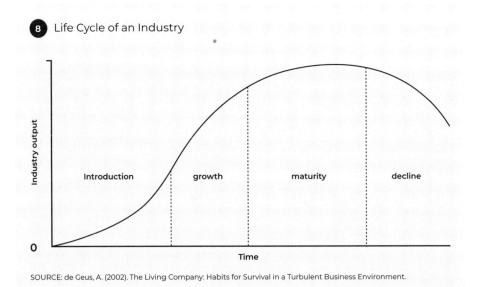

8 Life Cycle of an Industry

SOURCE: de Geus, A. (2002). The Living Company: Habits for Survival in a Turbulent Business Environment.

true for all companies and types of businesses regardless of how strong or large they may appear. As money manager and global investment strategist Barton Biggs said, 'If you're wealthy, just remember "nothing is forever" and pay attention to markets. They know more than they can tell.'

It may surprise you to learn that most businesses are bad businesses. In the developed world, data shows that the chances of a start-up surviving its first five years of operation are just 50 percent. Although 80 percent of businesses survive their first year, 50 percent fail by their fifth anniversary. And only around 30 percent are still around to celebrate their tenth.

The idea of 'creative destruction', first advanced by the noted economist Joseph Schumpeter in 1942, is still relevant today. Creative destruction says that no business is unassailable and that, ultimately, every impassable moat surrounding a business today will eventually be drained or crossed and the business within destroyed. If we look back in time, we can see that this is the case. For example, of the hundreds of companies listed on the New York Stock Exchange in 1911, only one, General Electric, is still in business (and only just!) over 110 years later.

Business theorist Arie de Geus studied the life expectancies of companies of all sizes and was very surprised to find that the average Fortune 500 company had a life expectancy of just forty to fifty years. This is interesting. The Fortune 500 is a list of the 500 largest companies in the US – the largest economy in the world. These businesses represent, arguably, the best of the best. De Geus found that it took between twenty-five and thirty years from formation for a highly successful company to earn a spot on the Fortune 500. He also found that it typically took just twenty more years for that same company to cease to exist. His conclusion was sobering: the average Fortune 500 business is already past its prime by the time it makes the list.

None of the companies that comprise the current DJIA, known as components, existed when the index began back in 1896. In fact, when I look back at the previous largest companies in the world over any ten-year period, it always amazes me how quickly those companies have declined or been usurped by competitors.

Although the rate of change in the business world today has arguably accelerated compared to Schumpeter's time, as Buffett remarks, 'The key to investing is not assessing how much an industry is going to affect society, or how much it will grow, but rather determining the competitive advantage of any given company and, above all, the durability of that advantage.'

Most cars in the future will have non-combustion engines. Most likely, they will be electric. Therefore, the EV industry is going to change society significantly. However, from an investment perspective, the real question is what part of the auto industry, if any, has a durable competitive advantage to monetise this transformation and reward its investors? Will it be the original equipment manufacturers (OEMs) such as Tesla or a parts supplier such as CATL (batteries), or an entirely new business that develops self-driving electric cars?

Business Longevity Identifiers

Value investors need a way of identifying business longevity. In my experience, the three simplest ways are:

- Economies of scale
- Network effects
- First mover advantage

Economies of Scale

Economies of scale are the cost advantages that are gained as companies get larger and produce more, thus allowing them to negotiate their input costs down and increase production through efficiencies that reduce their marginal cost of production.

In today's knowledge-based economy, increasing returns through economies of scale is still advantageous. Products such as computers, pharmaceuticals and aircraft are expensive and complicated to design and manufacture, requiring large initial investments in research, development, and tooling. But once sales begin, incremental production is relatively cheap. A new aircraft engine, for example, typically costs between $2 billion and $3 billion to design, develop, certify, and put into production. Yet each subsequent unit costs between $50 and $100 million to produce. Therefore, unit costs fall and profits increase as more units are produced. Many great businesses take advantage of strong economies of scale to widen and deepen their moats against marauding competitors.

Businesses that survive over long periods of time usually have very wide and deep moats that keep their competitors at bay and their profits to themselves. In general, as Buffett would say, 'They can be run by idiots, which is important, as one day they will be.'

Network Effects

In today's widely interconnected world, economists have recognised a new effect called the 'network effect', which is having a significant impact on many business models. The network effect is the phenomenon by which the value or utility derived from a good or service by a user depends on the number of users of compatible products. The more users, the greater the value. Do you know anyone who doesn't use Microsoft Word no matter what computer or operating system they use? Or what about Apple? That company is now synonymous with the smartphone. People will often not even ask what brand of phone you own; they will ask you what model of iPhone it is. This is an example of the network effect at work. In Apple's case, the more people using iPhones, the bigger the network gets and the more developers develop apps for it, making it even more useful, which further increases demand and increases the network.

As more and more people buy or use a product, it becomes more valuable, and others will feel more compelled to use it, thus establishing a self-reinforcing moat around the business.

First Mover Advantage

First mover advantage is a constant source of debate between economists and business school professors. Some MBA courses teach that you should let others lead and learn from their mistakes once they have proved the market is viable and profitable. This strategy is tied to the free-market assumption that the company with the best product always wins, regardless of when it entered the market.

However, in technology or high-knowledge businesses, this may not be the case. First movers in this space may capture the market in such a way that a new and potentially superior late arrival cannot gain a commercial footing. Investors need to understand that the best product doesn't necessarily always win if the market has already been captured by an incumbent. Especially if that incumbent also enjoys network effects.

This concept of 'lock-in' was first noted by the economist Alfred Marshall during a period of immense technological change (the Industrial Revolution of the 1800s). In his *Principles of Economics*, published in 1890, he noted that 'if firms' production costs fall as their market share increases, a firm that by good fortune gained a high proportion of the market early on would be able to best its rivals; whichever firm first gets off to a good start could corner the market.'

Each of these three factors – economies of scale, network effects and first mover advantage – create wide and deep business moats that protect businesses from competitors and extend their longevity.

Observing where a company is in the business cycle can help value investors. This deeper insight allows us to be better prepared to take advantage of opportunities that arise during periods of market panic or euphoria. If the market is panicking, for example, but we know that a stock is in its growth phase, this may be a confirmatory buy signal. If the market is euphoric but a stock is moving into decline, this may be a perfect time to rebalance our portfolio and take advantage of that euphoria. This aligns seamlessly with our goals as contrarian value investors.

Market Cycles

In addition to business cycles there are also market cycles – the recurring patterns of economic expansion (bull markets) and contraction (bear markets).

These market cycles create the extremes that provide value investors with opportunity. For every peak there must be a trough, and vice versa, as we oscillate around the mean. Cycles are self-correcting, and peaks will either collapse under their own weight or be knocked back by unanticipated external events. When you hear people saying 'This time is different,' run! What goes up too quickly must come down – and the descent is usually much faster.

The further we go to either extreme, the faster the rebound. Like the action of a pendulum, markets frequently overshoot in alternate directions, never quite coming to rest at the mean.

This pendulum swing creates a no-man's-land between the extremes of 'rich' and 'cheap' in an individual stock or sector. [FIG. 9]

In no-man's-land there is no need for action; we may not even know whether the pendulum is closer to 'rich' or 'cheap', but at the extremes of

9 Mastering The Market Cycle

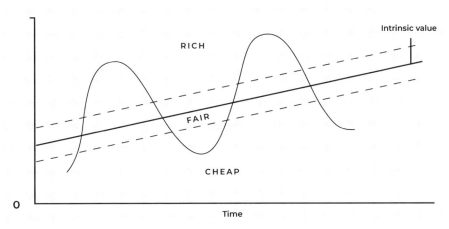

SOURCE: Marks, H. (2018). Mastering The Market Cycle: Getting the Odds on Your Side.

either swing it will be clear to us from the actions of those around us (greed or panic) that now is either the time to add to cheap businesses or rebalance away from those valued too richly.

I think there are two main reasons why markets will always be cyclical in nature. The first is greed. It is in our very nature to always want more and to push markets to positive extremes, or 'bubble territory'.

However, these excesses must always be corrected. When we look at the past, no business, economy or market

Bubble Territory

'Bubble territory' refers to a situation where the price of an asset (or even an entire sector or market) exceeds its fundamental value by a significant margin, thereby creating the conditions for a speculative bubble.

has ever moved upwards or downwards in a vertical line. The investor who understands market cycles adds a very valuable string to their bow if they are skilled at hunting for good returns.

The second reason is that the collective memory of all investors participating in the market is relatively static. New investors join who have never seen a bubble or a crash, and old ones leave who have seen too many. As the economist John Kenneth Galbraith wrote, 'Extreme brevity of the financial memory keeps market participants from recognizing the recurring nature of these patterns and thus their inevitability.' If only more participants were better educated in market history, perhaps the markets would be less cyclical.

Mean Regression Revisited

You have to be more [wary] as markets go higher and conversely get more excited as markets go lower. [This is similar to Buffett's advice 'To be greedy when others are fearful and fearful when others are greedy.']

— Howard Marks, co-founder and chairman of Oaktree Capital Management

As discussed in Chapter 3, regression to the mean is one of the most powerful forces in business and financial markets. Like gravity, it is inescapable. Regression to the mean, also known as mean reversion, ensures that periods of high returns are followed by periods of lower returns, and vice versa. It's essential to understand this phenomenon not only when it comes to risk but also for cycles. How mean regression occurs in markets, though, can vary substantially. It can happen if there are no more incremental buyers during a time of market euphoria, which leads to a crash. Or when an external shock, such as the Covid pandemic, causes confidence to fall and markets to reprice. However, the most common way is through the dynamics of competition.

A business or sector making extraordinary profits will inevitably attract competitors keen to secure a slice of the excess returns. First there was Pizza Hut, then, two years later, Domino's. First there was Uber, then, three years later, Lyft. A competitor offering a similar product or service seeks to carve market share and profit from the incumbent. This competition lessens the overall profitability of the incumbent, and the process continues as further newcomers enter the industry (e.g. Papa Johns and Bolt). Profitable companies or industries attract competition, and this leads to mean reversion of profit margins. The same forces push out underperforming competitors in loss-making industries; less competition can mean higher profits for the remaining companies, and so the cycle begins again.

From this process, what economists call 'theory of the firm', we can deduce two general rules. The first is that overvalued stocks must eventually underperform undervalued stocks because profitable industries generating huge profits attract competition. Meanwhile, competition in loss-making industries pushes businesses out until the industry overall becomes profitable again. Therefore, the stock prices of undervalued stocks are likely to rise over time, and the stock prices of expensive stocks fall – regression to the mean.

The second is the importance of moats. Highly profitable businesses generating extraordinary profits can only retain those levels of profit if they enjoy the protection of significant barriers to entry either into the industry or in creating or delivering the product or service. Without a significant and defensible moat, highly profitable businesses will quickly revert to the mean as their profits are eaten away by competitors.

We contrarian investors can take advantage of mean regression. We know that undervalued stocks with low returns on equity or falling profits tend to eventually beat the market, while hot stocks with high returns and growth tend to lag the market over time – remember J.P. Morgan's analysis on IPOs in Chapter 4. This is because stock prices always revert to their intrinsic value over time. That is, expensive stocks go down and undervalued stocks go up. When we perform our financial analyses, we need to remember that returns on equity and earnings growth rates also regress to the mean. In other words, high returns on equity will go down; high rates of earnings growth will slow; low returns on equity will rise; and low or negative earnings growth will tend to improve. A great deal of statistical and empirical evidence supports these trends. This should give an investor an additional level of comfort when undertaking a contrarian investment strategy.

Managing Market Cycles

No victory is everlasting; no defeat forever: 'the pendulum swings.'
– Benjamin Disraeli, UK Prime Minister 1874–1880

When it comes to media speculation about markets, it is always important to remember that it is just that: speculation. As billionaire fund manager Michael Steinhardt wrote:

> Only when everyone says the market will fall does it then turn, i.e. the point of maximum bearishness is the turn. Time and time again, in every market cycle I have witnessed, the extremes of emotion always

appear, even amongst experienced investors. ... Euphoria is a sign of a market top, fear is, for sure, a sign of a market bottom. ... When the world wants to buy treasury bills, you can almost close your eyes and get long stocks.

The amplitude of market cycles can be prolonged. The DJIA fell 90 percent to its nadir during the crash of 1929 and the subsequent Great Depression. It took twenty-five years and an 825-percent gain to get back to where it had been (or ten years if allowing for dividends reinvested). Future crashes will not be carbon copies of what has happened in the past. But as the maxim that has been attributed to Mark Twain reminds us, 'History never repeats itself but it rhymes.' Similarly, philosopher George Santayana wrote, 'Those who cannot remember the past are condemned to repeat it.' One thing is certain: there will be constant change in the constituents of any index. In 1970, IBM seemed unstoppable. In 1990, Microsoft made the technology industry quake in terror. Companies grow older; success breeds complacency; and the departure of top talent in search of new challenges after exercising pre-IPO options on equity is inevitable. Therefore, having conviction in your investment process, especially when the market performance is leaving you behind, is critical.

For contrarian investors, it is a fact of life that if we want to outperform the market or an index over time, we must be doing something different. Inevitably, there will be periods, sometimes extended periods, when we underperform that market or index. As Buffett wrote after he had been called a dinosaur for missing the tech bubble of the late nineties, only to see it pop in 2000, 'I will not abandon a previous approach whose logic I understand even though it may mean foregoing large, and apparently easy profits to embrace an approach which I don't fully understand, have not practiced successfully and which, possibly, could lead to a substantial permanent loss of capital.' Now, *that* is the courage of one's convictions!

If a particular sector gets hammered and you don't have any companies from this sector in your portfolio or watchlist, sometimes an alternative strategy is required. As Howard Marks reminds us,

> If we don't change our investment stance as these things change, we're being passive with regards to cycles; in other words, we're ignoring the chance to tilt the odds in our favour. But if we apply some insight

regarding cycles, we can increase our bets and place them on more aggressive investments when the odds are in our favour, and we can take money off the table and increase our defensiveness when the odds are against us.

As the March 2022 Covid crisis sell-off of the S&P 500 showed, we experienced a technical bear market (−20 percent) and subsequent recovery (+25 percent) within thirty-three days. The fastest-ever recovery; the historical average recovery period is thirteen months. [FIG. 10]

There were specific reasons why this recovery was so fast, namely, government stimulus and support packages, both of which alleviated fears in the market. It was a potent reminder that we must be prepared to act fast. It takes significant time to research individual equities, especially in a relatively unfamiliar or beaten-down sector, especially when business conditions are changing rapidly. However, if you believe the sector overall represents value at its current levels, the best strategy may be to take a 'basket approach' whereby, instead of selecting one company, you buy a basket of three to five individual companies that you think represent the best overall value.

I used this strategy when the oil price briefly went negative for the first time in history (21 April 2020) during the Covid pandemic. During this time,

10 Performance of Financial Assets in America from 1800 to 2024

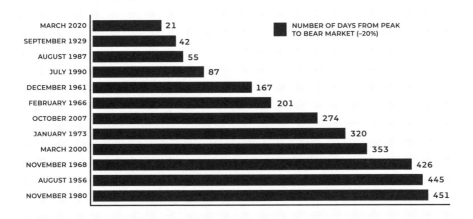

SOURCE: BoA Research Investment Committee, Bloomberg

all US shale producer stock prices tanked, and the sector went off some 70 percent from its pre-pandemic highs. I had done some research into the oil and gas sector and, in particular, the dynamics of US shale oil producers. The technology interested me, even though I try to steer clear of capital-intensive and cyclical sectors. At the time of the crash, I purchased the three least-indebted US shale producers that I liked the most. My reasoning was that the oil price could not stay negative forever and the last shale producer left standing would be able to earn extraordinary profits and buy the best assets off their weakened or bankrupted competitors for a song.

The last man standing was likely to be the one that had the least amount of debt and the lowest extraction costs. As I didn't know the sector well enough, I bought three stocks. Fast forward two years, and although most of the shale producers did not go bankrupt, my selected three were able to capitalise on the situation with their share prices increasing by a combined 240 percent. You never really know a business until you own it, and as I got to know the three companies better, I sold two of them and reinvested the proceeds into the third (Marathon Oil) which I came to recognise was by far the best operator in the sector.

Of course, this strategy presents stock selection risk, as we don't know enough about the companies; therefore, having a few eggs in the basket, as opposed to one, offers a better chance to mitigate risk. When faced with this type of unique situation, a concentrated value investor is unwise not to take advantage of great companies going on sale.

Sense-Checking Market Moves

To arrive at a conclusion, you must ask yourself questions such as, Are investors appropriately sceptical and risk averse or are they ignoring risks and happily paying up? Are valuations reasonable relative to historical standards? Are deal structures fair to investors? Is there too much faith in the future?

— Howard Marks, co-founder and chairman of Oaktree Capital Management

John Maynard Keynes wrote about the tendency of even the most inde-pendently minded investors to succumb to the random price action of the market, especially during bubbles and panics, and how we rationalise our behaviour:

1. We assume that the present is a much more serviceable guide to the future than a candid examination of past experience would show it to have been hitherto. In other words, we largely ignore the prospect of future changes about the actual character of which we know nothing.
2. We assume that the existing state of opinion as expressed in prices and the character of existing output is based on a correct summing up of future prospects.
3. Knowing that our own individual judgement is worthless, we endeavour to fall back on the judgement of the rest of the world which is perhaps better informed. That is, we endeavour to conform with the behaviour of the majority or the average.

These points are as valid today as they were when they were written in 1937. The longer the bull (or bear) market continues, the more it becomes the norm and the favourable (or unfavourable) conditions are projected forward via earnings expectations. From this perspective, it is easy to see how bull and bear markets gather momentum the longer they last, becoming self-fulfilling prophecies.

There is always one market pundit or analyst who will correctly predict a significant move either up or down. Of course, if you throw enough darts at the dartboard one will eventually hit the bullseye. We already know that the future is unknowable, despite the number of market commentators who will constantly and confidently predict as if it were otherwise. This one lucky pundit is soon on the front cover of every investor magazine and touted around TV shows as the next investment sage. People hang off their every word as they continue to 'predict' the future. Everyone, including the man of the moment, completely forgets that they can't possibly know the future. As mentioned in Chapter 3, people love certainty. People, therefore, also love people in positions of authority or who are recognised as experts because they can tell them what to do or what will happen. (More on authority bias in Chapter 8.) We investors need to remember that the most important philosophy to follow is our own.

The market is a tool for you to use, but its behaviour should not drive your actions. We are the master, and the market is our servant – not vice versa. This quote from *The Intelligent Investor* captures the essence perfectly:

The true investor can take advantage of the daily market price or leave it alone, as dictated by his own judgment and inclination. He must take cognizance of important price movements, for otherwise his judgments will have nothing to work on. Basically, price fluctuations have only one significant meaning for the true investor. They provide him with an opportunity to buy wisely when prices fall sharply and sell wisely when they advance a great deal. At other times he will do better if he forgets about the stock market and pays attention to the operating results of his companies.

It is also wise to recognise that regardless of how robust your investment process is, your portfolio will still be subject to the vicissitudes of the market. As value investors, we can expect significant performance deviation from any benchmark for considerable periods of time, as academic and billionaire fund manager Joel Greenblatt points out:

> Looking at just the top-quartile (best performing 25 percent) of managers over a recent decade, almost all of these top performing managers (96 percent) spent at least one three-year period during that decade in the bottom half of the performance rankings. Even more telling, 79 percent spent at least three years in the bottom quartile (bottom 25 percent of managers) and a staggering 47 percent spent at least three years in the bottom 10 percent. In other words, even the best performing managers go through long periods of significant underperformance.

These results make perfect sense to contrarian investors. Only by seeking to do something different from the index can we hope to outperform it. As a result, there will always be periods of time, sometimes extended, where our strategy is out of favour and underperforms.

I believe that the very best investors have an inner calm that is almost impossible to disturb regardless of cycles or market price action. It is not that they don't care about 'paper losses' or 'perceived underperformance' relative to a benchmark across extended periods of time. It's just that they don't allow this to pollute their investment process.

This emotional fortitude is often gained via direct experience when we are young. Witnessing the ups and downs of family finances or of those we know well when we are growing up – or experiencing financial hardship ourselves – can have a particular effect on a child's cognitive make-up. I can still remember the yellow walls of the ground-floor office in Australia where I did my homework after school and where I was when I first learnt of a significant blow to our family finances. My mother knocked on the door and said she needed to speak to me. She told me that my father's business had failed and that, therefore, they could no longer afford to send me to the select school I was attending (Sydney Grammar). Even now, I can vividly remember the awful feeling of my thirteen-year-old self's small world disappearing. The dread of having to go back to my old local high school and never seeing my friends again. I think there are certain events in our lives, both positive and negative, that determine our paths in life. This event was certainly mine. I never wanted to be in a situation again where money decided whether or not I would be able to continue living my life the way that I wanted to. In my case, the headmaster awarded me a scholarship, so I was able to remain at my school. I will always be grateful for that act of kindness.

People who make their own money often have a resilience to loss as well as hardship, as they believe that they can do it all again if required. This is certainly true for me – on both counts. Not only through experiencing my parents' entrepreneurial ups and downs but also my own. Failure began early for me, with 'The Console Club', which I founded at age seven to trade PlayStation and Nintendo 64 games with my friends at school. Parents paid £5 as 'insurance' for their child to rent a game for one week. If they returned the game in good condition, they got their £5 back. However, there was always one kid who damaged the game, so I had to buy a new game to replace it out of my savings. Alongside learning that reputation is key when building a business, it also taught me the lesson about sizing my 'insurance float' right – as, otherwise, you will be out of business quick!

My second business was an online retail store established in Australia when I was eleven years old. It generated over $1,000 a month in profit. I got electronic toys and gadgets shipped from Shenzhen, China, to Sydney and then sold them on eBay; I was 'buying wholesale and selling retail'. However, as the business got more successful, my orders got larger and larger, and they needed to be prepaid. After almost eighteen months of running this business, I sent my biggest prepayment yet – and the goods never arrived! My supplier had taken the money and disappeared! It taught me a very valuable lesson:

do business only with people that you like, admire and trust. Experiencing failures early and learning from them has been an essential part of my development as a businessman and an investor.

When looking for the best investment managers, I believe we want people who understand the value of money but are not enthralled by it. We want people who can separate whatever is going on at work from what is going on at home and who can separate the noise in their portfolios and associated fund performance from their own sense of self-worth. The investors who truly understand their own emotional make-up and can use it to their advantage are the ultimate contrarians.

Summary

Resilience and perseverance are essential character traits for success in life and markets. We need these qualities to survive the cycles. Every successful investor or businessperson has endured their own personal cycles. The key to their success has been the ability to keep going, keep learning, and keep evolving, so they thrive in the face of adversity. They are the ultimate contrarians. Only by learning from failures and disappointments can we put this new knowledge to work and rise to the next peak, leading to even greater success in the long run.

I will leave the final words on market cycles to financial journalist Maggie Mahar:

> A history of financial cycles cannot pretend to protect investors against losses. As everyone knows, history is a poor teacher, and human beings poor students in the classroom. Nevertheless, if one truly thought that men and women were doomed simply to repeat their mistakes, only misanthropes would write history – and only masochists would read it.
>
> In truth, a knowledge of history is an investor's best defence against error. Despite all the financial engineering that attempts to eliminate risk, cycles appear to be as inevitable as the seasons. Investors who understand these cycles are more likely to survive the winter of a bear market and to avoid its final phase – despair. They know that eventually, summer always returns, and more than that, they know that somewhere on the planet it is always summer.

CHAPTER 6: DIFFERENT INVESTMENT APPROACHES

Never adopt permanently any type of asset or any selection method. Try to stay sceptical, open minded and flexible.

> – Sir John Templeton, fund manager of the Templeton Growth Fund

Clearly, there are many different investment approaches, but from a value-investing perspective it's definitely worth knowing about three of the main ones:

1. Active vs. passive investing
2. Growth vs. value investing
3. Diversification vs. concentration

Active vs. Passive Investing

Paradoxically when 'dumb' money acknowledges its limitations, it ceases to be dumb.

> – Terry Smith, founder and CIO of Fundsmith

When successful investors discuss active versus passive investing, the vast majority advocate in favour of passive investing for the individual investor. They all acknowledge that to be successful in the investing space in the long run is a very difficult task. Research also indicates that it is difficult to improve on the results delivered by broadly diversified index investments. Economists have rigorously shown that the financial markets are not perfectly efficient, as discussed in Chapter 4.

But opportunities certainly exist for active investors. Some stocks will, at times, sell for prices that are low relative to their intrinsic value, and others will, at times, be overvalued. In his 2017 paper titled 'Do stocks outperform Treasury Bills?' Professor Hendrick Bessembinder concluded thus: 'The results in this paper imply that the returns to active stock selection can be very large, if the investor is either fortunate or skilled enough to select a concentrated portfolio containing stocks that go on to earn extreme positive returns.' Buffett and his eight investors of Graham and Doddsville also demonstrated that huge outperformance of any passive index is achievable over time.

Here we will examine what separates active and passive investing.

As we have already established, markets are zero-sum games – for every winner, there is a loser. In fact, when you subtract the frictional costs – management fees, custody/brokerage/settlement charges, slippage and bid–offer spread – each time you trade, it's clear that participating in markets is a significantly negative-sum proposition. In other words, the odds are stacked against you. And this does not even include the tax costs of portfolio churn, in which most fund managers engage. The net result is that most investors do not make the same return as the benchmark. They will often substantially underperform it.

To select a well-diversified portfolio of great businesses and manage them well over time is essentially a full-time job. Most people do not have the time to do this while also doing their normal day job. Yet investing is still widely recognised as the way to build long-term wealth. The solution: enter the world of passive investing. Index funds promise to track the selected benchmark, for example, the S&P 500 or FTSE 100. Some funds such as Vanguard have millions of investors, and the economies of scale that this generates allows them to provide their services for almost no cost. This is a phenomenal deal for investors, as the S&P 500, for example, has returned roughly 8 percent per year since inception and all the investor has had to do is not touch it. Which, as we have already seen for most investors, is all but impossible!

Alongside index funds, you have mutual funds and ETFs that select benchmarks and attempt to outperform them. These funds typically charge an annual fee based on a percentage of the assets under management (AUM). Unsurprisingly, the evidence suggests that this group of funds significantly underperforms their passive benchmarks over time. According to one widely credited study by Arnott et al., '95% of active investors lose to the passive alternative, dropping an average of 3.8% per annum relative to the equivalent index fund' (in this case, the Vanguard 500).

Both financial theory and real-world experience teach that most actively managed assets fail to exceed market returns. On average, investors lose by the amount of transaction costs incurred and management fees paid. I am yet to receive marketing material for a fund that wasn't 'top-quartile' – but how can everyone be top quartile? Any investor considering a fund needs to take extra care to check these claims. Over what period are they referring? Against which benchmark? Against which peer group? And top-quartile according to which study or external data provider? As has been attributed to the former UK Prime Minister Benjamin Disraeli, 'There are three kinds of lies: lies, damned lies, and statistics.' Fund marketing materials are another example where caveat emptor applies!

Passive Investing

The art of investment has one characteristic that is not generally appreciated. A creditable, if unspectacular, result can be achieved by the lay investor with a minimum of effort and capability; but to improve this easily attainable standard requires much appreciation and more than a trace of wisdom.

– Benjamin Graham, father of value investing and author of *The Intelligent Investor* and *Securities Analysis*

The above quote from Ben Graham neatly sums up the advantages of passive or index investing. If you are an index investor, you will not be the next Warren Buffett; you will not beat the market, but you can ensure you get the same return as the market over time, or very close to it (minus a few basis points). This approach requires two things. The first is steadfast conviction, that is, not selling when the market has gone down by half; the second is a recognition of your abilities as an investor. It takes a certain inner strength to acknowledge and accept that you can't beat the market and to instead choose not to even try. If you have no more than a passing interest in investing, or if you can't or don't want to dedicate full-time effort to it, then passive indexing makes sense. As mathematician and billionaire hedge fund manager Ed Thorpe says, 'You don't even have to do any work and you're ahead of maybe 80% of the people who do otherwise. … An index such as the S&P 500 will "probably" rise in the long run.'

If you do decide that indexing is the correct way for you to invest, I would follow billionaire fund manager Terry Smith's advice that a 'broadly-based index fund is often the best investment you can make in the equity markets'.

Be careful not to conflate exchange-traded funds (ETFs) and index funds. ETFs usually allow constant dealing, whereas index funds may only allow one trade per day. (To be clear, once a day is more than enough.) Index funds almost always cost less than ETF providers. Vanguard in particular, which was set up by the father of index investing, Jack Bogle, is especially well known for its cut-price fees. It is set up as a not-for-profit, so all income is reinvested to lower the fund charges – potentially the greatest philanthropic gift ever given by an individual to the masses. For a final piece of advice, David Swensen of the Yale Endowment wrote that 'sensible investors avoid the brokerage community, opting for the lower-cost, self-service alternative'. Remember this the next time someone approaches you to manage your wealth.

Academic and billionaire fund manager Joel Greenblatt has also published several books in which he has attempted to help amateur investors to beat the market. One of the interesting areas that he has explored is whether there is a smarter way of index investing than, say, just buying the S&P 500 Index and holding it for fifty years. Is there a value-investing approach to index investing?

Greenblatt's comparison of indexes that were fundamentally weighted (i.e. the most undervalued stocks had the highest weightings, and the most over-valued stocks had the lowest) with market capitalisation-weighted indexes (i.e. indexes such as the S&P 500 which apply weightings based on company size) found that the fundamentally weighted indexes had outperformed by 213 basis points per year over the forty-two years of data covered by his study. The indexes themselves broadly contained the same stocks; the weightings given them made the difference.

As Greenblatt wrote, 'An index that doesn't systematically own too much of the overpriced stocks and too little of the bargain-priced ones should provide us with even better long-term investment returns than the market-cap weighted indexes. Since market cap weighting, flawed as it is, appears to handily beat most active managers over time, that's pretty exciting.'

Active Investing

In any sort of contest – financial, mental or physical – it's an enormous advantage to have opponents who have been taught that it's useless to even try.

– Warren E. Buffett, chairman of Berkshire Hathaway

Given that the management fees associated with an active fund eat significantly into an investor's real returns and that over the long term, passive investing has been shown to outperform most active funds, active portfolio management starts on the back foot. You need to be an exceptional investor to consistently outperform the index over a significant period, especially in light of all the costs involved in trying to do so. When he was the CIO of the Yale Endowment, David Swensen used a portion of the endowment to pioneer investing through active asset managers. He found that the dispersion of returns – the 'performance gap' – between the top quartile of managers and the rest was about 10 percent per annum. Therefore, as an active investor, you need to select a fund in the top quartile to really outperform, but it is very hard to accurately determine which funds will be in the top quartile. This is also valuable for active portfolio managers themselves to realise: that any excess returns enjoyed by the industry are shared amongst a handful of firms at the very top. But as I have just mentioned, it is not always easy to know in advance which funds will be top-quartile performers.

All the evidence around investing points to patience being critical for exceptional returns. Activity is almost always detrimental to investment performance. If you are a portfolio manager at an asset management company with teams of analysts providing new stock ideas every day, you feel like you 'have to do something'; otherwise, what is the point of having the teams of analysts? Plus, when the boss asks for an update, you need to be able to explain what you've been doing for the past three months. You will almost certainly be putting your career at risk if your answer is 'Nothing.' Your investors may also call for an update and ask why your fund has underperformed the benchmark by 1.5 percent during the quarter. If you tell them that your current stocks are undervalued and you are not going to chase performance by selling them to buy today's hot new issues, the investors may very well pull their funds. This describes what Munger calls the 'institutional imperative'. He says, 'The institutional imperative in fund management is that fund managers must always be seen to be doing something; how else can they justify their fees?'

Fees are a particularly sensitive subject, because they can have a very pernicious effect on investment returns over time. This fact is well recognised by those who work in the industry. Very few active managers have all or most of their net worth invested in their own funds. Seth Klarman points out that this misalignment of managers with their investors leads to what is known as the principal–agent problem. Proposed by Michael Jensen and William Meckling, both former professors at the University of Rochester, the idea is that when managers of a fund don't have their own money invested or senior executives of a business are not shareholders, they don't have skin in the game. They may, therefore, make decisions that benefit them but not the investors or shareholders; their behaviour and actions may not be aligned with the best interests of the principals of the business or the owners of the capital. Thus, the principal–agent problem. Economist Paul Rosenstein-Rodan tells the story of Roman construction and the motivating nature of having 'skin in the game' or the 'tremble factor': 'In the building practices of ancient Rome, when scaffolding was removed from a completed Roman arch, the Roman engineer stood beneath. If the arch came crashing down, he was the first to know. Thus, his concern for the quality of the arch was intensely personal, and it is not surprising that so many Roman arches have survived.'

The only fair system that I have seen for active managers is the original 1950s model that Buffett created for his original hedge fund, the Buffett Partnerships. He charged no management fee, and the costs of running the fund, such as accounting and legal, were split between all the investors on a pro rata basis. Buffett did not take a salary, and his performance fee of 25 percent was applied only after he had achieved a set minimum return for his investors. He also applied a high-water mark: if he made 10 percent one year but lost 10 percent the following, he could not charge a performance fee until the fund was back above its previous high. Finally, he also invested his liquid net worth into the fund alongside his investors' money.

Buffett was explicit about the rules for investing with him from the outset and stated very clearly that the fund was for long-term-oriented investors only. In my eyes, this was perfect alignment of a manager with his investors. So close was the alignment that Buffett did not call them his 'investors'; he referred to them as his 'Partners', as they were in business together, as equals. Under this structure, Buffett compounded at over 30 percent per year for twelve years, with no leverage. Why do so few use this structure today? Personally, I think the answer is greed. At my own fund, we have used the original Buffett Partnerships as the model for our own structure.

As Buffett and his fellow investors from Graham and Doddsville have shown, with the correct investment strategy, it is possible to outperform the market. Once they have identified an exceptional fund manager, an investor would be foolish not to invest as much as they could with them.

In the end, it comes down to temperament and knowledge. Terry Smith illustrates this point when he tells the story of the infamous 1877 argument between art critic John Ruskin and American artist James Whistler over Whistler's painting *Nocturne In Black And Gold: The Falling Rocket*. Ruskin thought the painting was hideous and too expensive. He wrote in a review that he had 'never expected to see a coxcomb ask two hundred guineas for flinging a pot of paint in the public's face'. Whistler sued for libel. In court, Ruskin's counsel asked Whistler how long it had taken him to paint the work. His response was two days, which prompted the lawyer to ask, 'The labour of two days is that for which you ask 200 guineas?' 'No,' Whistler replied, 'I ask it for the knowledge I have gained in the work of a lifetime.' The point here is that all 'overnight successes' involve 'a lifetime of work', and a superior active investor will, and should, charge accordingly.

Summary

A low-cost index fund is the most sensible equity investment for the great majority of investors.

— Warren E. Buffett, chairman of Berkshire Hathaway

As mentioned previously, humans are social animals. We all like to believe that we are better than average. The investor who is willing to accept the average result over the long term through indexing and not be distracted when their neighbour doubles their money in a week by speculating is a truly exceptional individual. Such an investor will significantly outperform most investors over time. That said, the proliferation of index investing over active management will lead to more opportunities for the active managers who remain. As Howard Marks points out, 'Value Investing is about investing in undervalued companies; indexers buy all companies regardless of value. Therefore, as indexing grows as a percentage of the market, so value investing for those who remain true to it will perform better.'

Markets need active investors as a price-discovery mechanism. Passive investing is price-agnostic. If too great a proportion of the market is no longer focused on the relative value of each underlying business, won't this have a significantly distorting effect on the market? Li Lu, the billionaire fund manager of Himalaya Capital and the only external investor ever to have been seeded with capital by Charlie Munger, does not think we are at a tipping point – yet. He points out that the discipline of value investing has always been a very small part of all investors active in the market and that the advent of index investing may well give rise to more opportunities for true value investors.

Value vs. Growth Investing

Value and growth are joined at the hip.

— Warren E. Buffett, chairman of Berkshire Hathaway

In my opinion, the perennial debate of growth versus value is unnecessary. They are two sides of the same coin. Growth is a function of value that is incorporated in the projection of future earnings for the business, which we discount back to the present. Growth simply means higher earnings in the future that we need to adjust for and discount back to their present value today. Hence, the two are very closely related.

One of the most successful value investors of recent times is Nick Sleep of the Nomad Partnership, although he has closed his fund after deciding to manage his own money exclusively. During twelve years of operation, Sleep compounded at around 20 percent per annum net of fees. He has subsequently released his investor letters for public consumption, and they are well worth reading. His success came from recognising that there is no distinction between value and growth and that an optically expensive stock can, in truth, be cheap. This occurs when the future turns out to be significantly better than forecast because either the growth of a business is only just starting to accelerate or the length of its runway is not well recognised. The portfolio that he ran with partner Qais Zakaria started with about thirty similarly sized positions. However, over time, Amazon, Berkshire Hathaway and Costco, the best performing positions, came to dominate the portfolio, representing 90 percent of assets. This is concentrated value investing in its purest form. They let their winners run and allowed them to compound at well above market rates for a significant period.

Fund manager Bill Miller says that the growth–value distinction is not so much about the companies themselves but really a way to describe different types of investment managers. Value managers make valuation the critical driver in their approach. Growth managers focus on growth and underweight valuations. Miller was controversial among value investors because many saw the tech companies he was buying in the 1990s and 2000s as growth stocks, not value plays. He countered this argument with his belief that technology could be analysed on a business basis and that intrinsic value could be estimated. Using a value approach in the tech sector is a competitive advantage in an area dominated by investors who focus mainly or exclusively on growth and are, therefore, often ignored by those who focus on value.

Another important point: not all growth is created equal. For a start, there is organic growth generated internally and there is growth gained through acquisition. There is also growth financed by debt and growth financed by positive free cash flow. All should be weighted differently from an investment perspective because they impact value in different ways. Growth benefits investors only when the business can invest at enticing incremental returns. In other words, only when each dollar used to finance the growth creates more than a dollar of long-term market value. As Miller said, 'Growth is always a component in the calculation of value, constituting a variable whose importance can range from negligible to enormous and whose impact can be negative as well as positive.'

Indeed, growth can destroy value if it requires cash injections in the early years of a project or enterprise that exceed the discounted value of the cash that those assets will generate in later years (as usually occurs in empire-building projects by poor capital allocators, i.e. management). As Miller concludes on the subject, 'Market commentators and investment managers who glibly refer to "growth" and "value" styles as contrasting approaches to investment are displaying their ignorance, not their sophistication. Growth is simply a component – usually a plus, sometimes a minus – in the value equation.'

For me, the distinction between value and price is more important than that between growth and value. As Buffett once said, 'Price is what you pay, value is what you get.' Through his concept of 'Mr Market', Ben Graham taught us that price fluctuates more than value because it is humans who set prices in the short run. We investors must always remain aware of our own fallibility and the irrationality of markets. Cheap stocks can get cheaper; richly priced stocks can become richer; margins of safety can be miscalculated; and value can fail to materialise.

That said, historically, the strategy of buying the cheapest stocks in the market on various metrics relative to buying the most expensive stocks in the market on the same metrics has provided exceptional returns. This makes sense, as, often, the most expensive stocks are the hot stocks of the day or momentum plays, and they trade far above even the most optimistic futures. The cheap stocks are often relegated to the waste basket, ignored because they

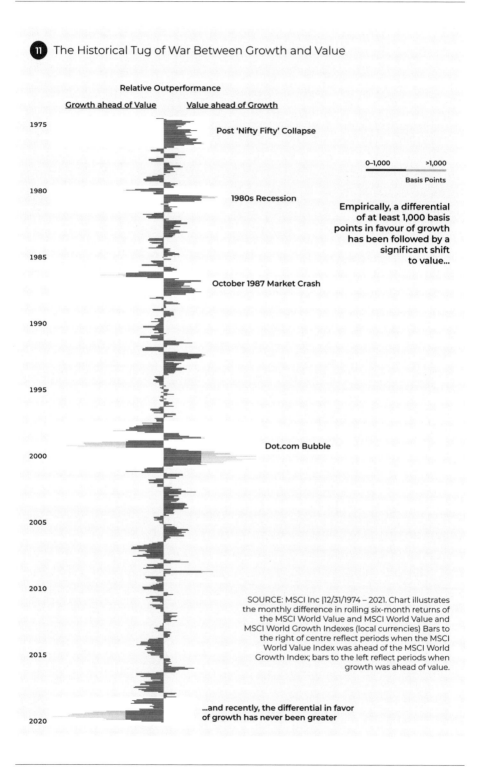

11 The Historical Tug of War Between Growth and Value

Relative Outperformance

Growth ahead of Value   Value ahead of Growth

1975

Post 'Nifty Fifty' Collapse

0–1,000   >1,000

Basis Points

1980

1980s Recession

Empirically, a differential
of at least 1,000 basis
points in favour of growth
has been followed by a
significant shift
to value...

1985

October 1987 Market Crash

1990

1995

Dot.com Bubble

2000

2005

2010

SOURCE: MSCI Inc |12/31/1974 – 2021. Chart illustrates
the monthly difference in rolling six-month returns of
the MSCI World Value and MSCI World Value and
MSCI World Growth Indexes (local currencies) Bars to
the right of centre reflect periods when the MSCI
World Value Index was ahead of the MSCI World
Growth Index; bars to the left reflect periods when
growth was ahead of value.

2015

...and recently, the differential in favor
of growth has never been greater

2020

are not sexy and trade far below intrinsic value. Obviously, if their earnings improve, their upside is significant relative to expectations.

Eugene Fama and Kenneth French, economists who believed that a firm's size and price were important inputs into how a firm should optimise its capital structure (mixture of debt and equity), have constructed indexes for growth and value and calculated their relative performance. Their research shows that value prevails over time, and the earlier you catch it (the smaller the company), the larger will be the upside. But you must be patient; growth can outperform value for significant periods of time. [FIG. 11]

Fama and French noticed in their research that smaller firms tended to outperform larger firms and cheaper firms tended to outperform richer firms. That is, if you bought shares in small businesses trading below their tangible book values, you tended to outperform people who bought shares in larger businesses trading far above their tangible book values. Ibbotson Associates, an investment firm that applied the so-called Fama–French Three Factor Model to funds they were managing, popularised the findings of this research.

Summary

Choosing between growth investing and value investing is not an either/or decision in most cases. Although growth investing focuses on companies with high growth potential and value investing looks for undervalued companies, growth always plays a part in the assessment of value.

To me, growth is just part of the value-investing equation in the assessment of a business's intrinsic value. Don't get bogged down in the terminology. In my experience, success often depends on picking your battles wisely.

Diversification vs. Concentration

'Tis the part of a wise man to keep himself today for tomorrow, and not venture all his eggs in one basket. [Motteux translation, 1700]

– Miguel de Cervantes, Spanish writer and author of Don Quixote

According to financial theory, diversification is the only 'free lunch' in markets. By owning a variety of financial assets or asset classes that align with your expected return, you are likely to enjoy a better return relative to the risk of volatility or portfolio variance taken. [FIG. 12]

This table by Robert Hagstrom illustrating the effects of diversification shows that with a single equity security in the portfolio, the risk that the annual return on the portfolio will deviate from the annual return of the market has a standard deviation of 49 percent. Adding a second security reduces the risk to 37 percent, a substantial reduction but still almost twice that of the market at an annual standard deviation of 19 percent. A portfolio containing twenty securities eliminates 85 percent of the idiosyncratic or market risk. A portfolio with thirty securities eliminates 88 percent of the market risk – just 3 percent more. Hagstrom concludes that, 'The additional gains beyond 30

12 Effect of Diversification

Number of Stocks in Portfolio	Expected Standard Deviation of Annual Portfolio Returns (%)	Ratio of Portfolio Standard Deviation to Standard Deviation of a Single Stock
1	49.24	1.00
2	37.36	0.76
4	29.69	0.60
6	26.64	0.54
8	24.98	0.51
10	23.93	0.49
12	23.20	0.47
14	22.26	0.46
16	21.94	0.45
18	21.20	0.45
20	21.68	0.44
25	21.20	0.43
30	20.87	0.42
40	20.46	0.42
50	20.20	0.41
400	19.29	0.39
500	19.27	0.39
1,000	19.21	0.39
Infinity	19.16	0.39

SOURCE: Hagstrom, R.G (2000). Latticework: The New Investing.

securities are minimal, and the cost of acquiring and monitoring those securities likely outweigh the benefits of any further risk reduction.'

This makes intuitive sense, but where are the thirty securities?

When we look at investor portfolios in any country or region, the results
are the same: there is always a significant home-country bias. In other words,
investors tend to prefer securities from their own country because of the bias
of familiarity, which we will explore in Chapter 8. This is not exactly surprising. Often investors will feel that they know such stocks better because they
are more familiar with them. For example, they recognise the local supermarket chain in their country or a domestic mobile phone service provider.
However, for an investor who is looking for genuine diversification, home-
country bias makes little sense. Global GDP in 2024 is approximately $100
trillion, so if you live in the UK, which has a GDP of roughly $2.5 trillion,
and you limit yourself to only UK equities, you are exposing yourself to just
2.5 percent of the world economy. Even though the UK has many multi-
national companies, it's clear that such a portfolio would not be optimally
diversified. It would also not be exposed to many parts of the world where
the returns could be substantially higher than those in the UK. The same goes
for investors in all other countries.

If diversification is the only free lunch in finance, why don't more
investors embrace an international investing mentality? Many US investors
would say they have no need for international diversification, as the US has
historically been host to the world's best-performing equity markets. It is
true that US markets have outperformed others, but as David Swensen of
the Yale Endowment pointed out, 'The lack of correlation between foreign
markets and the US market provides a valuable diversification opportunity
for investors.' If we graph the S&P 500 against the MSCI EAFE (an index of
twenty-one developed countries excluding the USA) over the last fifty years,
we can see that on a ten-year rolling basis, the S&P 500 only outperformed 52
percent of the time. It is this lack of positive correlation which makes securities from different countries valuable additions to any portfolio to improve
diversification. [FIG. 13]

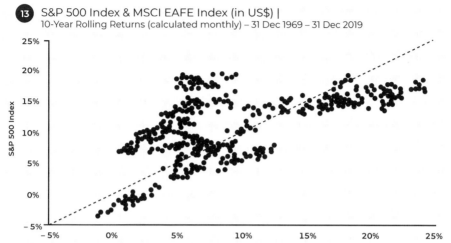

13 S&P 500 Index & MSCI EAFE Index (in US$) |
10-Year Rolling Returns (calculated monthly) – 31 Dec 1969 – 31 Dec 2019

The vertical axis represents the ten-year annual rolling returns for the S&P 500 while the horizontal axis is a line of demarcation separating periods of outperformance from periods of underperformance. Plot points above the diagonal axis are indicative of the S&P's relative outperformance, while points below the diagonal axis are indicative of its relative underperfomance.
SOURCE: Bloomberg and MSCI

The Power of Concentration

*Behold, the fool saith, 'Put not all thine eggs in the one basket'
– which is but a matter of saying, 'Scatter your money and your
attention.'*

– Mark Twain, American writer and humorist

Throughout investment history, all successful investors have embraced the concept of portfolio concentration. John Maynard Keynes wrote:

> As time goes on, I get more and more convinced that the right method in investment is to put fairly large sums into enterprises which one thinks one knows something about and in the management of which one thoroughly believes. It is a mistake to think that one limits one's risk by spreading too much between enterprises about which one knows little and has no reason for special confidence. … One's knowledge and experience are definitely limited and there are seldom more than two or three enterprises at any given time in which I personally feel myself entitled to put full confidence.

Keynes should know. He had made – and lost – two fortunes speculating on macro events by 1932, and then he transitioned full time to concentrated value investing to make (and, more importantly, keep) his final fortune.

Instead of increasing the number of positions, he instead advocated for diversifying in terms of the types of stocks held, or sectors, to create 'a balanced investment position, i.e. a variety of risks in spite of individual holdings being large, and if possible opposed risks'. Regarding investment time horizons, Keynes also proposed '[a] steadfast holding of these in fairly large units through thick and thin, perhaps for several years, until they have fulfilled their promise or it is evident that they were purchased by mistake.'

Later in the 1940s, Ben Graham proposed a portfolio of ten to thirty holdings as the ideal number. Phil Fisher, one of Buffett's mentors, wrote voluminously on the subject. He surmised that because the 'perils' of concentration and the 'delights' of diversification were so widely acclaimed by even non-investors, investors would, in fact, practise excessive diversification, which is an 'evil of the other extreme'.

The problem is that when investors have many eggs in many baskets, they don't know enough about each 'egg' or cannot spend enough time checking how each 'egg' is doing. Beyond a certain point, it is not the quantity of stocks held but their quality and your understanding of them that matters. In Fisher's words, 'It never seems to occur to them, much less to their advisors, that buying a company without having sufficient knowledge of it may be even more dangerous than having inadequate diversification.' The next problem is that the majority of market returns come from a very few great businesses. For example, the 'Magnificent 7' is a nickname given to the group of US stocks (Alphabet, Amazon, Apple, Meta, Microsoft, Nvidia and Tesla) that have accounted for a great deal of growth in the S&P 500 during the 2020s.

When you recognise a great company, you need to own a meaningful amount of it. Pursuing a policy of diversification for diversification's sake may mean you own too small a piece of that great company for it to make a meaningful difference to the overall performance of your portfolio. The maths is simple, but it is counterintuitive: if you invest in four companies, and three of them go to zero but the fourth is a 5×, the return on the portfolio is 50 percent.

Fund manager Seth Klarman expanded further on Fisher's thoughts to describe how diversification can be achieved through the selection of the individual stocks themselves. For example, an investor with ten stocks all in the financial sector clearly has less diversification in their portfolio than an investor who owns ten stocks operating in ten different industries. Some stocks are more correlated to interest rates; some are more correlated to the commodities cycle; and some are more correlated to inflation. Depending on what your views of the market risks are, you can find a way to hedge those risks in your equities portfolio without having to use other instruments.

A certain amount of diversification is necessary in case of a black swan event, but beyond that, increasing the degree of diversification into companies or markets that you know less and less about is likely to cause, as Buffett calls it, 'deworsification'. Fund manager Michael Steinhardt has pointed out the limits of portfolio diversification across different asset classes: 'I was also wrong to think that because I held positions in various global markets, my portfolio was truly diversified. If so, it might then have provided some reduction in the overall risk. In times of stress, inevitably, markets that are not normally correlated suddenly are.'

On this point, Joel Greenblatt is unequivocal: the historical returns clearly show that the strategy of putting all your eggs in one basket and carefully watching that basket is less risky than academics would suggest. If you assume, based on history, that the average annual return from investing in the stock market is approximately 10 percent, history also shows us that the chance of any year's return falling between −8 percent and +28 percent is about two out of three. Obviously, there is still a one-in-three chance of falling outside this incredibly wide thirty-six-point range. These statistics hold for portfolios containing 50 or 500 different securities. If there are eight stocks in your portfolio, the range widens a little further to −10 percent to +30 percent. Not a significant difference from owning 500 stocks. As Greenblatt says, 'The fact that you can drive a truck through any of these wide ranges of expected returns should lend comfort to those who don't hold fifty stocks in their portfolio and strike fear in the hearts of anyone who thinks owning dozens of stocks will assure them a predictable annual income.'

The historical returns of stocks are a matter of public record, and that record makes for somewhat grim reading. In the US, on a yearly rolling basis, on average four out of seven stocks underperform the return on rolling one-month US. Treasury Bills. As a group, a single-digit number of exceptional businesses pull up the market averages, contrary to the commonly held view that many exceptional businesses are dragged down by a few laggards. [FIG. 14]

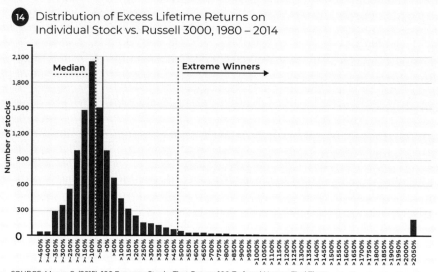

14 Distribution of Excess Lifetime Returns on Individual Stock vs. Russell 3000, 1980 – 2014

SOURCE: Mayer, C. (2015). 100 Baggers: Stocks That Return 100-To-1 and How to Find Them.

What is notable from the chart is that during the thirty-four-year study period, the median return of all the stocks was negative. Think about that for a minute. There were far more losing stocks than winning ones. In fact, the index return would have been negative but for the fat right tail of the distribution of extreme winners which pulled the index into positive territory overall.

When I look at any rich list, there are two things I find striking about it: first, almost every individual on it is concentrated in a single stock or business; the second thing is the lack of short-sellers. A short-seller is someone who sells stocks on the assumption that the share price will drop, so that they can buy them back more cheaply to lock in a profit. Shorting, as we will discuss in greater detail in Chapter 14 ('Investment Mistakes and Warnings'), is not the way to go to add diversification to your portfolio.

As Munger himself says, 'The great personal fortunes weren't built on a portfolio of fifty companies. They were built by someone who identified one wonderful business. With each investment you make, you should have the courage and the conviction to place at least 10 percent of your net worth in that stock.' As concentrated value investors, we are only looking to invest in the very best businesses once we have built in sufficient margin to cushion ourselves in case we are wrong. As fund manager Peter Lynch explains it,

'The more right you are on any one stock, the more wrong you can be on all the others and still triumph as an investor, and you can expect to be wrong at least 40% of the time.'

Fund manager Mohnish Pabrai advocates making '[f]ew bets, big bets, infrequent bets – all placed when the odds are overwhelmingly in your favour.' He says this in recognition of the fact that exceptional investment opportunities are found very rarely and that when you identify them, you need to have the conviction to back up the truck. For the final point on the subject of portfolio concentration, I will hand over to Buffett, who in a talk with business school students concluded the following:

> Really outstanding investment opportunities are rare enough that you should really have a go at it when it comes around, and put a huge portion of your wealth into it. I've said in the past you should think of investment as though you have a punch card with 20 holes in it. You have to think really hard about each one, and in fact 20 (in a lifetime) is way more than you need to do extremely well as an investor.

Summary

A lot of great fortunes in the world have been made by owning a single wonderful business. If you understand the business, you do not need to own very many of them.

— Warren E. Buffett, chairman of Berkshire Hathaway

Diversification, much like leverage, is a double-edged sword. On the one hand, sufficient diversification guards us against unforeseen calamities. On the other, it condemns us to mediocrity, at best. If you do not know how to analyse businesses or do not have a passion for business and investing, the advice from successful investors is unequivocal: buy and hold a low-cost passive index fund.

For active managers, as fund manager Michael Steinhardt says, 'Diversification is a hedge against ignorance,' and as value investors we are better off owning fewer stocks that we know a great deal about. By carefully selecting the stocks in our portfolio and managing the correlations between them, we can combine the best aspects of both concentration and diversification.

Fund manager Seth Klarman concludes that '[d]iversification, after all, is not how many different things you own, but how different the things you do own are in the risks they entail.' Variance of returns is a given, even more so for concentrated value investors. Most investors will see this volatility as excessively risky and run away. The most successful investors have enough of their own capital in their funds (permanent capital) and understand their strategy well enough that they can endure the greater volatility of returns. They are variance-seekers, attempting to maximise the upside variance and minimise the downside.

CHAPTER 7: COMPOUNDING

Compound interest is the eighth wonder of the world. He who understands it, earns it; he who doesn't, pays it.

— Albert Einstein, German-born theoretical physicist and Nobel Prize winner

I first discovered the joys of compound interest when I was comparing fixed deposit rates between various bank accounts in an English lesson when I was sixteen years old (thank you, Shakespeare!). By this point I had started, run, and worked for several businesses. My last one, delivering newspapers when we lived in Copenhagen, Denmark, alerted me to the idea that there had to be a way to make the money I had accumulated from my various business ventures work for me. What struck me was how even a small change in the interest rate, when compounded over a long-enough period, gave completely different results. Take the following example of three hypothetical savers:

1. Susan invests $5,000 per year from age 25 to 35 (10 years), then stops investing. Each year, she earns 7% until the age of 65.
2. Bill invests $5,000 per year from age 35 to 65 (30 years), earning 7% per annum.
3. Chris invests $5,000 per year from age 25 to 65 (40 years), earning 7% per annum.

When you look at the number of years of contributions, you would correctly presume that Chris would do best as he invests for the longest time (forty years) and the most money ($200k in total). But who would come in second, Bill or Susan? Most people assume that Bill, with twenty years' worth of extra contributions and a total of $150,000 invested (compared with just $50,000 for Susan over ten years), would end up with the most money. This intuition is wrong. Susan is second — which shows how underappreciated the power of compound interest is. The earlier you start, the greater the advantage. [FIG. 15]

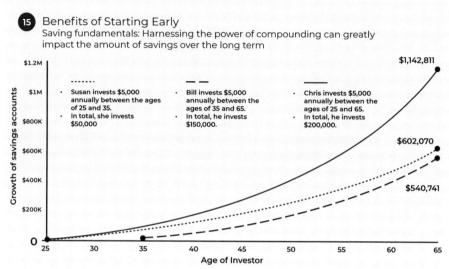

15 Benefits of Starting Early
Saving fundamentals: Harnessing the power of compounding can greatly impact the amount of savings over the long term

SOURCE: J.P.Morgan Asset Management. The above example is for illustrative purposes only and not indicative of any investment. Account value in this example assumes a 7% annual return. Compounding refers to the process of earning return on principal plus the return that was earned earlier.

When it comes to compounding, there are only three variables that matter:

1. How long is your runway? (i.e. how long will you be able to compound?)
2. What is the rate at which you will be able to compound your capital?
3. How much capital will you start with and how much can you add along the way?

What struck me from the chart was the importance of accumulating and investing your savings as early as possible to allow them to compound for as long as possible. When asked what he would like engraved on his tombstone, in a nod to the awesome power of compounding, Warren Buffett replied, 'Here lies the oldest man that ever lived.'

Rule of 72

The first rule of compounding is to never interrupt it unnecessarily.

— Charles T. Munger, vice-chairman of Berkshire Hathaway

For those who understand them, compound interest tables are fascinating to examine. In the one below, you can see exactly what returns you would get on a lump sum earning different rates of interest compounded over different periods or vice versa (i.e. how long it would take to earn certain returns on a lump sum for different rates of compounded interest). [**FIG. 16**]

This table can help us understand and verify the simple shortcut known as the 'Rule of 72'. Essentially, when you are given a rate of return, dividing 72 by that rate gives you the approximate number of years it would take compound interest to double your money. Thus, for a rate of return of 10 percent, it would take about 7.2 years (seven years and three months).

It also works the other way around. As Munger says, 'Invert, always invert.' Inverting the equation gives us the return we would need to double our money in a certain number of years. For example, if we wanted to double our money in five years, we would need an approximate rate of return of

16 Compound Interest Table

						RATE OF RETURN						
Period	4%	5%	6%	7%	8%	9%	10%	12%	14%	16%	18%	20%
1	1.04	1.05	1.06	1.07	1.08	1.09	1.10	1.12	1.14	1.16	1.18	1.20
2	1.08	1.10	1.12	1.14	1.17	1.19	1.21	1.25	1.30	1.35	1.39	1.44
3	1.12	1.16	1.19	1.23	1.26	1.30	1.33	1.40	1.48	1.56	1.64	1.73
4	1.17	1.22	1.26	1.31	1.36	1.41	1.46	1.57	1.69	1.81	1.94	2.07
5	1.22	1.28	1.34	1.40	1.47	1.54	1.61	1.76	1.93	2.10	2.29	2.49
6	1.27	1.34	1.42	1.50	1.59	1.68	1.77	1.97	2.19	2.44	2.70	2.99
7	1.32	1.41	1.50	1.61	1.71	1.83	1.95	2.21	2.50	2.83	3.19	3.58
8	1.37	1.48	1.59	1.72	1.85	1.99	2.14	2.48	2.85	3.28	3.76	4.30
9	1.42	1.55	1.69	1.84	2.00	2.17	2.36	2.77	3.25	3.80	4.44	5.16
10	1.48	1.63	1.79	1.97	2.16	2.37	2.59	3.11	3.71	4.41	5.23	6.19
11	1.54	1.71	1.90	2.10	2.33	2.58	2.85	3.48	4.23	5.12	6.18	7.43
12	1.60	1.80	2.01	2.25	2.52	2.81	3.14	3.90	4.82	5.94	7.29	8.92
13	1.67	1.89	2.13	2.41	2.72	3.07	3.45	4.36	5.49	6.89	8.60	10.70
14	1.73	1.98	2.26	2.58	2.94	3.34	3.80	4.89	6.26	7.99	10.15	12.84
15	1.80	2.08	2.40	2.76	3.17	3.64	4.18	5.47	7.14	9.27	11.97	15.41
20	2.19	2.65	3.21	3.87	4.66	5.60	6.73	9.65	13.74	19.46	27.39	38.34

SOURCE: Collins, J.L. (2016). The Simple Path to Wealth: Your Road Map to Financial Independence and a Rich, Free Life.

72 ÷ 5 = 14.4 percent. That is, if we compounded our money at 14.4 percent for five years, we would double our starting capital.

The best example I have heard that encompasses both the power of compounding and the Rule of 72 was given by fund manager Mohnish Pabrai to a class of business school students in 2017. Below is the abridged version of the conversation, where he recounted an example from a previous Buffett Partnership letter:

> In 1626, which is almost 400 years ago, it's widely rumoured that the Dutch bought the island of Manhattan from the Native Americans for $24. Buffett wrote about this story to his Buffett Partnership investors in the late 50s making the point that if you look at the value of even undeveloped land in Manhattan today, one would think that the Native Americans got taken.
>
> But let's just say that the $24 was given by the Indians to their Chief Investment Officer and the Chief Investment Officer was told to invest this amount for the benefit of the tribe. Let's say for argument's sake that our investment officer wasn't too bright and only managed a 7% annual rate of return.
>
> If you are compounding at 7% a year, Rule of 72, in 10 years, your money is going to double. 100 years is 10 sets of doubles or 2^{10} which is roughly 1,000×. So if you had $24 in 1626, it was $24,000 in 1726, and then it was $24 million in 1826, and it's $24 billion in 1926, and it will be $24 trillion in 2026.
>
> Basically, if the Indians had gotten a 7% annualized return, they'd be at $24 trillion by 2026. What would the cost of undeveloped land in Manhattan be in 2026. I don't know, but I do know that the total wealth of every man, woman and child in the United States is about $100 trillion. And if everything is worth $100 trillion, the Island of Manhattan, even with all its buildings is way under $26 trillion.
>
> So, the Indians actually negotiated quite a good deal. The problem is they had an incompetent Chief Investment Officer, who couldn't bring the bacon home. And of course, we are going to make sure that such incompetence is permanently banished!

That's the power of compounding. You must start early and never interrupt it.

Declines and Return Drags

One of the only things that interrupts the compounding cycle is a loss. When we experience a loss, the maths works against us. If you lose 5 percent of your capital, it takes an approximately equivalent gain to return you to where you were before the loss. If you lose 10 percent, you need an 11 percent gain to recover. If you lose 20 percent, you need a 25 percent gain; lose 50 percent and you need a 100 percent gain. Lose 80 percent and you need a 225 percent gain to get back to where you were before the loss! Losses compound, too. The bigger the loss, the bigger the gain needed to recover. As billionaire hedge fund manager David Einhorn joked, 'What do you call a stock that's down 90%? A stock that was down by 80% and then got cut in half.' The deeper the hole we find ourselves in, the harder it is to climb out.

Value investors will only buy businesses with a significant margin of safety, but the maths does show that we need complete faith in our portfolio holdings to ride out these declines and where possible to add when they are falling. However, not all stocks that fall will recover. The J.P. Morgan *Agony and Ecstasy* study found that since 1980, 40 percent of all stocks experienced a 70 percent decline, from which they never recovered. So, it is imperative that you invest only when you truly understand the business.

Fees and taxes are the two other main causes of a reduction in our compounding rate. Fees reduce the size of the assets that are compounding and can make a significant difference over time. Taxes do the same. Taxes are usually due on income received and when assets are sold for a gain – another reason why low portfolio turnover is usually a strong indicator of better returns for investors!

Deferred taxation for taxable investors is essentially an interest-free loan from the government without a fixed repayment date. To explain the point, Buffett asks us to imagine what happens if you buy a $1 investment that doubles in price each year. If you sell the investment at the end of the first year, you would retain a net gain of $0.66 (assuming you're in the 34 percent tax bracket). Let's say you reinvest the $1.66 and it doubles in value by the second year-end. If the investment continues to double each year, and you continue to sell, pay the tax, and reinvest the proceeds, at the end of twenty years you will have a net gain of $25,200 after paying taxes of $13,000. If, instead, you were to purchase a $1 investment that doubled each year and is not sold until after twenty years, you would gain $692,000 after paying taxes of approximately $356,000. By reducing portfolio turnover, we can have more money invested, and thus our returns will be higher than would otherwise be the case. David Swensen of the Yale Endowment emphasises the point that for taxable investors, minimising the tax drag on their portfolios is essential, as taxes impair wealth creation.

The table below, from James M. Poterba's study of *Taxation, Risk-Taking and Household Portfolio Behaviour*, shows the pernicious effects of tax impairment on wealth creation in action. For stocks, the pre-tax return for the seventy years of study data is 12.7 percent but this reduces by 27 percent to 9.2 percent after tax. The tax effect on the returns of bonds is even higher – a 38 percent reduction in overall returns, as we have to pay income tax as soon as it is received versus capital gains on stocks (which, however, we can opt to defer). [FIG. 17]

A separate study by Arnott and Jeffrey published in *Journal of Portfolio Management* analysed the pre- and post-tax returns investors received for variable rates of turnover in their portfolios. [FIG. 18]

The results are particularly eye-opening in today's environment of increasing short-term holding periods for equities. These results show that to achieve

17 Taxes Materially Reduce Investment Returns
Pre-Tax and After-Tax Returns (Percent) 1926 to 1996

Asset Class	Pre-Tax Return	After-Tax Return	Tax Burden
Large stocks	12.7	9.2	3.5
Long-term goverment bonds	5.5	3.4	2.1
Treasury bills	3.8	2.2	1.6

SOURCE: James M. Poterba; 'Taxation, Risk-Taking, and Household Portfolio Behaviour '
NBER Working Paper Series, Working Paper 8340 (National Bureau of Economic Research, 2001), 90

18 Portfolio Turnover Reduces After-Tax Returns (Percent)

Turnover Rate	Pre-Tax Return	After-Tax Return
0	6.0	6.0
5	6.0	5.4
10	6.0	5.0
25	6.0	4.4
50	6.0	4.1
100	6.0	3.9

SOURCE: Arnott and Jeffery, Journal of Portfolio Management 19, no.3 (1993): 19.

high after-tax returns, investors need to keep their average portfolio turnover ratio somewhere between 0 and 10 percent per year. If they gravitate to more portfolio activity than this, it can result in a 25 to 50 percent lower net return after taxes have been paid!

Summary

The power of compounding is particularly important when we are searching for businesses to include within our portfolio. We already know most of the gain in equity markets over time comes from a few stellar performers. We call these the '100 Baggers' – stocks which, had you invested and held onto, would have made you one hundred times your money. Even capturing the returns from one of these companies in your concentrated portfolio would likely have led to a vast outperformance against any index over time. The question then becomes for how long and at what rate would a company have to compound its share price to achieve a return of 100× on your initial capital? [FIG. 19]

This graphic is worth bearing in mind when comparing the growth expectations already baked into the current stock price versus what you think they should be and, therefore, what you expect your returns to be over time versus the market. I have always set myself specific return expectations for each of my portfolio holdings. Not only does this give me something concrete to work towards but it also helps to narrow the field of investments that are able to achieve my return goals.

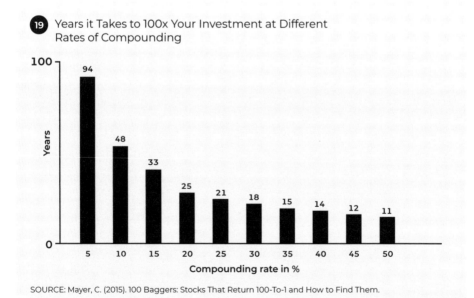

19 Years it Takes to 100x Your Investment at Different Rates of Compounding

SOURCE: Mayer, C. (2015). 100 Baggers: Stocks That Return 100-To-1 and How to Find Them.

For example, if I want to double my money within five years, the Rule of 72 tells me that I must compound at no less than 14.4 percent per year. Therefore, I should not be investing in businesses that are not also able to compound their share price (through a combination of earnings growth and multiple expansion) at the same rate or higher per year.

Setting an overall returns objective helps value investors to filter out the noise and focus only on those businesses that they believe can fulfil their return expectations.

CHAPTER 8: THE PSYCHOLOGY AND BIOLOGY OF INVESTING

The world makes much less sense than you think. The coherence comes mostly from the way your mind works.

— Daniel Kahneman, Israeli-American cognitive scientist, Nobel Prize winner, and author of *Thinking, Fast and Slow*

The modern world is nothing like the past. Our living conditions today are almost entirely unrelated to the world we were born into and significantly different to when human beings first emerged from their caves. Unfortunately, as Professor Nigel Nicholson once said, 'You can take the person out of the Stone Age, but you can't take the Stone Age out of the person.'

It's easy to forget how recent a concept 'financial markets' really is. As financial historian Niall Ferguson points out, 'The New York Stock Exchange opened in 1817, less than 10 generations ago. Index Funds are only 50 years old. If you were to plot the two-million-year-old history of Homo sapiens on a single day, modern portfolio theory would appear at 11:59:58.'

We are, therefore, trying to run new software on Stone Age hardware and wondering why it leads to trouble. We are trying to figure out how to function in the modern world, including investing successfully, using a brain that hasn't evolved a great deal since the woolly mammoths roamed the tundra. The result is a mixture of conflicting modes of thinking and learned behaviour known as cognitive biases and behavioural heuristics that make it extremely hard for us to be objective and rational about pretty much anything.

Charlie Munger spent a great deal of his time writing and speaking about the impact cognitive biases and heuristics have on our everyday lives, as well as on investment decision-making. The most famous of his works (and a must read) is his speech titled *The Psychology of Human Misjudgement*. Head of Consilient Research and investor Michael Mauboussin describes what Munger identified as the evident disconnect between hardware and software:

Human beings' primary motivation over the past two million years has been to pass our genes onto the next generation. Simple rules of thumb like 'if you hear something in the bushes, run' had aided our efforts in doing this. If it turned out that the noise wasn't a sabre-tooth tiger but only wind, no harm no foul. The 'run first, ask questions later' attitude is something that helped us survive in the field, but too many people have been unable to suppress this primal instinct from their investment decisions. This has and will continue to create a wedge between investment returns and investor returns. Running at the first sign of trouble in financial markets is dangerous because it's almost never a sabre-toothed tiger and the 'no harm no foul' rules don't apply to stocks.

Our actions are frequently the result of our biology, for example, the automatic fight, flight or freeze response to potentially dangerous situations discussed by Mauboussin. This response is governed by the amygdala, a small region of our brain that kickstarts the fight, flight or freeze response. Designed to react immediately and instinctively to threats, the amygdala is the reason we panic and sell when the market takes a tumble. Only to feel stupid when it rallies a few days later. Resisting this instant risk assessment software is incredibly difficult because the hardware it runs on has not evolved enough to recognise that it's almost never a sabre-toothed tiger!

Scientists used to believe that sensory signals from the five senses travelled first to the thalamus, where they were translated into the language of the brain and sent to the neocortex for appropriate response. If the neocortex detected a threat, a 'risk message' would be sent to the amygdala for an 'act now, think later' response. But that isn't what happens. Instead, there is a neural emergency exit connecting the thalamus and the amygdala which means that a small portion of every sensory signal goes straight to the amygdala across a single synapse – bypassing the 'thinking brain' all together. Psychologist and emotional intelligence guru Daniel Goleman talks of this when he tells the story of a friend jumping into a canal to save a toddler. He wasn't even cognitively aware of the toddler until he was in the water, fully clothed. Something about the situation triggered his amygdala and made him react before the rest of the message reached his neocortex.

As touched on in the Introduction, we learn through experience and develop increasingly conditioned responses as we grow up. By the time we are adults, we have a vast repository of conditioned responses to risks both real and imagined. These conditioned responses act as mental shortcuts, known as heuristics, which allow us to immediately assess threats. Heuristics save time, which is crucial in dangerous situations involving sabre-toothed tigers, but they are automatic, and in the investing world, they lead to mistakes.

Psychologists Amos Tversky and Daniel Kahneman's prospect theory helped us better understand the irrationalities in our decision-making processes. They attributed these irrationalities to two very human issues. The first is emotions, which reduce our self-control – an essential part of rational decision-making. The second is our inability to fully understand the information or situations with which we are dealing. For example, the average person is terrible with numbers. When asked whether they are above- or below-average drivers, almost everybody will score themselves as being well above average, reflecting not just poor numeracy (only half of us can be above-average drivers) but also another well-known bias: overconfidence bias.

If you are reading this book, you may well consider yourself an above-average investor. But how did you come to that conclusion? Human beings are incredibly complex. Economic textbooks are based on our idealised cousin 'Homo Economicus'. The assumption is that all people make decisions rationally, based on all the available information, while considering their expected utility. But people are anything but rational. We will often act purely on impulse or emotion. Take envy, for example. The economic historian Charles Kindleberger wrote, 'There is nothing so disturbing to one's well-being and judgement as to see a friend get rich.' There is also nothing rational or logical about the emotion of envy. By extension, one could argue that all traditional economic theory is wrong, as it is based on an entirely false assumption that human beings are rational decision-makers!

The toll that emotions take on investor performance is often highlighted in academic literature, but Oxford Risk's study published in the *Financial Times* really brought the scale of the issue home to me. During normal market times, they estimated that the average investor lost 3 percent per year from emotionally driven decision-making, and the figure rose to 7 percent during times of significant volatility. These results occurred for two reasons: first, from investors crystallising small losses and then holding excess cash during normal times, and, secondly, during times of market panic. Selling their biggest winners and holding onto their losers, until the pain became too great and they switched mostly to cash and missed the subsequent recovery. Eventually to reinvest at a new all-time high. Investors flock to the most popular investment themes or funds, which usually correlates with short-term outperformance, just before they turn into long-term underperformance. We like running with the crowd.

Behavioural Economics Revisited

The economist Richard Thaler took the findings from prospect theory and applied them to economics. The result, as mentioned in Chapter 3, was a whole new field of study, behavioural economics, designed to shine a light on our biases – many of which can have an outsized impact on our investment results.

We have touched on some of these biases before. For example, we display risk aversion when we are offered a choice (and select the more conservative option) in one setting and then turn into risk-seekers when we are offered the same choice (but select the riskier option) in a different setting. The most common example of this is games of chance, such as coin-flipping contests, where we are poor at calculating the odds of both winning or losing and the actual amount of money at stake changes our perception of risk. For example, for a bet on a coin flip where you win $20 for heads or lose $10 for tails, most people will take it. However, most people will reject a flip where you win $500,000 for heads or lose $50,000 for tails.

We also have trouble recognising how much information is enough to make an informed decision. As Charles Koch, billionaire chairman of Koch Industries, describes,

> It is usually wasteful to develop detailed information beyond what is necessary to make good decisions. When evaluating an investment, unnecessary detail just distracts from the key drivers. Since it is impossible to predict outcomes precisely, trying to do so – as in making financial projections to several decimal points – is wasteful. Even worse, such attempts can create a false sense of confidence.

We also tend to pay excessive attention to low-probability events accompanied by high drama. For example, we will worry more about a plane crash because we saw one on the news, even though a plane crash is far rarer than a car accident. International risk expert David Ropeik calls this phenomenon 'the perception gap'. It's the inconsistency between how likely we perceive a threat to occur versus the actual danger it poses. Statistically speaking, it is much safer travelling by plane than car, despite almost everyone believing the opposite to be true.

Other cognitive biases that we should be aware of as value investors and against which we should incorporate counterweights within our investment process include:

- Anchoring bias
- Confirmation bias
- Disposition effect bias
- Hindsight bias
- Familiarity bias
- Endowment effect
- Excessive self-attribution bias
- Availability heuristic and recency bias
- Overreaction bias
- Mental accounting
- Gambler's fallacy
- Sunk cost fallacy

Anchoring Bias

Anchoring occurs when an initial piece of information or a first impression of something is used as the basis for our subsequent views, even if they are entirely unrelated. For example, if I say, '10,000,' and then ask you how much you think it costs to fly business class return from London to New York, your response will be higher than if I had said '1,000' and then asked the same question and lower than if I had said '100,000'. Hearing the initial number 'anchors' that number in your mind and influences your response; hence, anchoring bias. This is why restaurants always put an expensive bottle of wine first on their wine list – that first price influences you to order a higher-priced bottle. First impressions count. When it comes to making investment decisions, we need to be careful about the order in which we receive and review information.

At Gronager Partners, when we go through our investment process, one of our rules related to this bias is to look at the stock price and performance last – not first, as we are hardwired to do – as that can affect our judgement of intrinsic value.

Confirmation Bias

Confirmation bias has us purposely look for evidence that confirms our initial view while discarding any evidence that runs counter to it. Or as Warren Buffett says, 'What human beings are best at doing is interpreting new information so that their prior conclusions remain intact.' To counter this tendency in our investment process, Mohnish Pabrai advises that we must understand both the long and short views for each business we evaluate for inclusion in our portfolios and update both views regularly as new information arises.

Disposition Effect Bias

Disposition effect bias is closely related to the regret and loss aversion biases. In investors' minds, their portfolios are usually made up of winners and losers. Thanks to Kahneman and Tversky's research, we know that the psychological pain of a loss is about twice the magnitude of the joy of an equivalent gain. Therefore, investors prefer to sell their winners and will sell them often so they can bolster their self-esteem. Conversely, they prefer to keep their losers, often for a long time, so they can avoid the blow to their sense of self-worth or ego. This is particularly harmful for investors, because there is also a significant tax disadvantage from always selling winners (and paying tax on gains) and keeping losers (not making use of the tax deductibility of losses).

This makes no sense, but inexperienced investors do it all the time because they don't understand psychology. Hersh Shefrin and Meir Statman, both notable figures in behavioural finance, evaluated 10,000 anonymised client accounts from a brokerage firm and found ample evidence of the disposition effect bias during normal times, and even more evidence during times of exuberance. Most interesting to me was that they also found it during times of market panic! But this was probably because the dent to self-esteem would have been diminished by the herd mentality of everyone else selling at the same time. Again, we like the warmth of being part of a herd that is 'all wrong together', so we feel it's okay to take a loss and won't feel bad about it.

Hindsight Bias

As the adage goes, hindsight is 20/20. We have all been guilty of saying that something was obvious in retrospect. However, it can't have been that obvious; otherwise, we would have predicted it.

Investors need to be particularly wary of hindsight bias. Market news-letters tell us about how much we would have made had we bought a certain stock five years ago; the latest billionaire, who founded another company that's going to be a huge success; or the list of the biggest gainers in the market yesterday that we should have bought. Hindsight bias leads to regret, and regret pollutes decision-making and encourages irrational decisions. As the saying goes, 'Regret makes you want to shoot where the rabbit was, not where it is headed.' In other words, you must understand that whatever the opportunity was, it's gone. And chasing after it is never going to deliver results. Each day is a new day in which to find fresh opportunities, not to waste time chasing a rabbit that is long gone.

Familiarity Bias

Investing in things that are unfamiliar and less well known – despite, as we have seen, the often-obvious benefits of diversification and superior returns – takes most investors outside their comfort zone. As a result, many investors will over-allocate their portfolios in favour of their home countries (home-country bias), or companies they know well (familiarity bias).

Although it is excellent advice to never invest in anything that you do not understand, by not seeking to educate ourselves on the merits of companies that operate outside of our specific geography or the benefits of investing in different sectors, we are potentially missing out on great opportunities. We are also exposing ourselves to the ever-greater risk of loss through product or geographic concentration.

Familiarity usually encourages overconfidence, and suspicion of the unknown discourages change, innovation or learning as we stick with the status quo. Familiarity can also lead to a lack of impartiality in our investment decision-making process as we put too much faith in what we already under-stand or are familiar with.

Endowment Effect

As mentioned in Chapter 1, the endowment effect influences us to place more value on an object if we already possess it, or an idea if we know something about it. For concentrated and long-term investors, the endowment effect is a double-edged sword (we meet again, old friend/foe). On one hand, it makes perfect sense that we are more committed to our investment choices, because we know a lot about the companies we have chosen. On the other hand, the endowment effect can blind us to shifting fundamentals; thus, we hold on to a losing stock for too long. It can also blinker us to new investing opportunities that may be superior to the stocks we hold.

So long as we are objective in analysing new information regarding our holdings as it comes to light, the bar to selling a current investment in favour of a new, relatively unknown one must be high. The endowment effect can either help or hinder your investment process. Which one it is (help or hinder) will depend on your awareness of its influence.

Excessive Self-Attribution Bias

Everyone has an ego. Most of us believe we know more than we do. Over-confidence based on a sense of infallibility inevitably leads to serious mistakes. We tend to hold ourselves in excessive self-regard: when things go well, we attribute them firmly to our own brilliance; when things go badly, we prefer to blame some external event or person.

Overconfidence is a huge issue as it makes us think our circle of competence is wider than it actually is. Part of being an expert is being able to separate what you know, from what you don't know. The ability to simply admit 'I don't know' is essential and may be the key to superior investment performance by reducing mistakes in both size and frequency.

Availability Heuristic and Recency Bias

Psychological testing has shown that our brains perceive immediate and deferred rewards differently. As an example, let's look at the following net annual performance numbers for investors in funds for the last five years:

- Year 1: +10%
- Year 2: +1%
- Year 3: +90%
- Year 4: +6%
- Year 5: +32%

How would you describe those returns? Would you invest with this manager? And what would you infer about future performance?

Now, if I were to reorder them thus:

- Year 1: +90%
- Year 2: +32%
- Year 3: +10%
- Year 4: +6%
- Year 5: +1%

How do you feel about them now? No doubt, worse, as the performance numbers are declining.

How about if I were to put them in ascending order:

- Year 1: +1%
- Year 2: +6%
- Year 3: +10%
- Year 4: +32%
- Year 5: +90%

How do you feel about them now? Almost certainly better.

Even though the overall result of investing in any of the three funds would be exactly the same!

Psychologists call the feeling that recent success is superior to distant success the availability heuristic or recency bias. The brain perceives recent rewards more vividly. This is why bands always play their best song at the end of a gig. It's why the person who pitches last is statistically more likely to land the job than the one who went first. It is also why inexperienced investors prefer to buy the hottest stocks that everyone is talking about.

People also tend to give greater weight to recent events or new information. This can have a significant impact on our investing behaviour if we attach too much weight to the most recent information. However, a lot of that information is just market commentators coming up with content, which is almost always irrelevant. The effects of mark-to-market accounting and the frequency of reporting (quarterly earnings reports) can, therefore, have undesirable consequences on investor returns. As Nick Sleep, co-founder of the Nomad Investment Partnership, identified, 'The Pavlovian association of poor short-term results with long-term incompetence and confusion between the two can lead to disastrous decisions.' Short-term poor performance inevitably improves, and the panicked investor is left nursing the loss of exiting at a low and the pain of having missed the bounce. Even professional investors can fall into this trap.

The next time you receive a quarterly report, throw it in the bin!

Overreaction Bias

Overreaction bias relates to how we process new information or news. In general, when we receive bad news about our investments, we tend to overreact. We integrate bad news into our investment process much faster and extrapolate it much further into the future than we would good news. Overreaction bias influences us to sell a stock after a short period of underperformance.

Remember, the price of a stock – and, by extension, the price of your investment – rarely reflects the value of the underlying businesses. So long as the business fundamentals are steady or improving and we have purchased with a big-enough margin of safety, the price can do whatever it wants. We need to have the right temperament to incorporate adequate patience into our investment process, to allow enough time for the thesis behind our investment to be carried out. As Buffett quipped, 'Time is the friend of the wonderful business and the enemy of the mediocre.'

He also suggested the following:

I could improve your ultimate financial welfare by giving you a ticket with only 20 slots in it, so that you had 20 punches – representing all the investments that you got to make in a lifetime. And once you'd punch through the card, you couldn't make any more investments at all. You'd really have to think carefully about what you did, and you'd be forced to load up on what you really think about. So you'd do much better.

Adopting the '20 Slot Rule' for investing will certainly make your investment selection process far more robust.

Mental Accounting

One of the weird things we do around money is to compartmentalise it into different accounts – even if they are just mental accounts. You might have an account that your regular income goes into and which pays for your regular outgoings. You may have a savings account for emergencies. You may even have an 'anything goes' account. Most of us wouldn't splurge our monthly pay on a single item, or gamble with it, because we need it to live. A bonus, however, is different. We tend to value a bonus less, despite it being the same thing. Money is money.

It's important to properly examine how you think about money. A good way to start is by looking at your personal finances and your implicit approaches to risk-seeking and risk aversion in how you earn, spend, and manage your own money. How we decide to invest and manage our personal finances is closely tied to the way we think about money.

Gambler's Fallacy

Also known as the 'Monte Carlo fallacy', the gambler's fallacy is illustrated by the belief that if red (or black) comes up on a roulette spin more often than normal, that colour will be landed on less often in the future. For example, if the ball has landed on red five times in a row, everyone around the table will assume that black is next. This harks back to probability and how little we understand it.

Each spin of the roulette wheel is entirely independent, and the probability of red or black is always 50/50. You can read absolutely nothing into the result of the next spin based on the previous result. It's pure chance. The gambler's fallacy has us seeing a pattern in random events, and by confusing the two we believe we can predict the unpredictable. Big mistake. To co-opt

John Maynard Keynes, the roulette wheel of the market can stay irrational a lot longer than you can stay solvent.

Sunk Cost Fallacy

The sunk cost fallacy makes a cognitive appearance when an investor has spent a great deal of time researching a business. As they get closer to making a decision, they will stop seeing the business as a potential investment and instead view it as a definite investment. The reason for this is that they don't want to have wasted their time. The same concept applies when a project goes over budget; rather than admit they might have been wrong and cancel the project, managers will throw more money at it. Submitting to the sunk cost fallacy can often mean that even more time or money is wasted.

No matter how much time you spend on a potential investment, it's important to always consider it as such until all your research is done and you can objectively decide whether to invest or not. Once you've invested, you'll need to be mindful again of the sunk cost fallacy, so that you will buy more of the stock only if your investment process and follow-up assessments indicate that further buying is prudent. Not because you've already spent a lot of money on it!

Very few investments will make it past the value investor's filters, but that's okay. The more time I spend on an investment, the more I feel I learn. If I decide not to invest, I am always careful to note key things I learnt in my research that I can apply to future investments. Therefore, there is always something of value to take away from the time invested.

Influence and Manipulation

As well as better understanding cognitive biases and heuristics, it is also wise to appreciate how open we are to manipulation. According to Robert Cialdini, an expert on human behaviour, we are at the mercy of six basic but incredibly powerful drivers that will influence our behaviour unless we understand them:

1. **Reciprocity**: People feel obligated to return favours or concessions offered to them. This principle suggests that when we give something to someone, they will feel compelled to give us something in return.

2. **Commitment and consistency**: Once people commit to something, they are more likely to stick to it. This principle is based on the idea that we want to be consistent with our past behaviour and decisions.

3. **Social proof**: People tend to follow the actions of others, especially when they are uncertain about what to do. This principle suggests that we look to others to determine the correct behaviour in a particular situation.

4. **Authority**: People are more likely to comply with requests from someone who is seen as an authority figure. This principle suggests that we tend to obey figures of authority without questioning their commands.

5. **Liking**: People are more likely to be influenced by those they know, like and trust. This principle emphasises the importance of building rapport and establishing a connection with others we want to influence.

6. **Scarcity**: People tend to want things more when they perceive them to be scarce or in limited supply. This principle suggests that the fear of missing out (FOMO) drives us to take actions to obtain scarce resources or opportunities.

Looking through this list and seeing the behaviour influenced by each driver, it is easy to see how they can influence our investment process. There are also obvious intersections between these drivers of human behaviour and some of the cognitive biases we discussed.

We must be very aware of these drivers being used to our detriment. Did we get taken out to dinner by the (always) charismatic CEO of a business and afterwards decide that we liked the business and its management? If so, our liking and reciprocity tendencies may have been activated. Have we spent months investigating a company and investing heavily in the business only for the fundamentals to change? If so, and if we don't act on that change, it is possible we are being influenced by the commitment and consistency driver and not investment rigour. Investors who jump into hot stocks and run for the hills when they tumble are almost certainly driven by social proof – they are unsure what to do, so they follow what everyone else is doing. Their choice is also probably driven by a dash of authority, following market commentators and investment pundits who prophesy riches or doom. Or maybe FOMO or scarcity is driving their actions. In the end, all these examples show that investors must understand the basic drivers behind human behaviour and the associated cognitive and behavioural biases. We must learn how to identify them and then protect ourselves by compensating for them within our investment process.

Summary

Human nature desires quick results; there is a peculiar zest in making money quickly, and remoter gains are discounted by the average man at a very high rate. The game of professional investment is intolerably boring and over-exacting to anyone who is entirely exempt from the gambling instinct; whilst he who has it must pay to this propensity the appropriate toll. If he is successful, that will only confirm the general belief in his rashness, and if in the short run he is unsuccessful, which is very likely, he will not receive much mercy.

– John Maynard Keynes, English economist, philosopher and fund manager

As Kahneman concludes in his book *Thinking, Fast and Slow*, the most vital aspect of preventing biases is to be aware of them, and '[e]ach situation must be treated objectively rather than as a participant in it.' Kahneman's research, amongst others, has shown that these biases and behavioural heuristics are systemic in human nature. Yet it's always surprising to me how few investors pay any attention. They remain unaware of why they are making bad decisions or how to correct them in the future – a further demonstration of the excessive self-attribution bias!

While it is true that these behaviours are inherently human and, therefore, unavoidable, it is a mistake to assume that we are powerless against their influence. To be successful, we must understand how vulnerable we are to external manipulation and self-sabotage to be able to guard against it. This objective is every bit as important as our analysis of a company's financial statements and the assessment of the economic moat around their business.

Beware the various psychological traps that can emerge when investing in the market. Large market swings and significant changes in the value of our portfolios can easily trigger our baser instincts. The desire to sell in a crisis is deeply embedded in our psychology, but that is almost always the wrong thing to do. Paper losses cause us a discomfort that we instinctively want to escape. That is why we sell our winners instead. After removing ourselves from the perceived danger, the brain releases calming hormones into the blood, and we immediately feel better for it.

We tend to simplify things, and one such way is to project the present situation indefinitely into the future. This is why when markets are crashing we believe they will keep going down and when they are climbing that they will keep going up. Emotion-based decision-making leads to dramatic underperformance.

Despite it being drummed into every investor to not panic and to buy the dip, we are almost hardwired to do the opposite. The act of investing is uncomfortable unless you have an ironclad process for selecting securities with a significant margin of safety to weather any downturn. We investors should also have a specific set of rules to follow during periods of market turmoil to ensure we make decisions as objectively as possible without giving in to our emotions.

You need to be in the right mental space to make good investment decisions. Therefore, if you're not feeling a hundred percent, or if your personal life is in chaos, deal with those front-of-mind issues first. There is little hope of making good investment decisions if you don't. As Fidelity fund manager Anthony Bolton wrote, 'Dieting provides an apt analogy to investing. Most people have the necessary knowledge to lose weight – that is, they know that in order to lose weight you have to exercise and cut down your calorie intake. However, despite widespread knowledge, the vast majority of people who attempt to lose weight are unsuccessful. Why? Because they lack the emotional discipline.'

A core psychological component of successful investors is, therefore, developing emotional self-discipline and the inner mental strength and resilience to weather external factors which would otherwise make us stumble. Psychologist Roy Baumeister has studied this topic extensively. His research found that willpower is a limited resource. Constructing an investment process and managing our environment is the best way to support willpower.

For a start, make your decisions in relative isolation, free from interruptions and distractions. Don't give destabilising forces or bias triggers access to your decision-making process. Ignore the news. The media is there to capture eyeballs; it must be attention-grabbing or it won't achieve that outcome. It is always alarmist and biased to the negative because that's what gets attention. Following the news is one of the main reasons most people don't succeed as investors. Turn off the TV. You will be happier, and a better investor for it. Don't check your portfolio constantly. As fund manager Nicholas Taleb says,

'Why would I put myself in a position where I may have negative emotional reactions to this short-term drop, which sends all the wrong signals to my brain?'

Part of our process at Gronager Partners is not looking at stock prices during market trading hours. I want to be as objective as possible when I look at them and not see them ticking up or down by the second. I understand my own internal biases; to counteract them, I look at the changes in the value of our portfolio as infrequently as possible. I preset alerts on the market, our portfolio, and also on the stocks in our watchlist to tell me when they have risen or fallen by a certain percentage. I complement these preset percentage changes with a concrete action plan for what to do at that price. For example, if the price of one of our portfolio holdings drops 30 percent and the fundamentals underlying it haven't changed, I will increase the position. This way I don't sit glued to the screens watching the price-action chaos of the market. Buffett doesn't even have a computer in his office. Stan Druckenmiller, a more active trader than most, famously kept his Bloomberg terminal in another room, on a table with no chair, so it would take effort to look at his portfolio. Constantly watching moving prices feeds our need for action, but, as all the research suggests, the more active you are, the worse your performance will be.

Long-term value investors need to be mindful of all these drivers, cognitive biases and heuristics. I would strongly recommend you read Daniel Kahneman's *Thinking, Fast and Slow* and Robert Cialdini's *Influence* as two great places to start to better understand the minefield between our ears. Part of what makes great investors is understanding ourselves – our strengths, weaknesses and temperaments. Only by understanding this vast and complex field can we ensure that our decision-making process and, therefore, our investment process is as free as possible from undue and unappreciated interference.

PART TWO

CHAPTER 9: PERFORMANCE OF DIFFERENT ASSET CLASSES

Just keep accumulating knowledge. That's one of the beauties of the business that Charlie and I are in, is that everything is cumulative. The stuff I learned when I was 20 is useful today. Not in necessarily the same way and not necessarily every day. But it's useful. So you're building a database in your mind that is going to pay off over time.

‒ Warren E. Buffett, Chairman of Berkshire Hathaway

I find that the best way to begin to make sense of the various broad investment asset classes is to examine their relative performance over time. [**FIG. 20**]

Stocks have clearly trounced every other asset class over the long term, and that well-known 'investment' known as gold has barely kept up with inflation. Also displayed in the graph below is the Consumer Price Index

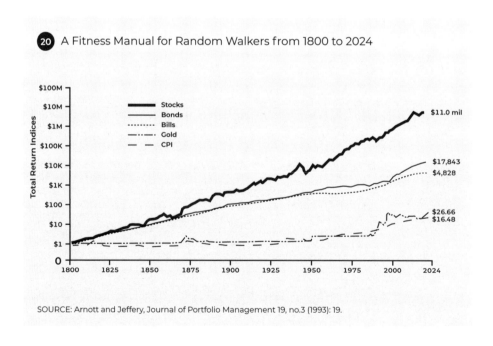

20 A Fitness Manual for Random Walkers from 1800 to 2024

SOURCE: Arnott and Jeffery, Journal of Portfolio Management 19, no.3 (1993): 19.

(CPI). Inflation is a macroeconomic concept that many people know but few understand. Even economists argue about its definition, how to measure it, and where it comes from. For our purposes, we can define inflation as 'the reduction of purchasing power that comes about through a general rise in prices'. David Swensen, the CIO of the Yale Endowment, liked to say that '[y]ou as an investor in an inflation-prone world want to be an owner – not a lender. Most of that commitment should be in publicly traded global equities.'

Essentially, stocks provide partial protection against inflation. They are better than some kinds of assets but are not a perfect hedge. Properly selected individual stocks should, at the very least, protect against inflation over the long term. In many instances, they also offer the chance of major gains in real purchasing power as well as in investment dollars. Therefore, it's important to include inflation so you can calculate an asset class's 'real return' – returns minus inflation. [FIG. 21]

As you can see from this inflation-adjusted graph of real returns, inflation, although it has often been low for extended periods of time, has had a significant effect on the actual returns received from the various asset classes. For example, the first graph in this chapter shows that a $1 investment in stocks in 1800 would have been worth $11 million in 2024, but this graph shows that,

21 Performance of Financial Assets in America from 1800 to 2024

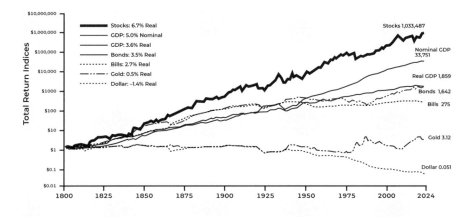

SOURCE: Siegel, Jeremy, Future for Investors (2005), Bureau of Economic Analysis, Measuring Worth

accounting for inflation, the real return actually dropped to about $1 million in 2024. *Now* tell me you don't care about inflation!

Ibbotson Associates undertook one of the most in-depth and widely referenced pieces of research on historical returns and inflation-adjusted returns. They examined how many times your money would have doubled over the eighty-year period from 1925 to 2005 if you had continuously invested in each asset class. [**FIG. 22**]

The real-world results mirror what the academic research suggests investors should have received. For example, to compensate the investors for the additional risk, investing in equities should provide a higher return than investing in fixed income. Also, within the equity asset class, smaller-capitalisation businesses are higher-risk propositions than larger-capitalisation businesses; thus, investors should be compensated accordingly. The two results that every investor should take from these studies are, first, that holding cash over the medium to long term is a guaranteed way to end up poor. Secondly, on every level, investing in equities over the medium to long term is the surest way to end up rich.

Yale's David Swensen took Ibbotson's research a step further as he tried to ascertain the best strategy for identifying areas where active versus passive management could further increase a perceptive investor's returns. He concluded

22 Equities Generate Superior Returns in the Long Run
Wealth Multiples for US Asset Classes and Inflation – Dec 1925 to Dec 2005

Asset Class	Multiple
Inflation	11 times
Treasury bills	18 times
Treasury bonds	71 times
Corporate bonds	100 times
Large-capitalisation stocks	2,658 times
Small-capitalisation stocks	13,706 times

SOURCE: Ibbotson Associates, Stocks, Bonds, Bills and Inflation, 2006 Year Book.

23 Dispersion of Active Management Returns
Indentifies Areas of Opportunity
Asset Returns by Quartile. Ten Years Ending 30 June 2005

Asset Class	First Quartile	Median	Third Quartile	Range
US fixed income	7.4%	7.1%	6.9%	0.5%
US equity	12.1	11.2	10.2	1.9
International equity	10.5	9.0	6.5	4.0
US small-capitalisation equity	16.1	14.0	11.3	4.8
Absolute return	15.6	12.5	8.5	7.1
Real estate	17.6	12.0	8.4	9.2
Leveraged buyouts	13.3	8.0	– 0.4	13.7
Venture capital	28.7	–1.4	–14.5	43.2

SOURCE: Data for marketable securities are from Russell/Mellon. The absolute return, real estate, leveraged buyout, and venture capital data are from Cambridge Associates. Real estate, leveraged buyout, and venture capital data represent returns on funds formed between 1995 and 1999, excluding more recent funds so that immature investments will not bias results downward.

that the larger the range (dispersion) of returns within a specific asset class, the greater the chance that an active manager would be able to outperform. The results from his study are shown above. [FIG. 23]

Swensen found that '[g]reater inefficiency in the market environment may not lead to greater average success.' For example, the median returns from leveraged buyouts and venture capital were far below those of US equities, despite being higher-risk strategies, because of illiquidity and higher fees. He concluded that '[i]n order to justify including private equity in the portfolio, managers must select top-quartile managers. Anything less fails to compensate for the time, effort and risk entailed in the pursuit of non-marketable investments.' This conclusion was particularly damning because what he was effectively saying was that most of the supposedly sophisticated private equity and venture capital funds underperformed a passive equity investment index such as the S&P 500. However, if you manage to invest with a top-quartile or preferably top-decile manager in private equity or venture capital, you will outperform. But as mentioned in Chapter 6, *every* marketing brochure for *every* fund claims to be in the top quartile, so the issue then becomes how to even begin selecting one?

Summary

No competitive field of investment seems to offer future prospects that are more attractive or contain a significantly lower element of peril than do common stocks.

– Phil Fisher, investor and pioneer in the field of growth investing

I've included a short description of all the major asset classes in Appendix B, but if you are investing for the long term, there is no asset class other than equities in which to allocate your capital. That is not to say that you shouldn't own other asset classes as a form of diversification, but, for long-term wealth creation, there is nothing better than equities.

You just have to have developed the correct temperament from Part One of this book and persisted long enough to achieve the superior long-term returns that are achievable.

CHAPTER 10: PORTFOLIO CONSTRUCTION

'How do I select great individual stocks to construct the ideal portfolio?' is the wrong question to ask. As Munger says, 'Invert, always invert.' The question investors should be asking themselves is rather 'How do I construct a great portfolio framework within which to select the ideal individual stocks?'

— Ardal Gronager, fund manager

Countless pages have been written about portfolio construction, some simple and some incredibly complex. No one strategy is correct for all. Every investor is unique; thus, every portfolio and asset allocation mix is unique. There are, however, guidelines to portfolio construction that will make sense for most investors and will help them to avoid unnecessary complexity and mistakes. Like so much in the field of investing, there is no 'right way', but there are plenty of 'wrong ways'. We will explore them in this chapter, so you can better identify and avoid them.

At Gronager Partners, we believe that the overarching portfolio construction needs to come before the individual securities selection process that goes into it. This should be entirely intuitive, and yet many investors we meet don't grasp the importance of first building a solid foundation of portfolio construction and management before selecting the individual securities that will sit within it. Rigorous portfolio construction is essential for long-term success. Therefore, this is where our investment process begins.

We have three rules for portfolio construction. We refer to them internally as the Three 'A's because following them ensures that our portfolio will be AAA-Rated:

1. Always invest within your own circle of competence.
   - Invest only in businesses of which you have a complete fundamental understanding and into which you would be comfortable investing all your net worth and not being able to sell for at least ten years.

- Investing is the broadest of intellectual disciplines. And as we know, all knowledge is cumulative. We can gradually expand our circle over time through continuous development and improvement of our own unique latticework of mental models. It is always better to be an inch wide and a mile deep than a mile wide and an inch deep.
- When in doubt, take a pass. There are about 45,000 listed equities around the world. There is no shame in having a large 'too hard' pile.

2. Always invest with a sufficient margin of safety.
   - Rule Number 1: Don't lose money.
     Rule Number 2: Don't forget Rule Number 1.
   - Although quantitative analysis is important, qualitative analysis should determine whether or not a business is exceptional.
   - Growth is a key input in the value equation.

3. Always allow 'Mr Market' time to take care of the rest.
   - Temperament is what sets apart the truly successful investor.
   - Patience and the ability to remove yourself from the noise of the market and judge investments dispassionately are the keys to long-term outperformance. Patience will stop you buying the top or selling the bottom.

It is important that we not only select our investments individually but also examine how they go together as part of a wider portfolio. No amount of knowledge of complex algebra and statistics will help you with your portfolio construction unless you put it to good use. This may sound obvious, but although most investors have a decent grasp of the merits and trade-offs between portfolio concentration and diversification, very few put it into practice through a well-thought-out and consistently applied strategy.

From experience or looking at history, it is clear that 'once-in-a-generation' financial crises seem to occur every five to ten years. Value investors need to have the mindset that the next one could occur tomorrow and know that their portfolios are robust enough to withstand it. As well as knowing what actions they would take to capitalise on the opportunity.

Asset Allocation

An investor asked whether Buffett's track record was statistically significant as he traded so little. Klarman answered that each day Buffett chose not to do something was a decision taken, too.

– Nick Sleep, co-founder of the Nomad Investment Partnership

In theory, having all your available funds always invested in the market is the optimal way to deploy capital. In other words, as soon as you receive new investor funds or a dividend, this should be deployed into your portfolio. As fund manager Barton Biggs describes the process, 'We put all our capital to work over the course of a morning. Our theory was that the right thing to do was to get where you wanted to be immediately. I still think it is the right way to handle new money.'

However, this misses one important issue. The number of great investments available at any one point in time is very limited. Unless you are happy to deploy additional capital into less-than-stellar ideas (something I would not recommend) or add them to your existing positions (a better option) you will be left with a portion of cash in your portfolio.

Holding cash in your portfolio can act as a drag on returns over time, but when looked at as an investment decision, it can make sense. If an over-priced market means there is a dearth of good investment ideas, holding cash can be seen as having a lower opportunity cost and higher potential return compared to deploying it into markets at elevated levels. Given Buffett's track record at Berkshire Hathaway, for example, it makes no sense to assign the value of cash held by Berkshire as cash with no potential for future return on it. As of mid-2024, Berkshire's market cap is $900 billion with $200 billion of cash and short-term securities (22 percent of the market cap!). Clearly, a multiple should be attached to this cash based on its future earnings potential when Buffett finds something suitably priced to buy. He does not see it as 'just cash' earning interest in the bank, but powder being kept dry, ready to be used in 20 percent-plus compounders in the future. As fund manager Ray Dalio explains, 'Knowing when to bet is as important as knowing what bets are probably worth making. You can significantly improve your track record if you only make the bets that you are most confident will pay off.'

In the inverse situation, that is, where you believe markets are far from their peak and you are still searching for the very best investment in which to deploy capital, it may make sense to take the cash and invest it in a low-cost equity index fund. This will allow you to capture some of the upward move in equities without putting yourself under additional pressure to quickly identify suitable investments. And if, as I recommend, you are already cultivating a watchlist, finding suitable investments will not be an issue.

The second reason for holding cash is for a rainy day. As any engineer will tell you, you want some excess capacity or a buffer built into the system. An amount of cash is always required for unexpected costs. Or to allow you to act quickly on a briefly available investment opportunity. Cash provides you with an added layer of protection against unforeseen market volatility, and having it allows you to capitalise on these dislocations while others are scrambling for it. As the saying goes, 'In times of crisis, cash is king,' and you certainly don't want to have to scrounge up cash by selling current investments at a loss due to unforeseen market moves (i.e. forced selling).

In my investing career, I have found it helpful to adhere to fixed rules during times of market volatility. These rules force me to act and reject my default condition, which is to do nothing. Doing nothing is significantly better for my long-term returns than selling, but it's during times of market stress that the greatest future returns can be found. I always have a minimum cash buffer in the portfolio of, say, 5 percent, which I invest in short-term government bonds. As markets rise and good investment ideas become scarcer, the interest and dividend income from my portfolio begins to accumulate as additional cash reserves if there are no longer any great opportunities to deploy it. The cash portion of my portfolio may then grow to 20 percent-plus of my overall portfolio.

When the markets fall, as they inevitably will, we will find investment opportunities. And even more the further they fall. We can never know in advance how far they will fall; all we know is that the average annual retracement in markets is about 14 percent. Thus, it makes sense to have rules for deploying your excess cash as the market falls to ensure that you don't try to bottom-pick or time the market, which, as we have discussed, is impossible anyway. For example, if your cash holdings are 20 percent of the portfolio, you could deploy them as follows: if the market falls 10 percent, invest half of your cash. If the market falls further, down 20 percent, invest half of your remaining cash. If the market falls further, down 30 percent, invest half of your remaining cash. And so on. Because the iterations of this strategy are 'endless', this ensures that we will never miss the investment opportunities presented by a pull-back. In other words, we will always be positioned to buy low and sell high and take advantage of the vicissitudes of the market.

It's also worth noting that keeping the cash portion of your portfolio in short-duration fixed income instruments (government bonds) has two advantages. First, it is as safe and liquid an investment as there is. In times of market stress, this is vital, as the equity portion of your portfolio will be less liquid. The second is that not only do bonds generate a steady income stream, but their returns are also often inversely correlated with the equities portion of your portfolio. This is true particularly during times of market panic when short-duration government bonds ('govvies') rally as investors flee to relative safety and away from more-volatile asset classes such as equities. To be clear, short-term corporate bonds are not recommended because during times of market volatility, their liquidity also tends to evaporate. In my experience, buying corporates over govvies is not worth the added risk, despite the likely extra yield pick-up.

Position-sizing, in terms of putting money to work, is also an essential element of portfolio construction, and I find that each investor has their own way of doing it. Some prefer to buy a 'toehold' position and build a larger or 'full' position from there (i.e. averaging in). Others like to buy their entire position as quickly as possible. There is not necessarily a right way, but there needs to be a clearly thought-out process behind your actions.

Lee Freeman-Shor, in his book *The Art of Execution*, provides detailed evidence that investors are not good at predicting which of their ideas will perform the best, let alone ranking their likely future performance from best to worst. On this basis, it makes little sense for us to allocate more capital to what we believe to be our best ideas. Even if you find one company that you believe is the best investment you have ever come across (overconfidence bias), it would be a mistake to allocate the capital you would normally reserve for two positions to just this one. Personally, I like to keep the capital allo-cation decision on position-sizing simple. I favour about a 5 percent 'full' position for each idea (a 5 × 20 portfolio) but am happy to have some slightly smaller starting positions if I find more good ideas than expected.

For watchlist stocks, I like to have a smaller position, usually 1 percent. I truly believe the words of fund manager Li Lu when he says, 'You never truly understand a business until you own it.' By owning even a small position, I am mentally far more engaged with that business. I switch from being an observer to a business owner and am far more likely to spend the requisite time to see if my watchlist companies need to be culled or promoted to full portfolio positions. Using a sports analogy, I think of my full portfolio positions, which are all initiated at approximately 5 percent, as my first team. They are the best of the best, with a proven track record, and are on the pitch playing the game. My watchlist stocks (1 percent positions) are the players warming up on the sidelines. They have everything going for them and are just waiting for an opportunity to be promoted into the first team.

I am happy to keep a company on our watchlist for many years so long as it presents the right investment characteristics, even if its price means there isn't a sufficient discount to intrinsic value to promote it to a full position. If we are wrong on the estimate of intrinsic value and the business ends up being a 100-bagger, at a 1 percent starting-position size, it can still have a meaningful impact on our overall portfolio returns. When we are doing investment research, we always look for exceptional businesses to add to our watchlist.

Creating an 'Anti-Fragile' Portfolio

The prudent, farsighted investor manages his or her portfolio with the knowledge that financial catastrophes can and do occur.

   – Seth Klarman, founder and chief executive of the Baupost Group

The best portfolio construction combines elements of concentration with diversification. On the one hand, we need enough diversification to be 'anti-fragile' so we can survive or even thrive in the toughest of market conditions. On the other, and to maximise returns, as fund manager Barton Biggs writes, 'The way to invest for superior performance is to have a few big bets in which you can develop an edge and that you have real conviction in.'

An anti-fragile portfolio can be achieved via diversification. Diversification means very different things to different people. To indexers, diversification may mean owning a little bit of everything, for example, tens of thousands of securities over various asset classes. For Charlie Munger, three positions was enough: Berkshire, Costco, and his investment in Li Lu's fund. Buffett has 99 percent of his net worth solely in Berkshire stock, and that has been the case for over fifty years! Of course, Berkshire is a conglomerate and is, therefore, not one position but an aggregation of many businesses, providing significant real-world diversification to its owners.

Diversification in some form must play a key role in any successful long-term investment strategy. This may seem counterintuitive to concentrated value investors. However, given what we know about the uncertainties of investing and the impossibility of predicting the future, having all our money invested into one single position, no matter how well we know it, likely represents an overly risky proposition.

Once we have committed to running an equity-biased long-term portfolio as the best way to maximise our returns, we must accept that the degree of correlation between our portfolio and the market will be larger than one that is diversified across more asset classes. That said, we can reduce the correlation between the positions in our portfolio by ensuring they operate in different industries and geographies. Just because the oil and gas sector, for example, represents the best 'value' or 'screens the cheapest' relative to other sectors does not mean we should only own a hundred oil and gas stocks. This may look diversified based on the number of positions, but they will be highly correlated with one another. As billionaire hedge fund manager Bruce Kovner wrote, 'Beware correlation of positions; if you are running eight different but highly correlated positions then you are in effect running one position at eight times its normal size.'

Our objective is to minimise the amount of correlation between our equity positions by diversifying between companies operating in different industries and geographies. However, this is never achieved at the expense of how good they are relative to each other as investments. In other words, don't include substandard investment opportunities in your portfolio just because it reduces the portfolio correlation. If a significant portion of your portfolio is already concentrated towards a certain industry (as a rule of thumb, I use 25 percent) and there are no other equally good investment opportunities outside this sector, the correct decision may be to sit on cash instead of becoming more exposed in one sector.

Thus, as your investment opportunities become focused in only one sector, your portfolio will likely hold an increasing proportion of cash (short-term government bonds) which will increasingly reduce your correlation with the equity market, during times of overvaluation.

Conversely when there are investment opportunities aplenty, usually after a significant market drop, we reverse the strategy and reduce our allocation to non-correlated short-term government bonds and invest the proceeds into the more correlated equity positions to take advantage of the market-fall. Although on paper this may seem risky as we are increasing the degree of correlation in our portfolio during times of market stress, the margin of safety present in the securities that we are buying should more than compensate for this.

Your individual capacity to be resilient during equity market downturns should dictate the degree of diversification in your investment portfolio. This is where a great deal of intellectual honesty and self-awareness as an investor becomes essential. There is no point in having a 90 percent equity portfolio and 10 percent fixed income if, when the equity market halves, you sell all your equities in a blind panic and buy more short-term government bonds just when they are at their most expensive! As David Swensen of the Yale Endowment wrote, 'Sensible individuals take care to distribute assets across a range of investment alternatives. The act of diversification provides a free lunch of enhanced returns and reduced risk, increasing the likelihood that an investor will stay the course in difficult market environments.'

Like our individual investments and the requirement for their prices to include significant margins of safety, we need our overall portfolio to incorporate a margin of safety against all known bad outcomes – and ideally some unknown ones, too.

We also know the investment theory on diversification and how it can help us on our quest for superior returns. All that is required is to incorporate it into our portfolio construction process. For me, the saying 'To finish first, you must first finish' comes to mind when people talk to me about diversification. To be a professional investor, you must love being in the game. A leveraged single-stock 'portfolio' is the single surest way to ensure you won't be playing the game for long. We professional investors want to be in the game forever and, therefore, must not make decisions that could bring our participation to a sudden end. Constructing an anti-fragile portfolio is key to long-term investment success.

A Word on Leverage

A leveraged portfolio forces you to act irrationally when markets are irrational, as opposed to acting rationally when markets are irrational.

— Mark Lasry, co-founder and chief executive of Avenue Capital Group

Leverage in your life (e.g. credit card debt), in your portfolio (e.g. buying on margin), and in your portfolio businesses (e.g. through bond issuance) introduces fragility. Buying things you cannot reasonably afford today by borrowing is to be avoided, however tempting it may seem. Whether it's borrowing to buy a shiny new car, to buy additional stock for your portfolio to try to increase your returns, or the management team of the business you own engaging in value-destroying and expensive debt-funded M&A. Leverage truly is a double-edged sword. In good times, it makes you look smart by enhancing your gains, but in bad times it can easily decapitate you. I have never been convinced of the merits of leverage in an equity portfolio. History tells us that it's possible for the broad equity market to decline 90 percent (the Great Depression). On that basis alone, you should never use leverage in an equity portfolio. Bill Ruane, one of the super-investors of Graham and Doddsville, stated, 'Do not borrow money to buy stocks ... You don't act rationally when you're investing borrowed money.'

Economist John Maynard Keynes famously described the pernicious effects of leverage when he wrote,

> It is rare, particularly with leveraged securities, that one can endure a substantial decline without being a victim of it. Even if one has great confidence in a position, which then declines substantially, the process by which the loss is experienced is always so unnerving and detrimental that the position is a victim of the decline itself. Price creates its own reality. Obviously, dramatic declines often end with liquidations at the bottom. This is the insidious impact of panic and leverage.

If you want to survive, let alone thrive, in both life and investing, my advice is do not leverage. Period!

Portfolio Concentration

We believe that a policy of portfolio concentration may well decrease risk if it raises, as it should, both the intensity with which an investor thinks about a business and the comfort level he must feel with its economic characteristics before buying into it.

— Warren E. Buffett, chairman of Berkshire Hathaway

As mentioned in Chapter 1, when we look at any list of the richest people in the world, they overwhelmingly tend to be entrepreneurs who started their own businesses and concentrated the vast portion of their net worth in those businesses. This allowed their wealth to compound and grow. However, what we often see when they get older is they sell out. Interestingly, these billionaires very rarely continue to have 95 percent-plus of their net worth in a single business, even one they know and thoroughly understand, for the rest of their lives. Why do even they consider this to be a risky strategy? Conventional wisdom would have us believe that the first stage of getting wealthy is to concentrate, but once we are wealthy, conventional wisdom then suggests our preoccupation should move to diversification. This is the second stage, where people move from the wealth accumulation or concentration stage to the wealth preservation or diversification stage at the end of their lives. It's worth exploring exactly where this logic comes from.

As mentioned in Chapter 7, J.P. Morgan Asset Management published a very interesting paper called 'Agony & Ecstasy' wherein they investigated whether switching from an accumulation strategy to a wealth preservation strategy generally made sense for wealthy individuals. Of course, we need to take the conclusions with a pinch of salt as their motivation was to induce business owners to sell and look for new investments – all very lucrative for J.P. Morgan. Nonetheless, some of the findings are insightful. [FIG. 24]

It is interesting to see on that table what we know intuitively: that faster-moving sectors (e.g. information technology) have higher rates of catastrophic loss than slower-moving sectors (e.g. utilities or consumer staples). This is worth thinking about when we look at the sector split of companies across our portfolio.

A second takeaway from their research is that the return on the median stock since its inception versus an investment in the Russell 3000 Index

Total % of Companies Experiencing 'Catastrophic Loss'
1980–2014

Sector	Total % of companies experiencing "catastrophic loss" 1980-2014
All sectors	40%
Consumer Discretionary	43%
Consumer Staples	26%
Energy	47%
Materials	34%
Industrials	35%
Health Care	42%
Financials	25%
Information Technology	57%
Telecommunication Services	51%
Utilites	13%

Around 40% of all stocks experienced catastrophic declines, when defined as a 70% decline from peak value with minimal recovery. This is a subjective cutoff point; many concentrated holders would see smaller permanent declines as equally unacceptable and as risks that should be mitigated against. The outcomes based on a variety of thresholds suggest that for many concentrated holders diversification should be a central part of wealth management planning.

SOURCE: FactSet, J.P. Morgan Asset Management

(which encompasses essentially all US-listed businesses of a reasonable size) was −54 percent. [FIG. 25]

Two-thirds of all stocks underperformed versus the Russell 3000 Index, and the absolute returns for 40 percent were negative. This confirms

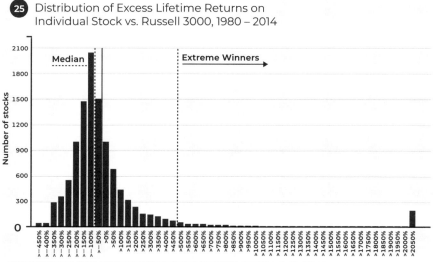 Distribution of Excess Lifetime Returns on Individual Stock vs. Russell 3000, 1980 – 2014

SOURCE: Mayer, C. (2015). 100 Baggers: Stocks That Return 100-To-1 and How to Find Them.

something we already know: most of the market gains are accounted for by a small number of very significant outperformers. These exceptional performers compensate for the lacklustre performance of the rest. This highlights for me that we must invest in only the very best businesses. As Buffett opines, 'The business world is divided into a tiny number of wonderful businesses – well worth investing in – and a huge number of bad or mediocre businesses that are not attractive as long-term holdings.'

In a concentrated equity portfolio of, say, ten stocks, over the long term most of the excess return generated over the market – that is, most of the 'alpha' – in the portfolio may come from just one of the holdings. In other words, three stocks may significantly underperform, four may do as well as the market, two may outperform the market, and one superstar may go up many multiples compared to the rest. Thus, if you were to cut any of your winners too early, you could significantly reduce the returns of your overall portfolio.

The J.P. Morgan study concludes by pointing out that since 1980, over 320 companies were deleted from the S&P 500 for business distress reasons, which implies a lot of turnover. This should not be a surprise. Capitalism is based on competition, creative destruction, and reinvention. While globalisation has expanded the opportunities for individual companies, it has also increased their competitive, regulatory and operational risks. This circles back to the importance of a business having a large, defensible and preferably expanding economic moat to ensure its longevity.

For long-term value investors utilising a concentrated strategy (in terms of number of holdings) but diversified across sectors and geographies, one or potentially several positions will likely grow over time to represent a larger and larger proportion of their overall portfolio. Personally, I don't cut my winners, especially the outlier positions, unless their valuations lose all connection to an optimistic reality.

The very best businesses can deliver huge upside surprises. The key is to ensure that your investment thesis remains intact as they grow to become a larger proportion of your portfolio. If they grow to such a size that they are affecting your judgement and you are worrying about their every move, clearly, the position has become too large and should be cut back. Cutting back acknowledges your psychological limitations and is absolutely the correct thing to do. A position should never become so large that it interrupts your sleep at night. If you know the business as well as you should and your thesis remains intact, you should have nothing to worry about. Worry can be a red flag.

Many investors view the J.P. Morgan paper as an advocate for overdiversification. However, if you fully foster the contrarian investor's mindset, you will see it differently. Value investors see the data presented as clear evidence of the possibilities for outperformance that are available through concentration and superior stock selection. As Charlie Munger wrote, 'A few major opportunities, clearly recognizable as such, will usually come to one who continuously searches and waits, with a curious mind that loves diagnosis involving multiple variables. And then all that is required is a willingness to bet heavily when the odds are extremely favourable, using resources available as a result of prudence and patience in the past.'

Summary

To beat the market over the long term, you need to be doing something different. Why do most investors start their investment process with individual securities selection instead of portfolio construction? If an investor does not know what their return objectives are, and the level of volatility they will need to accept to achieve them, how can they construct a portfolio that will meet their return objectives, that they will stick with through thick and thin? At Gronager Partners, we invert the process; we believe that the foundation of portfolio construction must come before the process of selecting individual securities. Foundations first; everything else second.

We don't play to win a game without first understanding the rules. In the game of investing, the rules change constantly; thus, our investment process must evolve with them. There are, however, three rules for portfolio construction that have stood the test of time. We referred to them at the start of this chapter. It's worth reminding ourselves of the Three 'A's:

1. Always invest within your own circle of competence.
2. Always invest with a sufficient margin of safety.
3. Always allow 'Mr Market' time to take care of the rest.

The research on the benefits to your returns from position concentration combined with geographic and sectoral diversification is well known. However, understanding your own temperament as an investor in terms of how you will behave given a certain type of portfolio construction is even more important. The key is to have faith in your portfolio foundations so you don't panic when the market goes against you. First, you need to understand what you own; it must sit well within your circle of competence. Secondly, you need to build enough anti-fragility into your portfolio to allow you to sleep soundly; therefore, you need to incorporate a big-enough margin of safety. Thirdly, be patient. Let the market do its thing. Allow these three rules of portfolio construction to form the foundations of your portfolio construction and you will be well on the way to AAA-Rated, long-term investment success.

CHAPTER 11: THE ART AND SCIENCE OF INVESTMENT SELECTION

Although the future is unknowable, it is not unimaginable. The entrepreneurial idea that carries on and brings profit is precisely that idea which did not occur to the majority. It is not correct foresight as such that yields profits, but foresight better than that of the rest. The prize goes only to the dissenters, who do not let themselves be misled by the errors accepted by the multitude.

— Ludwig von Mises, Austrian economist

Successful stock-picking seems simple, but it's certainly not easy. Many novice investors believe that they just need to invest in sectors or industries that will revolutionise the world, such as electric cars, then sit back and watch the money roll in. The reality is radically different. Even if you can identify a revolutionary sector or industry, you need to be able to predict the individual long-term winners within it. And even then, you must ensure that this 'revolutionary' future is not already fully incorporated into the no doubt wonderfully high price you will likely have to pay for the business.

As Buffett wrote, 'There's a lot more to picking stocks than figuring out what's going to be a wonderful industry in the future. ... I do not think the average person can pick stocks.'

If you look at the top ten companies in the world today (2024) listed by market capitalisation, eight of them are American:

1. NVIDIA
2. Microsoft
3. Apple
4. Alphabet (Google)
5. Amazon
6. Saudi Aramco
7. Meta (Facebook)
8. Taiwan Semiconductor Manufacturing Company (TSMC)

9. Berkshire Hathaway

10. Eli Lilly

How many of these companies do you expect to be around in thirty years' time? Half? A quarter? If history is any guide, the answer will be zero. If we go back thirty years and repeat the exercise, not one company in the 1994 top ten by market cap has made it into today's list.

Clearly, finding a growing industry or sector is just part of the puzzle for potential outperformance. Being able to identify companies that have re-invention programmed into their corporate DNA so they can successfully adapt to an ever-changing world is also critical. We must also have the same 'evolvability' as investors, applied to our own investment processes. As Howard Marks puts it, 'One's investment approach must be intuitive and adaptive rather than fixed and mechanical.'

In my experience, the investment situations that offer the most asymmetric risk/reward are those where the market gets confused between risk and uncertainty. We have already defined risk as the probability of a permanent loss of our capital; this is very distinct from price volatility, which is usually made up entirely of noise. Markets, however, view price volatility as risk. Therefore, if there is uncertainty around a business, the price action can become very erratic, as there is nothing that 'Mr Market' dislikes more than uncertainty. In these situations, a value investor who is patient, methodical and impartial can extract enormous value by identifying that there is far less risk in a situation than the market price is currently reflecting.

Every investment is made based on imperfect knowledge, as no amount of research can ever make us one hundred percent certain of a successful outcome. The degree of uncertainty in a situation is what we are compensated for when we purchase a security, through the discount it is trading at relative to our estimate of its intrinsic value. Value investing is about identifying those situations where the market is overweighting the discount required for the perceived uncertainty that we are willing to bear. These opportunities arise when we are comfortable with the risk and capable of seeing through the uncertainty.

When it comes to the volume of information required to make an investment, each of us will have our own threshold depending on the situation. I would, however, caution you against automatically believing that more information is better. As Seth Klarman says, 'Information generally follows the well-known 80/20 rule: the first 80 percent of the useful information is gathered by the first 20 percent of the time spent.'

We need a system or an approach that allows us to assess the right information at the right time to either discard potential investment opportunities or push them further through our investment process. As Buffett described in his 1996 Letter to Berkshire Shareholders,

> Your goal as an investor should be simply to purchase, at a rational price, a part interest in an easily understood business whose earnings are virtually certain to be materially higher, five, ten, and twenty years from now. Over time, you will find only a few companies that meet those standards – so when you see one that qualifies, you should buy a meaningful amount.

The Individual Securities Selection Process

The stock market is filled with individuals who know the price of everything, but the value of nothing.

– Phil Fisher, investor and pioneer in the field of growth investing

As discussed in Chapter 1, there is no fundamental difference between buying a business outright and buying a piece of that business in the form of shares of stock. 'When investing,' Buffett says, 'we view ourselves as business analysts, not as market analysts, not as macroeconomic analysts, and not even as securities analysts.' This means that Buffett works first and foremost from the perspective of a business owner.

We do the same at Gronager Partners, and I recommend you do that, too. We must look at every company holistically, examining all quantitative and qualitative aspects of its business, its financial position and its purchase price. We look for companies that we understand that have favourable long-term prospects, are operated by honest and competent management, and, most importantly, are available at attractive prices.

Implementing the 'owner's mentality', that is, viewing the purchase of a single share of a business as the equivalent to buying the entire business, can often be difficult. Because of this, I like to ask myself a single question that helps me tap into the ownership mindset when I'm evaluating any potential investment: If I had the total market capitalisation of the company in cash today and could only buy one stock with the money, would I buy the entirety of this business or would I buy something else?

To properly answer this question at Gronager Partners, we have developed a five-step process through which we run every potential investment idea. This is our Individual Securities Selection Process:

- **Step 1**: Identifying investment opportunities
- **Step 2**: Circle of competence test
- **Step 3**: Quantitative analysis
- **Step 4**: Qualitative analysis
- **Step 5**: Investment decision

A picture is often worth a thousand words. I visualise our individual securities selection process as an inverted funnel. People are often surprised by this because it is 'upside down', but I explain that we as value investors are bottom-up stock-pickers, not top-down macro-analysts. Therefore, it makes sense that we start with the widest end of the funnel at the bottom and work our way up to the top. Most investors are always looking for reasons to say 'Yes!' and invest. We take the opposite stance; instead, at every stage

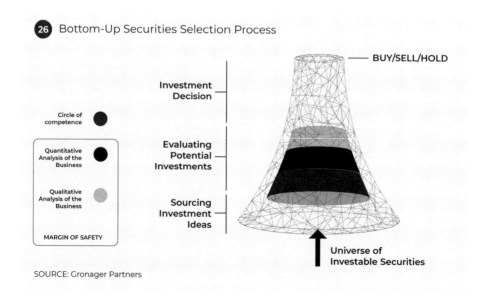

26 Bottom-Up Securities Selection Process

SOURCE: Gronager Partners

of our investment process, we always look for reasons to say 'No!' There are always more investment opportunities than there are exceptional businesses. Therefore, being a harsh grader is a requirement for successful securities selection. [FIG. 26]

Step 1: Identifying Investment Opportunities

There are two rules of fishing. Rule no. 1: 'Fish where the fish are.' Rule no. 2: 'Don't forget rule no. 1.'

Charles T. Munger, vice-chairman of Berkshire Hathaway

As mentioned previously, there are about 45,000 listed equities globally. If you were to spend just one hour analysing each company (with no break or sleep), it would take you over five years to go through them all. How, then, do we go about narrowing down the investable universe to *our* investable universe? As with many aspects of investing, there is no 'right way' of doing it, but there are certainly many 'wrong ways'. But before we began Step 1, we established the foundations of our portfolio construction, so we already know at this point what sort of securities meet our portfolio criteria – whether they be asset classes, sectors or individual stocks.

There are many ways of reducing the intake into our funnel, but here are some of the methods that we use at Gronager Partners that have stood the test of time:

- 'Starting with the "A"'s' – a reference to the way Buffett used to find investments by flipping through printed *Moody's Manuals*, investor manuals that sorted businesses alphabetically. This method involves manually assessing every investment that fits within our investable universe in a particular market and eliminating them one by one.
- 'Cloning' – reverse-engineering the investment thesis behind the highest-conviction ideas of other renowned investors. These are easily googleable for investors with AUM over $100 million.
- The media – reading newspapers, trade and industry journals, investor forums, interviews, podcasts, and conference proceedings.
- Screening – using metrics such as return on capital employed (ROCE) or gross/operating/net margins to narrow down our investable universe.

As we have seen, to generate superior returns, your investment process must be geared towards finding outlier investments that have an asymmetry between risk and return that is in your favour. There are only ever likely to be a few securities in the market at any one time which clearly demonstrate these characteristics – which is why we have a concentrated portfolio. However, there are certain situations in the market which historically have been better fishing spots, and there are ways to identify them. These include, but are not limited to the following:

- Bankruptcy/reorganisation/distressed situations
- Low-risk/high-uncertainty situations
- Loss-making businesses
- Capital-allocation decision analysis
- Corporate spinoffs
- Market/company screening
- Thematic investment ideas
- Cloning or reverse-engineering investments
- Parallel investments
- Emerging markets

Bankruptcy/Reorganisation/Distressed Situations

If a sector is under pressure or a company has gone bankrupt in a stressed sector, this is usually a good place to start looking at both the bankrupt company as well as its major competitors to see if they offer value. A company in the bankruptcy process may be restructured, and if the equity is not wiped out, new equity investors can earn a very good return. Hence, we need to identify what the company is 'worth' both as a going concern and if sold off piecemeal. This usually requires a thorough understanding of the capital structure and claims against the businesses versus the assets available to satisfy them. (Equity holders always get paid after everyone else!)

It is also worth noting that companies that emerge from bankruptcy rarely repeat the same mistakes. The pain of and ingrained lessons from failure may make the company stronger over the long term. However, additional work needs to be done to analyse whether the business model has changed sufficiently to make it a worthwhile investment going forward.

In my experience, anything that has the word 'distressed' attached to it usually has the same effect on most investors as seeing a label on a piece of fruit that says 'toxic'. Many times, such a reaction may be justified, but given the complexity associated with most distressed investing situations, along with the small pool of investors who examine them carefully, they can present compelling opportunities for value investors. Billionaire founder of the Blackstone Group Steve Schwartzman says of distressed investing, 'If something's easy, there will be plenty of people willing to help solve it. But find a real mess, and there is no one around.'

Every distressed investing opportunity is unique, but I have found that a few broad frameworks can lead to consistent success. We have established already that to be a successful investor you must foster a contrarian mindset. When others are running away, you must remove all emotion and rationally evaluate the situation. The two sides to this mindset are summarised by Buffett. First,

> None of this means, however, that a business or stock is an intelligent purchase simply because it is unpopular; a contrarian approach is just as foolish as a follow-the-crowd strategy. What's required is thinking rather than polling. Unfortunately, Bertrand Russell's observation about life in general applies with unusual force in the financial world: 'Most men would rather die than think. Many do.'

There is clearly no point in taking a contrarian attitude to every investment, as the market is often correct.

Buffett goes on to say, 'The best thing that happens to us is when a great company gets into temporary trouble … We want to buy them when they're on the operating table.' Being able to rationally evaluate and project the long-term potential of a great business when it is going through a period of turmoil, while being able to see through the near-term problems when others are emotional and panicked, is the aspect of contrarianism that we are after.

Never is investing with a margin of safety more important than when it comes to investing in a distressed business. As famed investor Anthony Bolton wrote, 'It is an important observation that the first bad news (such as the first profit warning) is rarely the last.' Things can and often do get worse before they get better, which is why having a complete understanding of the business and building in plenty of downside protection is so important. There are different ways of doing this. Billionaire investor Sir Jim Goldsmith advocated buying only companies that had hard assets which could be liquidated if the company entered bankruptcy – this is what Buffett was doing when he bought the Washington Post Company. Billionaire property investor and businessman Sam Zell followed similar reasoning when he recommended that investors 'target good asset-intensive companies with bad balance sheets. We like asset-intensive investments because if the world ended, there would be something to liquidate.'

Bolton however, suggests that if a company is distressed, this usually means it has a falling free cash flow (FCF) and a declining multiple. As such, focusing on businesses where there are foreseeable catalysts that could reverse the slide in a company's FCF can lead to outsized gains as this would likely also lead to multiple expansion. He does however, caution that '[e]xperience suggests that industry-wide sell-offs represent better hunting grounds for potential opportunities than do company-specific crises. A single company may stumble in a way that makes recovery of value impossible, but entire industries disappear quite rarely.'

If a sector such as the oil and gas industry comes under pressure due to an unforeseen collapse in the oil price, for example, it is worth spending the time to look, not for the stock that has fallen the most, but the very best businesses in the sector – at a discount. We don't know how long, in this case, the oil price will be low, but we do know that individuals and companies will still require oil in the future, so we want to find the lowest-cost producer coupled with the best management that will be able to take advantage of reduced competition as weaker businesses disappear. The example of the shale oil producers that I highlighted in Chapter 5 is a good example of this strategy working well.

Low-Risk/High-Uncertainty Situations

As explored in Chapter 3, markets hate uncertainty, and when the outlook is deemed 'highly uncertain', they will often discount the stock price more than makes sense from the fundamentals of the business. This can throw up opportunities offering asymmetric risk/reward. For example, a highly cyclical business such as refining or shipping may have a low price/earnings ratio (P/E) and appear to be loss-making, but it may still have lots of cash on the balance sheet. In other words, such businesses are less risky than they may appear from looking at simple metrics. Another example would be a commodity producer for which the current commodity input prices (for example, iron ore in the case of a steel manufacturer) are at historic highs, but the output price for the product (steel) is at a cyclical low – but the company you're looking at is the lowest-cost producer. In this case, the baby may have been thrown out with

Price/Earnings Ratio (P/E)

Often called the price or earnings multiple, the P/E ratio helps assess the relative value of a company's stock. It is calculated by dividing the share price by the earnings per share (EPS).

A multiple can be used to show how much investors are willing to pay per dollar of earnings. Say you are analysing a stock with $5 of EPS that is currently trading at $50 per share. This stock has a P/E of 10 ($50/$5) which means that investors are willing to pay a multiple of ten times the current EPS (or ten years of current earnings) to own the stock.

the bathwater if the whole sector has been written off unfairly with a low P/E multiple. Our lowest-cost producer is primed to gain market share as its competitors go out of business.

In fact, many companies are given low P/E ratios by the market due to limited earnings visibility; for example, a business that has several of its largest contracts up for renewal. In situations like these, we need to assess how fast our payback period is (i.e. how long it would take the company to earn back its market cap) through our own projected earnings and assess whether this represents good risk/reward, despite what may be the cyclical nature of the industry within which it operates. The market often gives almost no chance that contracts will be renewed, but deeper analysis might show that the producer had renewed at least 80 percent of its contracts in the past, thus warranting a significantly higher multiple. Again, low risk, high uncertainty.

Loss-Making Businesses

A business that has gone from profitable to loss-making (or is loss-making and on the way to profitable but has undershot market expectations) is usually fertile ground for potential investment ideas. Markets tend to go from euphoric to overly pessimistic in the blink of an eye – and nothing accelerates this process faster than a loss-making business. In these situations, we are looking for catalyst(s) that would make the company profitable and evaluating the likelihood that they will occur. An example would be if new management has been brought in or if a viable turnaround plan has been implemented. A consistent return to profitability can very quickly lead to a significant re-rating of the stock, which provides the double returns benefit of growing earnings and also an increase in the P/E multiple.

Investor Sir John Templeton said the best way to find bargains was to study the assets that have performed most dismally over the past five years, then assess whether the cause of those woes is temporary or permanent. Most people are naturally drawn to investments that are already successful and popular, whether it's a high-flying stock, fund, or a rapidly growing economy. But if a sunny future is already reflected in the price of the asset, it's probably a sucker's bet.

Capital Allocation Decision Analysis

How well management allocates capital is one of the key questions to answer for any potential investment. If a company is profitable but does not pay a dividend, it can be worthwhile exploring why. What is the business doing with the profits that it generates? Does it have significant internal growth opportunities that will expand its compounding engine? Or is it wasting the capital on large corporate overheads or value-destructive M&A?

If it is pursuing growth opportunities, you need to dig deeper to work out how likely they are to come to fruition and whether the businesses expansion strategy makes sense. As a rule, we want expansion of existing lines of business or clearly adjacent businesses that are directly related to its current successful operations. For example, an electric car manufacturer expanding to make electric scooters would fall within these guidelines. An electric car manufacturer moving into property development would not. In general, the market places a higher value on organic or internally generated growth over time than inorganic or acquired growth, usually from M&A.

Corporate Spinoffs

Spinoffs can be potential diamonds in the rough, especially if senior management jumps ship to run the new business. As Charlie Munger reminded us, human beings are incredibly straightforward. To understand how we behave, all we must do is look at the incentives. If a highly rated and highly paid executive leaves the mothership to lead a spinoff business, this is often a good indication for further exploration of the spinoff. That executive is not going to walk away from a secure job with a generous compensation package, regardless of how many stock options they will get in the new entity, if they are not supremely confident that the move is going to be significantly more lucrative for them (risk/reward in action again).

Management of the spinoff will, however, be tight-lipped about future opportunities until the establishment of the spinoff is completed and the price of their options has been set. In the meantime, there is uncertainty, which could magnify the opportunity. Although the mothership company may be well known, the new spinoff has not existed as a separate public entity before; hence, that uncertainty will be priced into the opportunity in the early stages. You only find out about the true potential of the rocket-ship spinoff once management are fully separated and their options vested, thus aligning them with their new investors and giving them free rein to drive the business forward.

Market/Company Screening

I am not a big fan of screening to select investment ideas because that tends to be a heavy-handed tool. An example of screening would be filtering the entire market to find the hundred companies with the lowest P/E ratio so that you can investigate them. This approach risks missing many exceptional businesses that have negative or very low earnings because they are investing everything back into the growth engines of their business to maximise long-term shareholder returns (e.g. Amazon). That said, certain screens can work well to alert us to possible overvalued or undervalued sectors or companies within our investable universe. In general, within my investment universe, I will look at:

- Stocks making new fifty-two-week highs and lows
- Stocks with the highest and lowest dividend yields
- Stocks conducting the largest share buybacks
- Stocks with the largest volumes of insider buying
- Stocks with the highest return on capital employed (ROCE)

In a similar vein, the following list was compiled by the investment advisors at Tweedy, Browne who are one of the most successful long-term value-investing shops in business. They looked at investment criteria that have worked in the past to identify investments that significantly outperformed over time. Their research indicated that the best future returns came from stocks that had:

- A low price in relation to their asset value
- A low price in relation to their earnings

- A significant pattern of purchases by one or more insiders (officers and directors)
- A significant decline in the stock's price
- Small market capitalisation (<$500 million)

Thematic Investment Ideas

Although we have somewhat discredited the idea that we can pick a sector that we know will be revolutionary and therefore primed for extreme growth, we can still use this knowledge to try to identify businesses in the value chain where the benefits of this growth may not have yet been priced in. I call this way of sourcing ideas 'thematic'.

One of the best sources of thematic ideas is the news. For example, the news is currently full of articles about artificial intelligence and how it's going to revolutionise the world. Looking at AI as an example of thematic investing, we should ask ourselves, Who are the big players in the space? Who are the challengers? What goes into 'producing' AI in terms of hardware, as well as software? What companies are in the supply chain? What companies are producing something that everyone else in the sector is going to need?

As you can see, each theme will throw up opportunities for research that go far beyond the main players. Each theme can spin a plethora of potential investment ideas that are all worth considering to establish if we can find value at any point in the production pipeline. All of this can be triggered by the simplest of things, such as a newspaper article that interests you. Besides, all knowledge is cumulative, and you never know when what you have read may become the seed of a new investment idea. As money manager Barton Biggs puts it, 'The trick is over time to develop a knowledge base. Then, out of the blue, some event or new piece of information triggers a thought process, and suddenly you have found an investment opportunity.'

I would add that if you come across an outstanding product or service in everyday life, it may also be worth investigating. The reality will often be that the company you identify in this way will already be highly valued, as they would likely have had to achieve great success for you to come across them. But this is not always the case, especially if the company isn't in a sexy or fashionable industry. If it is already highly valued, research the various suppliers of the components of the product to see if their prices have adjusted significantly to account for the expected demand. I get almost all my investment ideas from sources available to everyone. All that is required is to take the time to read and think through the implications of what you come across. Follow your interests!

Cloning or Reverse-Engineering Investments

Fund manager Mohnish Pabrai admits he's 'a shameless copycat'. He is more than happy to admit that almost everything in his life has been copied or 'cloned' from others and that he's not had an original thought. Yet, by 'cloning' Buffett and Munger, among others, he has achieved excellent returns. From 2000 to 2018, his flagship hedge fund returned a staggering 1,204% versus 159% for the S&P 500 index. The portfolios of other exceptional and like-minded investors is a rich seam of investment ideas worth mining.

Phil Fisher recommended this approach, too: 'If I knew their financial minds were keen and their records impressive, I would be disposed to listen eagerly to details they might furnish concerning any company within my range of interests that they considered unusually attractive for major appreciation.'

We humans, as we have discovered, are full of contradictions, and most of the time it is these irrationalities that lead us to make poor decisions in life and markets. To me, there is no clearer example of this than our attitude to 'cloning' or copying others. From childhood it is drilled into us not to copy each other during tests; not to copy each other's homework; and not to make fun of others in the playground by copying or impersonating them. It's hardly surprising, therefore, that even when we grow older (and, hopefully, a little wiser), copying ideas rather than coming up with original ideas ourselves is frowned upon. In some professions such as art or music, this may be right. But for investing, it's completely wrong.

Think of the most successful businesses or investors. Do you really think their every thought or action taken was the result of an original idea? Imitation is the sincerest form of flattery, and this is what many of the great businesses and businesspeople of our time have embraced. Think of Sam Walton, who founded Walmart in 1962. How did he compete with industry giants such as J.C. Penny and Woolworths to become the largest bricks-and-mortar retailer in America? One of his secrets was that he went into his competitors' stores, copied their best practices and procedures, and combined them into the unique formula that is Walmart. He was never shy about it, either. One famous story tells of how he had forgotten to bring his tape measure with him when he visited a competitor's store to check the width of the aisles, so he lay across the aisle himself to work out the width that way!

The very best ideas in both business and investing are often already all around us. For most of the world, Christmas comes only once a year. Only then do we find out whether we have gold or a lump of coal in our stockings. But in financial markets, we can see what the best investors in the world have in their 'stockings' four times a year. It is our job to look through their portfolios and ascertain what they consider to be gold. I am, of course, talking about 14 February, 15 May, 14 August and 14 November, which are the deadlines (forty-five days after quarter-end) for investment managers to file their 13-Fs with the SEC. 13-Fs are a quarterly filing required of all individuals and entities that have $100 million or more invested in US equity markets. A quarterly filing lists the updated positions of the managers and is made available to the public, free of charge. What a gift!

You might be concerned that looking at 'out of date' position movements is pointless because this information is already reflected in the price, and the filings show only long positions. Yet a 2008 study by professors Gerald Martin and John Puthenpurackal, *Imitation is the Sincerest Form of Flattery*, looked at the results of following this strategy. Using the information contained in the 13-F filing of Berkshire Hathaway as an example, they found that if you had simply copied the changes in Berkshire's portfolio holdings between 1976 and 2006, you would have beaten the S&P by 10.75 percent annually over thirty years – and it would have taken you half an hour, four times a year!

To be clear, this is not a strategy that I am advocating; I am simply trying to plant a seed in your mind. That when it comes to investing, what you have been conditioned to believe about copying is wrong. Copying, or 'cloning' as Pabrai calls it, can be very beneficial to your financial well-being, and it can be a vital component in any investor's toolkit. It is certainly a great way to find investment ideas to analyse.

Parallel Investments

New investment ideas may also come from what I call 'parallel investments'. An example: if you had an exceptional business in your portfolio that operated only in the USA, it may be worth seeing if there are any similar businesses operating in other geographies around the world. They may even be at an earlier stage in their lifecycle, operating in a developing market, and, therefore, represent better value. Often, I find that a superior business model will be widely recognised and, therefore, copied by similar businesses operating in other markets where valuations can be lower.

It is relatively common for a business in an emerging market to clone the business model of a successful company in a developed market. This does not necessarily mean that such businesses can be treated as substitute businesses for inclusion in your portfolio, but investing in them could lead to potentially superior alternative investment opportunities. These businesses would still need to have passed through your securities selection process.

Finally, comparing ratios and relative performance data between similar companies operating in different markets over time can sometimes give us an idea of what obstacles might lie in the path of smaller or less-mature parallel investments and how long the runway ahead of them might be.

Emerging Markets

William 'Willie' Sutton was one of the most infamous criminals of the twentieth century, plying his specialist profession of robbery for over forty years. During his career, he stole an estimated $2 million (about $40 million today). Long before computers, he was stealing bags of money from banks. The story goes that when he was caught, he was asked by a reporter why he robbed banks – and that he famously replied, 'Because that is where the money is.' The idea behind this simple and logical conclusion has become known as Sutton's Law, which first emerged in the field of medicine (when diagnosing, one should first consider the obvious). Essentially, the most obvious reason is usually the correct one. Today we could ask investors why they are often falling over themselves to invest in emerging markets. No doubt, the incredulous reply would be 'Because that's where all the money is!'

Emerging markets are a general term used to describe a group of countries that have a low GDP per capita when compared to developed markets. But their GDP is often growing fast, in contrast to developed markets, which have a significantly higher GDP per capita but are often growing at a much slower rate. Emerging markets tend to have younger populations and lower but growing literacy and numeracy rates. They are considered 'emerging' in that they are like an engine that is firing on only half of its cylinders: the best is arguably yet to come. For developed markets, they are already relatively rich, and although their growth is often slower in percentage terms because they are growing from a significantly larger base, the net change in GDP can be enormous. For example, although the US economy seems to grow at a normalised rate of only 3 percent per year, because it is the world's largest economy it's adding the equivalent of Taiwan's GDP every year. And Taiwan's economy is the twenty-first-largest in the world!

Of course, investing in emerging markets is far from a certain one-way bet. David Swensen of the Yale Endowment cautions that, in general, emerging markets operate within less-evolved legal and regulatory frameworks. Any investor looking for investment ideas in emerging markets should, therefore, insist on a higher return (a larger discount to intrinsic value) to compensate for the risks involved compared to investing in markets where the relevant laws and regulations are more robust.

Sam Zell, I think, captured the spirit of investing in emerging markets best when he wrote, 'In emerging markets, you're trading the rule of law for growth. If you think you can count on receiving justice in a foreign courtroom, you should think again. So, the first question is always "Who's your partner?" By that I mean "Who is going to watch your interests on the ground every day?"' When investing, we need to look for management alignment, preferably investing in entrepreneurial, founder-led enterprises operating in non-controversial industries and with strong track records of returns to shareholders.

As emerging-market countries move higher up the value chain and become more developed, this transition is often accompanied by ratings agency upgrades of their sovereign and corporate debt. Along with inclusion into various equity benchmarks, which can direct large flows of passive capital into their markets. The reduced borrowing rates that accompany ratings upgrades mean that upgrades are usually specifically targeted by countries and that they will, therefore, do their utmost to ensure the smooth development and functioning of their capital markets to win over the agencies. The reforms that often accompany this effort are usually to the benefit of public investors, including, ultimately, through lower corporate borrowing rates. Therefore, such reforms should be eagerly anticipated.

During times of economic turmoil, emerging markets can be particularly hard-hit, as the previously large and beneficial capital flows reverse even faster than they came in. Given the more limited pool of operators in emerging markets, this can lead to interesting investment opportunities for the enterprising value investor. During times like these, some of the 'net-net' companies that Ben Graham used to search for can (forgive the pun) 'emerge'. As fund manager Nick Sleep advised, when looking for net-nets, one should focus on asset-intensive

Net-Net Companies

Net-net is a value-investing technique in which a company's stock is valued based solely on its net current assets per share. Net-net value is calculated by deducting total liabilities from the adjusted current assets.

industries where the business is easy to understand and the company's stock is demonstrably trading below the replacement cost of its assets. Sleep found several of these around the world in the form of cement companies.

Although some investors believe that you must have an on-the-ground presence to fully understand these businesses, I disagree. Investing in emerging markets is more to do with your mindset than your location. What makes a great business is universal; just because you do not speak Thai and have never lived or even visited Thailand doesn't mean you can't identify good Thai businesses. The small number of Western institutional investors operating in these markets tend to adopt the same investment criteria and speak to the same bank analysts, as well as each other, and develop an unhealthy level of group think. Separating yourself from the herd can have clear benefits. In my experience, a 'specialist' on Thai stocks may not appreciate that, say, Indonesian stocks are trading at much more favourable relative valuations with better long-term prospects, so their lack of a more holistic regional and world view can limit their outlook.

Nick Sleep and I also agree that because these markets tend to be dominated by momentum-focused short-term retail investors, the sheer volume of herd behaviour can present some very interesting investment opportunities. When fear strikes these markets, liquidity can evaporate, and where previously there were only buyers at any price, there are now only sellers at any price. The availability of cheap leverage tends to exacerbate this issue, leading to margin calls and forced selling, which causes more margin calls, and so on. Thus, emerging markets can provide opportunities that are often far cheaper than expected – a value investor's dream!

This concludes Step 1, where the objective was to identify potentially exceptional investment opportunities. Next, in Step 2, we need to apply the circle of competence test to the opportunities we've identified.

Step 2: Circle of Competence Test

Knowing what you don't know is far more important than being brilliant.
— Charles T. Munger, vice-chairman of Berkshire Hathaway

Once you have a list of investment ideas, next, you need to determine whether each one is within your circle of competence.

Remember, your circle of competence almost always begins with the markets or sectors that you are most interested in and already have the most knowledge about. When Buffett talks about investing only in things that you understand, he's talking about investing only within your circle of competence.

So, do the investment ideas you've identified in Step 1 sit within your circle of competence? If the answer is a firm 'Yes', the idea can proceed to Step 3 of the securities selection process: Quantitative Analysis.

If the answer is 'No' and you have no interest in the area or you have any doubts about the business itself, the opportunity should be discarded. Being able to quickly discard an opportunity is a blessing because it gives you more time to focus on the ones that look the most promising.

If the answer is 'No' but you are fascinated with the sector and are willing to become an expert in it before making any investment decisions, then it can stay on your list to be explored further. Defining the boundaries of your circle of competence in absolute terms can be hard. For me, if I have any doubts that a potential investment sits firmly within my circle, I will always err on the side of caution and discard it.

Assuming the investment idea passes muster, it's on to Step 3.

Step 3: Quantitative Analysis

Interestingly enough, although I consider myself to be primarily in the quantitative school ... the really sensational ideas I have had over the years have been heavily weighted toward the qualitative side where I have had a 'high-probability insight.' ... So the really big money tends to be made by investors who are right on qualitative decisions but, at least in my opinion, the more sure money tends to be made on the obvious quantitative decisions.

– Warren E. Buffett, chairman of Berkshire Hathaway

Quantitative analysis is the thorough and deliberate evaluation of all the numbers and financial ratios behind the business, including the balance sheets, income statements and cash flow statements, for as many years as possible.

Quantitative analysis is a key pillar of the individual securities selection process for any value investor. That said, the weighting that it should be given relative to qualitative analysis or other factors is largely a personal decision. Some investors rely entirely on quantitative factors as they argue that they are less subjective or open to interpretation or error. Others will focus predominantly on the qualitative characteristics of a business *because* they are the most subjective, as the differences of interpretation are what lead to a divergent investment thesis.

At Gronager Partners, we do not attribute a very high weighting to the quantitative analysis of a business; we attribute most of our weighting to the qualitative analysis that follows it. However, for a business to be able to proceed to the qualitative analysis, a thorough quantitative analysis of the business is still a prerequisite, the reason being that numbers can be looked at dispassionately and, therefore, we are likely to be able to retain the most objectivity regarding whether this is an idea worthy of additional investigation or not.

When performing our quantitative analysis, I judge the overall results against a baseline expectation that I have regarding them. At a minimum, the results should provide us with an in-depth understanding of the business and its key drivers. In my experience, the most common reason why a potential investment is rejected at this stage is because the accounts are unclear or seem to be obfuscating the true performance, both of which are impassable red flags for us. If there are pages and pages of incomprehensible notes to the financial statements, we assume the business is trying to hide something, so we discard the idea and move on.

Once we are satisfied with the quality of the financial statements, we can move on to generating the metrics for the business, using company and market data which is almost always readily available. Interpreting the ratios and metrics allows us to look at the business against our own expectations, compared to its industry, market geographies and comparable businesses, so we can put them into context. Again, the limited room for interpretation of a company's financial metrics and ratios is useful, as it minimises emotion during the evaluation and ensures that this stage of our securities selection process remains as objective as possible.

Remember, investing is an emotion-laden journey which leaves us open to errors caused by behavioural as well as cognitive biases. Quantitative analysis helps to de-emotionalise the valuation process as the numbers (should) speak for themselves. Thorough quantitative analysis can therefore help to provide a solid platform on which to build our more subjective qualitative analysis. If we have allowed ourselves to get swept up with a market bubble, ratio analysis, especially when evaluated against previous years or industry averages over time, should help to highlight that we are either at or heading towards a market extreme. Always remember that 'This time is different' are four of the most dangerous words in investing.

My rule is that if I am going to invest the time to fully examine the qualitative factors of a business, each new potential investment needs to pass the 'smell test' regarding its financials. Every business is different, but if enough red flags are raised from the quantitative analysis, the business is discarded.

At Gronager Partners, a full quantitative analysis of a business encompasses:

- Financial statement analysis
- Tangibles vs. intangibles analysis
- Business model evaluation
- Intrinsic value estimates
- Earnings power analysis
- Quality of earnings evaluation
- Retained earnings strategy
- Dividends vs. stock buyback analysis
- Capital structure evaluation
- Comparable and sectoral analysis

Financial Statement Analysis

Financial statements are a snapshot of a business at a set point in time. They record everything up to the date of record of the report. They tell us about the past, not the future. As mentioned in Chapter 3, investing based on historical financial statements is like driving a car whilst looking in the rear-view mirror. They show you where we have been but not where we are going.

Caution should always be taken when reading financial statements. As billionaire entrepreneur Michael Bloomberg said, 'A good accountant with a creative mind can make numbers paint any desired picture. No one understates revenues and profits when they're trying to show off. Presumably, the financial situation is always equal to or worse than stated.' His statement reminds us that management are often incentivised to ensure that the accounts represent the rosiest picture possible to maximise their individual compensation at year end. External auditors are similarly incentivised, as they are hired and fired by management based on their ability to 'sing from the same hymn sheet' as them. As a result, we should not weight any single financial report too heavily and instead focus on the degree of change over time – over, say, five years. As Munger once quipped, 'Financial returns don't always coincide with the time it takes our planet to circle the sun.'

In this respect, one of my preferred methods of analysis is to take the last ten years of financial statements and review the balance sheets, income statements and cash flow statements in conjunction with one another and evaluate the changes year on year and over five-year rolling periods. This allows me to get a sense of the key business drivers. If you look at the year-on-year percentage change of any metric, you can often spot areas that warrant further investigation.

Although not perfect, financial statements are the most objective data that we can get about a company and its performance, so ignoring them because of their shortcomings is foolish. Nothing is perfect. What we are looking for as value investors is whether the business is an exception to the rule that states that most listed companies are mediocre. That should be apparent to us through the correct analysis and interpretation of the financial statements over time. As mentioned in the introduction to Step 3, one easy way to pass on a potential investment is if the financial statements are too complex to understand. In my experience, the approachability and ease with which financial statements can be read (or not) can tell us a lot about not only how the business is doing but also who is running it.

Tangibles vs. Intangibles Analysis

Earnings and book value no longer mean what they used to. Tangible assets such as factories and railway tracks were the foundations of business value in Graham's time. As Buffett wrote,

> Tangible assets like the Coca-Cola bottling plants can be bought and sold, so are straightforward to value. The difficulty arises with valuing intangibles such as Coca-Cola's 'brand name' as this is self-generated rather than purchased and therefore is not recognised in the company's balance sheet. This can lead to an investor having an incomplete view of the business if they do not understand the value of the Coca-Cola brand.

Intangible spending by companies – for example, research and development (R&D) – has been on the rise for decades, particularly in developed markets where businesses have become more service-oriented. Investments are outlays today in the expectation of higher cash flows tomorrow. Whereas tangible investments are recorded as assets on the balance sheet, intangible investments are treated as an expense on the income statement.

This means that a company that invests most of its free cash flow into intangible assets, for example, a pharmaceutical company researching a new drug, will have lower earnings and book value than a company that invests the equivalent amount into tangible assets (e.g. a storage business purchasing additional warehouses), even if their cash flows are identical. It is important, therefore, to acknowledge, especially in developed service-oriented markets, that earnings and book value are losing their ability to represent true economic value.

Simply screening businesses based on P/E ratios may cause you to miss many superior investments. To counter this disconnect, we need to examine each opportunity and its business model individually to accurately assess if there is a significant gap between the market price and our own assessment of intrinsic value, especially when R&D spend is high.

Business Model Evaluation

Certain businesses such as Amazon look to continuously recycle a significant portion of their profits back to their customers through lower prices or faster delivery. Therefore, we should always beware of discounting a business with low or falling profit margins from being an attractive investment. This is certainly true in Amazon's case, where enormous capex or lowering prices can build an unassailable moat to safeguard future profits. This business model, dubbed 'Scale-Economies-Shared' by fund manager Nick Sleep, is incredibly powerful. In general, I have found it can be helpful when you think you have found such a business to compare it to its major competitors to see if low or falling margins are endemic to the sector or whether the business is using a differentiated strategy to capture market share.

Over the long term, however, sustainably high gross margins are the single most important factor in the long-term performance of a business. Research has shown that if a company starts with a high gross profit margin, it tends to maintain it. Conversely, if it starts off with a low gross profit margin, it will tend to stay low. In the language of statistics, gross margins tend to persist.

When it comes to business models, I try to answer the following five questions:

1. Is the business simple and understandable – can I explain the business model in a single paragraph?
2. Does the business have a long track record and how has it changed over time?
3. Is the business model (temporarily) losing money or have profits dipped (recently, or further in the past?) and if so, why?
4. What margins does the business have (gross, operating and net), and what has been the trend over time?
5. Does the business have favourable long-term prospects?

Intrinsic Value Estimates

According to Berkshire Hathaway's *Owner's Manual,*

Intrinsic Value can be defined simply: It's the discounted value of cash that can be taken out of a business during its remaining life. The calculation of intrinsic value, though, is not as simple. As our definition suggests, intrinsic value is an estimate rather than a precise figure, and it's additionally an estimate that must be changed if interest rates move or forecasts of future cash flow are revised.

When it comes to calculating the intrinsic value of a business, I like to estimate a range of bull, bear and base case scenarios.

Bull, Bear and Base Case Scenarios

The bull case scenario is an optimistic view of the business's continued financial trajectory. The bear case scenario is a pessimistic view of the business's continued financial trajectory. The base case scenario assumes that everything will unfold mostly as expected (somewhere in between the bull and bear scenarios).

The process itself is more art than science as it requires an investor to use their best judgement to forecast the outcomes for both the future earnings and terminal value of the business as well as interest rates to discount these future cash flows back to the present. None of these things can be projected with certainty. As concentrated value investors, we have no insight into the future path of interest rates, and as mentioned previously, business is messy. There is no way for management to accurately forecast the earnings for even the next quarter, so our ability to forecast twenty years into the future is non-existent. This is why we always invest with a significant margin of safety. It is also why calculating a range for the intrinsic value is the best way to keep us from developing a false sense of security around our estimate.

Some businesses have more stable cash flows than others throughout the business cycle and longer observable track records. Forecasting the intrinsic value of a long-established utility company, for example, is easier than forecasting for a new social media company with highly variable cash flows and a relatively unknown track record.

This comes back to our circle of competence. If we do not believe we can understand the business (i.e. it is not within our circle of competence and we do not believe we can reasonably expand our circle to encompass the business we are investigating – always a risky proposition), then we should not be making estimates of its intrinsic value. We should not expect every business to fall within our circle of competence; most won't. Nor should we expect the intrinsic value of every business we research to be 'easy' to calculate. However, these qualifications do not hinder our chances of long-term investing success in any way. As Munger puts it, 'We have no system for estimating the correct value of all businesses. We put almost all in the "too hard" pile and sift through a few easy ones, and our track record has still been pretty good.'

Earnings Power Analysis

Long term, we are most interested in a company's earnings power and growth as the key determinants of a company's value. As Munger writes,

> Growth is always a component in the calculation of value, constituting a variable whose importance can range from negligible to enormous and whose impact can be negative as well as positive. ... Growth benefits investors only when the business in question can invest at incremental returns which are enticing – in other words, only when each dollar used to finance the growth creates over a dollar of long-term market value. In the case of a low-return business requiring incremental funds, growth hurts the investor.

To establish a company's earnings power, I find it useful to plot on a chart the following metrics over time (preferably a rolling five-year basis) so that I can visualise how the performance has evolved:

- Earnings growth
- Sales growth
- Profit margin
- Return on book value
- Change in book value
- Return on capital employed (ROCE)
- Return on invested capital (ROIC)
- Ratio of sales to invested capital

When looking at the results, it's important to be able to identify a positive trend over time. Some factors are more important for one business and less important for another. Therefore, we need also to consider what factors are important to a particular business to determine whether the trends identified are of value.

A final note on earnings power comes from fund manager Terry Smith, who suggests that attention must also be paid to the industry of the company you are assessing, to ensure that it is also growing. A growing industry is important because it should allow the business in question to continue to reinvest a portion of its cash flow at high rates of return even if its percentage of market share remains constant.

Quality of Earnings Evaluation

Most of the ratios relating to business valuation are related to either the current earnings of the business or its future earnings potential. The most common ratio used is the price/earnings (P/E) ratio, which indicates the multiple of current earnings investors are willing to pay for the stock. Or, to put it another way, how many years it will take investors to earn back their purchase price should the company continue to operate in the future exactly as it does today. The problem, according to renowned economist Burton Malkiel, is that 'God almighty does not know the proper price-earning multiple for a common stock.'

High P/E ratios above, say, 16 (which has been the rough historical average for the S&P 500) normally indicate what investors define as 'growth stocks', where significant future growth of earnings is priced into the shares. Comparatively low P/E ratios (below 16) have historically been defined as 'value stocks', as they have typically been slower-growing businesses in more stable industries.

The earnings being achieved by a company today are what management should be reporting clearly to us in the financial statements. And management wants these earnings reported to shareholders to be as high as possible. At the same time, they usually like keeping the earnings they report for tax purposes as low as possible. No one likes paying taxes unnecessarily. It is therefore useful to compare the earnings that management reports both for tax purposes and to shareholders, as it is likely those reported for tax purposes will be closer to the truth. For example, in the US, we can compare the 'cash income taxes paid' footnote in a firm's 10K against what management have presented in the annual report to shareholders. Any wide discrepancy between the two that is not easily explainable is a red flag for me.

This brings us to a key point regarding the quality of earnings. Revenue growth can be manufactured through various means such as offering product or service discounts (front-loading), and management may focus on this and say that net income growth will follow. But you must remember that revenue growth is totally irrelevant if it does not feed through to the bottom line. This is why examining a company's profit margin over time is so important. We want to see stable or growing margins to indicate that any growth in sales is of sufficient quality to be feeding through to the bottom line and not actually pressuring margins.

When it comes to assessing earnings quality, most investors like to skip straight to dessert and simply look at earnings growth quarter over quarter or year over year. Management has cottoned on to this trend; therefore, earnings per share (EPS) is trumpeted loudly as the only thing an investor needs to know to assess whether management is doing a good job (i.e. has it increased from one period to the next?).

Earnings Per Share (EPS)

A measure of profitability that indicates how much profit each outstanding share of common stock has earned. It's calculated by dividing the company's net income by the total number of outstanding shares.

But EPS is too easily manipulated to be believed in isolation. For instance, management could have undertaken a share buyback during the period, thus reducing the number of shares outstanding and artificially inflating EPS. Equally often, management may retain some of its earnings (retained earnings); that is, it may not always distribute all the earnings to the shareholders. This leads to a steadily growing capital base on which more earnings should be made. Even if the business were to only hold this excess cash in short-term securities, the income return from them would inflate EPS, even though the returns being generated may be below what the shareholders could earn with the cash if it were returned to us. In both cases – a share buyback or retaining some earnings – EPS will not give us a full picture about how well the underlying business is performing.

There are other metrics that I find useful to look at when analysing the quality of earnings. One of these is return on assets (ROA), which eliminates some of the issues that arise when looking solely at return on equity (ROE). However, for businesses with large asset bases, this measure doesn't tell us anything about the value of those assets. For example, banks will tend to show low ROAs but high ROEs because most of their assets are in the form of loans, but this does not tell us whether these assets or loans have been issued wisely or not.

My preferred measure, depending on the business, is return on capital employed (ROCE) because it illuminates how efficiently a company utilises all available capital to generate each dollar of additional profit.

Some investors prefer to look at return on invested capital (ROIC); however, making ROIC comparisons over time is harder because the cost of capital expenditure can vary greatly and therefore, comparisons either over

Return on Assets (ROA)

Return on assets indicates how profitable a company is in relation to its total assets. It is calculated by dividing net income by total assets.

Return on Equity (ROE)

Return on equity is a measure of financial performance calculated by dividing net income by shareholders' equity.

Return on Capital Employed (ROCE)

Return on capital employed assesses a company's profitability and capital efficiency. It is calculated by dividing earnings before tax and interest (EBIT) by capital employed.

Return on Invested Capital (ROIC)

Return on invested capital assesses a company's efficiency in allocating capital to profitable investments. It is calculated by dividing net operating profit after tax (NOPAT – these accounting acronyms just keep getting better!) by invested capital.

time or between companies can be misleading. For comparison purposes, I prefer to follow Phil Fisher's advice and compare the companies' profit margin per dollar of sales over time, as that measure provides a more 'apples-to-apples' comparison.

Finally, there are two modifications that I use when calculating these ratios. First, many companies issue preferred stock in addition to general equity and debt. I prefer to exclude preferred stock from investors' equity and treat it as debt. Secondly, I prefer to invest in companies that are anti-fragile, and, as such, have less debt and more cash and short-term marketable securities on their books. Typically, I will exclude both when calculating the ratios, so as not to unduly punish a business for being conservatively run.

Retained Earnings Strategy

What a company does with its earnings is very important, as this is essentially the capital allocation 'scorecard' for management. We want to invest only in companies that have a rational capital allocator at the helm. When it comes to retained earnings (i.e. money that will not be returned to shareholders through dividends or buybacks but, rather, retained in the business to pursue growth opportunities), we want to make sure that the company has a good track record of using capital efficiently. Management should be creating at least one dollar of market value for every dollar that they have retained

– hopefully, significantly more. The results will tell us not only how rational management's capital allocation decisions are but also what the reinvestment potential or growth potential for the business may be, given the performance of past reinvestment. As we know, the greatest returns for investors come from investing in long-term compounders. In general, this requires the company to have a great business engine that can consistently absorb more capital and use it to produce high(er) earnings. This compounding over time leads to exponential returns for investors.

It is difficult to overstate the importance of a company's capital reinvestment ability. The correlation between investor returns and the capital allocation decisions made by management is significant. As a rule, businesses that are already generating impressive ROCE are good places to look for investment opportunities when it comes to long-term compounders. Once you've identified them, you need to determine the size of the addressable market and how high the barriers to entry are. Will those barriers prevent the business from continuing to reinvest capital? Will the business be able to continue reinvesting without cannibalising its margins through self-induced market saturation? What about when competitors enter the market?

Dividends vs. Stock Buybacks

As mentioned, businesses that generate cash flow beyond what they need for reinvestment purposes have five additional avenues for capital allocation:

1. Pay the funds out to shareholders in the form of a dividend
2. Retire/pay back debt
3. Spend the money on acquisitions
4. Hoard the money as cash
5. Buy back their own stock

The popularity of Option 1 for investors has varied greatly over the years and is often correlated with the government's prevailing income tax policy. Tax-exempt institutions such as charities are often agnostic and may prefer dividend income over capital gains as they can use these funds for discretionary spending. However, taxable investors usually prefer Option 5.

Option 5, the so-called 'cannibal' option is often the most lucrative for shareholders over the long term, and it has several advantages. Most importantly in my view, it prevents management from hoarding cash (Option 4) or from spending money on often expensive and potentially wasteful acquisitions or empire-building (Option 3). Dividends (Option 1) for taxable investors, such as you and me, are usually taxed as income, often at a higher rate than that for capital gains. As a result, many investors prefer share buybacks, which can have the added benefit of supporting the share price. Share buybacks have very low transaction costs, unlike, say, acquisitions, and are also increasingly accretive to earnings per share (EPS) as more shares are taken out of circulation.

A business that throws off a lot of cash but has no good growth opportunities to utilise that cash can still generate superior returns by buying back their shares. If we look at just two of Berkshire Hathaway's oldest holdings – Coca-Cola and American Express – in the last thirty years, they have each bought back about a third of their outstanding shares. Long-term holders of these shares like Berkshire have realised that continuing to hold on to them while the stock buybacks are going on allows their proportional ownership of those businesses to continue to increase year on year.

As many wily readers will no doubt have noticed, we need to exercise a note of caution here. Management will often buy back a large percentage of shares each year, as their compensation is based on achieving a specific share price/EPS goal (misaligned incentives again!). They may do this even when the shares are more than fully valued; if they do, this will damage the shareholder value.

Another common concern occurs when a large percentage of shares are bought back each year but the amount bought is similar in size to the number issued to fulfil stock awards to management. In such cases, the stock merely 'treads water'. It's always a good idea to verify the buyback claims of management by directly comparing the number of shares outstanding year on year. Remember, repurchasing stock is only rational if the intrinsic value of the company is higher than the market price.

When valuing a business based purely on the dividends paid, it is often appropriate to add the amount spent on stock buybacks to the amount distributed as dividends to show the cumulative cash return to shareholders. This is referred to as the total shareholder yield.

Capital Structure Evaluation

I am frequently surprised at how little attention equity-focused investors pay to the nuances of a company's capital structure when it comes to debt. Even though over 90 percent of bankruptcies are the result of non-business conditions, predominantly debt. As fund manager Peter Lynch reminds us, 'Companies that have no debt can't go bankrupt.'

As the common refrain goes, 'Debt is like an iceberg.' Equity investors will often look at the ratio of debt to equity to check that it's similar to the ratios of its competitors and that the interest expense to be serviced is not too high in proportion to current earnings. And that's all they'll do. But that's not enough.

The word 'credit' comes from the Latin 'credo' ('I believe'). Clearly, most equity investors have taken that as their motto, investing their funds based on faith. There is far more complexity to a company's capital structure on the debt side than on the equity side, and a great deal of time should be spent seriously examining its structure and the logic behind it, as well as its potential weaknesses. A well-thought-out and well-executed capital structure shows that management understand what they are doing, at least from a financial perspective. It also makes it more likely that they understand the importance of correct capital allocation decisions, which is to the benefit of shareholders.

Equity investors must be familiar with both fixed income and credit markets. This knowledge will, in turn, allow them to understand the nuances of a company's capital structure through the variety of financing options available that make up the business's capital structure, as well as their individual strengths and weaknesses. We value investors are looking to buy businesses with a margin of safety, and that is possible only if we really understand the capital structure of a business. I do not mind companies using conservative amounts of debt to enhance their business models and, therefore, our returns. But we would all do well to follow the advice of fund manager Terry Smith, who wrote, 'One of my basic tenets is never to invest in a business which requires leverage or borrowing to make an adequate return on equity.'

Debt is the number one cause of bankruptcies for companies; it often occurs when they fail to generate enough cash to pay the interest due on their borrowing or are unable to roll over their maturing debt. Of course, debt in and of itself is not necessarily a bad thing when it comes to a company's capital structure. For one thing, the interest on debt is often tax deductible, representing a 'tax shield' which can be set against the profits that the company must report for tax purposes. From management's perspective, they do not have to ask for the shareholders' permission to borrow, and debt is often good for optics because it improves many of the metrics on which investors typically focus, such as ROE. However, equity investors do not like their shareholdings to be diluted or to participate in capital raises. Therefore, if a business needs additional capital for investment purposes, above retained free cash flow, shareholders often prefer that the company borrow it.

Most investors presume that more debt automatically makes a company riskier than a similar company with less debt. In my experience, this can be a fatal assumption. The type of debt involved is often as important as the amount. There are essentially two types of debt. The first is bank debt. The name is a misnomer, as it doesn't have to have anything to do with a bank; the term encompasses all short-term, 'callable' borrowings of the company. Meaning the lender can, at any point, request repayment – which they will often do if they sense the borrower is in any kind of financial trouble. This is the riskiest type of debt, but it's also often the most frequently overlooked. Just ask former Lehman Brothers shareholders.

The second type is 'funded debt', which usually takes the form of non-callable long-term corporate bonds. The ratings agencies can upgrade or downgrade them based on their perception of the financial health of the issuers. However, so long as they continue to make their interest payments in full and on time, the lenders cannot demand immediate repayment of principal the same way that bank debt lenders can. Funded debt is, therefore, rightly seen as 'better' or at least 'less risky' than bank debt from a capital structure perspective. Provided the maturity profile of their funded debt is sensible (i.e. it does not all mature at the same time, but over a period of years), most companies can hold a reasonable debt burden without too much risk that it will push them into bankruptcy.

Regardless of the type of debt, however, if the borrower cannot make the interest payments or defaults on the repayment of the principal, lenders often have the power to force the company into bankruptcy. In bankruptcy, companies are often reorganised when there is more value to be recouped by having them continue operating as a 'going concern'. In extreme cases where the business is worth more dead than alive, they are liquidated or sold piecemeal for scrap for investors to recoup as much of their money as possible.

If there is anything left over after all creditors (mainly debt holders) have been repaid, this goes to the former shareholders, but there is rarely anything left.

What, then, are the quantitative characteristics of a company's debt that we should be looking at to ensure that our potential investment doesn't have a vulnerable capital structure? A few we have touched on already; first, we need to know precisely how much debt the company has and in what form (short-term versus long-term liabilities). I find it helpful to plot the maturity profile to visualise when the debts come due and in what size. Ideally, we are looking for a relatively even spread over two to seven years. Corporate debt issuers generally issue five-year maturity bonds, but some issue seven-to-ten-year debt. A significant amount of short-term funding (under twelve months) as a percentage of overall debt is a red flag for me.

We also want to look at the annual interest expense to see how much of the company's earnings are being taken up by interest payments. If there is not much left over, clearly, there is an increased risk of default should earnings fall or interest rates rise.

On a more granular level, it's worth examining the types of bonds issued. Are they interest bearing, zero-coupon, fixed or floating rates of interest? What is the current yield to maturity? If the bonds are trading above issuance price (par), their yield will be below the bond coupon, which is a sign that the market perceives the company as a 'better' credit risk now than when the bonds were issued. The inverse is true if the bonds are trading below par. It's interesting to contrast this price action with the share price – if the share price is rising but the bond price is falling (yield to maturity is rising) and/or the spread to similar debt issued by comparable companies is widening, this says that the equity markets and debt markets have differing views on the future prospects for the business. This would warrant further investigation. When in doubt, I always side with the debt investors, as they are often far more focused on protecting their principal than typical equity holders.

Comparable and Sectoral Analysis

When looking for investment ideas, it's important to look at the bigger picture or wider sector and not view the opportunity in isolation. It makes sense to compare the business with their competitors as well as industry averages. Exceptional businesses in an industry must be doing something different from

27 Comparables Analysis

	Stock	Lead Competitor(s)	Sector Average	Market Average
Gross Profit Margin				
Operating Profit Margin				
Net Profit Margin				
Cash Conversion Cycle				
Debt to Equity Ratio				
Interest Cover Ratio				
Free Cash Flow Yield (FCF divided by Market Value) i.e. cash generated after all costs except dividends paid				
Invested Capital Per Share				
Return on Capital Employed (ROCE)				
Return on Invested Capital (ROIC)				
Book Value Per Share				
Return on Book Value Per Share				
Sales per $ of Invested Capital				

SOURCE: Gronager Partners

the competition, and this is often evident when we compare their financials side by side with those of other businesses operating in the same sector. The table above offers a list of the metrics that I like to compare and use as the basis for further investigation. [FIG. 27]

Taking Pointers from the Investment Greats

From my experience, the best investors ask the right questions and spend a significant amount of time trying to answer them as objectively as possible. Thankfully, many of the world's most successful investors have provided us with some of the questions that they believe are the most important to ask.

Buffett, for example, simplifies the .quantitative aspects of what he is looking for in a prospective investment down to six things:

1. Does the company have a high ROE (i.e. the highest possible return for each dollar invested in the business)?
2. Does the company earn an above-average return on invested capital (ROIC) and what is the magnitude and persistence of that ability? In short, how much a business earns on the capital employed in its business determines the quality of that business.

3. Does the company have a low P/E? Also take care to adjust for companies with falling earnings (often overlooked by other investors), as they can be in some sort of temporary distress.
4. Does the company enjoy EPS growth?
5. Is the company's stock price low relative to its fifty-two-week range?
6. Does the company have a high book value?

David Einhorn, billionaire founder and president of Greenlight Capital Management, narrows his focus to just three key questions:

1. What are the true economics of the business?
2. How do the economics compare to the reported earnings?
3. How are the interests of the decision-makers aligned with the investors? (However, answering this involves a somewhat qualitative judgement that we will come to in Step 4.)

Our fellow investor Joel Greenblatt outlines four different valuation techniques in his book *The Little Book that Still Beats the Market*, each of which he uses depending on their relevance to the business in question:

1. He performs a discounted cash flow analysis, calculating the net present value of the company's estimated future earnings.
2. He assesses the company's relative value, comparing it to the prices of similar businesses.
3. He estimates the company's acquisition value, figuring out what an informed buyer might pay for it.
4. He calculates the company's liquidation value, analysing what it would be worth if it closed and sold all its assets.

Greenblatt takes the valuation process a step further by saying that although these quantitative-based valuation techniques by themselves can help to identify a good business, they don't always represent great stock investments. To determine good from great, he asks a further set of questions of the business under consideration:

1. How much will what I expect to happen be different from the status quo?
2. How long will it take?
3. What is the present value of the increase that I expect?

4. How much of this increase is already in the price that I will have to pay?

5. Is there enough difference between the market and my expectations if I am right, as well as a margin of error in case I am wrong?

At the end of the process, when you have identified which businesses warrant further qualitative assessment, it's important to conduct a 'sanity check'. Remember cognitive biases. Because by this stage you will have invested a significant amount of time researching the prospective investment, you may be more tempted to overlook red flags and continue with your investment process to ensure your time has not been wasted. We need to recognise this tendency of the sunk cost fallacy and deliberately put it aside, and assess the potential investment with objectivity on its investment merits alone.

Remember, all knowledge is cumulative, so nothing is ever wasted. Even if an idea is discarded, what we learnt from evaluating one company can be taken forward when evaluating the next. Inclusion of a business in your portfolio should be a rare event. If it becomes too common, then your investment criteria are not stringent enough. According to Munger, 'You have to be like a man standing with a spear next to a stream. Most of the time he's doing nothing. When a fat, juicy salmon swims by, the man spears it. Then he goes back to doing nothing. It may be six months before the next salmon swims past.'

Canadian fund manager Francis Chou adds, 'When there is hardly anything to buy, you have to be very careful. You cannot force the issue. You just have to be patient, and the bargains will come to you. If you want to participate in the market all the time, then it's a mug's game and you're going to lose.' Chou has been known to wait five years or longer before spearing a salmon he likes!

As a final test to ensure your objectivity, it can be useful to check your assumptions and estimates with an independent peer. The objective here is not to have someone deliberately disagree with your numbers, but more to give their opinion on whether they believe your bull, bear and base case estimates of intrinsic value are within a range that they also believe to be reasonable. Even if you opt not to do this, it is still worth taking some time to re-evaluate the assumptions that you made.

If the company passes the quantitative test, it's time for the real work to begin in Step 4: Qualitative Analysis.

Step 4: Qualitative Analysis

Successful companies innovate constantly – the products they offer,
how they sell them, or how they conduct operations.
    – Nick Sleep, co-founder of the Nomad Investment Partnership

The qualitative analysis of a business is exactly what it says on the tin: it is the process of assessing all the nuances of the business that we cannot understand from just looking at the numbers. In fact, looking at the numbers should have generated some qualitative questions regarding how the business operates. And vice versa: the qualitative answers that we ascertain about the business should enable us to better understand the quantitative prospects of the business. To perform this analysis requires in-depth research of all the publicly available data about the business, including annual reports, quarterly reports, management calls, annual general meeting (AGM) Q&A, newspaper articles, manager biographies, director conference calls and presentations, as well as industry analysis and competitor analysis, to name some sources.

At Gronager Partners, this is where the bulk of the 250-question checklist that I mentioned in Chapter 1 comes into play. These detailed questions seek to shine a light on all the critical aspects of the business from management's background to evaluating the size and stability of the business's competitive advantage and the defensibility of its moat.

Our qualitative questions broadly relate to six interconnected facets of the business:

1. Business complexity evaluation
2. Ownership analysis
3. Insider buying and selling review
4. Sectoral analysis
5. Media (on- and offline) review
6. Business attributes evaluation

Each of these facets, to a greater or lesser extent, touches on the subject of management. However, the evaluation of management is, in our view, so important to a successful investment outcome and so nuanced that it warrants its own chapter. We will explore the evaluation of management in greater detail in Chapter 12.

Business Complexity Evaluation

The first question I ask is often reasonably simple to answer: Is the business complex? Complexity comes in two different forms – bad and good. Bad comes first, as we always try to think about the downside before the upside.

Bad Complexity

Bad complexity is where the business itself seems needlessly complex or too complex to properly understand. Bad complexity is one of the key reasons firms fail. As Buffett describes it, 'Unlike the scoring system utilized in diving competitions, you are awarded NO points in business endeavours for "degree of difficulty."' Bad complexity is a red flag.

I often get asked what I do when I encounter a business that I think is good but cannot fully wrap my head around it to be comfortable enough to invest. The answer is that I *always* discard that business from further consideration. With around 45,000 listed businesses in the world, there is always another opportunity, and I don't waste any time on businesses that are too complex for me to fully understand. As fund manager Mohnish Pabrai puts it,

> If you don't have a good idea about what's going to happen in the industry, with the company's new product or services, or the effects of new technology on the company, then you can't really make good estimates for future earnings growth rates. If you can't do that, you have no business investing in that company in the first place!

In school, we are taught to never say something is too hard to understand and that to admit as much is admitting defeat. Saying 'too hard' is associated with the negative connotation that we are not smart enough to understand whatever it is. However, in investing, we should embrace the concept of throwing as many things as possible into our respective 'too-hard pile'. This frees up our time to examine and invest in businesses we truly understand and allows us to construct a well-informed view that is divergent from the market. As Buffett says, one of your single largest risks as an investor is investing in things that sit outside of your own circle of competence. It takes both humility and an ability to keep our ego in check to perceive where our individual competencies lie.

Good Complexity (Moats)

Good complexity comes in the form of a business moat that makes it hard for a competitor to replicate products or services. 'What,' asked Phil Fisher, 'can the particular company do that others would not be able to do as well?'

The concept of economic moats is not a new one, but it still attracts a great deal of heated debate. Mainly around how to identify and measure them, and how a company can sustain its moat over the long term. By using the term 'economic moat', we are really asking what a company's competitive edge is and whether it is durable, expandable, and sustainable. As mentioned in the opening of this chapter, not even the best companies in the world last forever. Once we acknowledge that every company will eventually fail, it's easier to search for frailties in the company's economic moat no matter how unassailable it may appear today.

A report by Credit Suisse suggested that it is possible to measure moats quantitatively by looking at the spread between a company's return on invested capital (ROIC) and its cost of capital over time. In my experience, though, this quantitative measurement doesn't capture all the nuances of an economic moat. I find it better to ask a qualitative question to explore the width and depth of the moat first: 'What would I need to start a new business to compete with this potential investment?' To answer this, I will need to really understand both the industry and its competitive dynamics. Clearly, capital is important, but it is not the only thing. We also need human capital. We may also require patents, or a strong brand name. What scale do we require to effectively compete and how much market share would we need to gain to achieve scale? Once we know the answer, we can try to quantify it by evaluating the costs of competition in terms of money but also the time and effort required to do so. This thought experiment allows me to conceptualise the business's moat and enables me to begin to quantify its size.

Next, we need to establish the durability of the moat. How long do we believe the firm can maintain its competitive advantage? According to Buffett, this relates closely to a firm's 'ability to raise prices in excess of inflation.' Put another way, how price inelastic is demand for the firm's product? Take Coca-Cola, for example. People who love Coke – and there are billions of them around the world – would still buy the drink if its price went up by one cent, ten cents or potentially even more. Coke has incredibly high price inelasticity.

Even if Coke doubled in price, I doubt it would convince a significant slice of their market to switch brands or products. Now *that* is a durable moat!

Buffett often remarks that he wants his managers focused on the moat around their business and every year to be working towards making it a little wider and a little deeper. How, then, can we measure the growth of the moat of a business? I'd argue that this is the hardest aspect to measure. For new products or services, if they quickly become indispensable to our daily lives (e.g. Netflix during the Covid lockdown), there is clearly a growing moat. In fact, the network effect makes this moat even more durable because, as more people join, the better and more varied the content becomes, which further drives subscription growth in a virtuous cycle. The larger the business grows, the harder it is for other businesses to compete. Over time, Netflix is clearly growing its moat.

For an older product like Coke, we want to ensure that over any rolling five-year period there is no impairment of the value of the brand. When I think of things that could make Coke stock go to zero, the main one that comes to my mind is if people were to associate the Coke brand with something harmful and, by extension, its products began to be seen as unsafe for consumption. No wonder Coke spends billions every year on advertising to associate itself with happiness and good times!

Coming back to the Credit Suisse study on business moats, the paper's authors offer some advice for finding companies with durable and growing moats: 'A clear understanding of how a company creates shareholder value is core to understanding sustainable value creation.' This comes through understanding the stability of the industry in which the company operates, the total profit pool available, and the business's current market share, along with the past trajectory of growth in gaining additional share. Finally, the authors stated that the culture of a firm was the most-referenced trait amongst firms that were successful over very long periods of time, leading them to conclude that culture could be 'a potential source of enduring competitive advantage.'

Essentially, a moat indicates whether a business has favourable long-term prospects. Favourable long-term prospects can come in many forms, such as selling a product or service that has no close substitute (e.g. the iPhone and the App Store – Apple) or a business that has significant pricing power through its brand and structure (e.g. franchises such as McDonald's). It might be through 'scale economies shared' (e.g. Amazon Marketplace), network effects (e.g.

Facebook/Meta) or businesses that are operating as virtual monopolies (e.g. Google searches – Alphabet).

What we don't want are commodity businesses that compete solely based on price for undifferentiated products, unless they are the lowest-cost producer by a significant margin (there is almost always an exception to the rule in investing!). Even then, care must be taken to ensure that they would thrive in a cost-cutting war in terms of gaining market share and not be driven out of business. One way to evaluate this is to examine the industry's fundamental operating principles and how the company differentiates itself from its competitors. Our objective is to establish whether the business in question possesses an economic moat that protects its supernormal profits from competition. If so, how robust is the moat and how long is the available runway in terms of future business growth?

Ownership Analysis

A surprising amount of useful investment information can be gleaned from looking at the stockholders register. Here we can see the composition of the shareholder base. Is it mainly founder, institutional or retail owners? The quality of the largest shareholders can tell us something about the business. For example, if we see large institutional investors, we can normally presume the company is already well followed and has passed through many due diligence filters – the inverse being the case if they are absent. It's important to distinguish between passive and active institutional managers, however, as passive managers are just following the index.

Of the active institutional managers, look for the ones you know and respect. These may be private equity companies that continue to own a significant stake in the business after taking it public or activist managers who are pushing the company to evolve in positive ways. Another research tactic I employ is to look for significant holdings of other value investors whom I respect and admire, provided the position is not a 'toehold' position and is a 'full' position in terms of size relative to their assets under management (AUM). Once identified, this gives me an additional layer of confidence that this business has made it through another respected manager's due diligence filters.

If they have been adding to the position over time, this is another favourable indicator. However, if they are reducing their position, I want to try and understand why. Is it because they have had an AUM outflow and this is position-trimming to match the redemption? Or is this a slow exit from the position, as they believe it was a mistake? In my experience, managers do not exit slowly; they cut a position quickly if they believe it was a mistake. Therefore, position-trimming is often the more likely conclusion.

For me, the businesses that I get most excited by (yes, even I am subject to emotions), when looking over the shareholder register, are founder- or owner-operated with management holding most of their net worth in the business. This 'voting with their money' when it comes to owner-operated and first-generation managed businesses is a potential sign of highly motivated and engaged ownership. As fund manager Nick Sleep highlights, 'First generation owners want to grow wealth, not reported profits, so are long-term thinkers,' and thus they are amongst the highest-quality managers a business can hope to have. In fact, Sleep's portfolio in the years before his retirement had, on average, 85 percent of the portfolio businesses run by founders or first-generation management. Skin in the game.

When management are, for all intents and purposes, the owners of a business, it often means that they fulfil all the qualitative due diligence that is usually required to ensure that they think, and are incentivised to act, like business owners. Engaged ownership and management is often one of the hallmarks of long-term business success. They are almost always willing to give up smaller, short-term profits to prioritise larger, long-term gains.

We are looking for owners who use their vision to steward the company in conjunction with the management team. It is often the owners who bring in valuable resources such as additional capital or financial expertise and new customer or supplier relationships to help the business succeed. Partnering as a 'co-owner' in these businesses can often result in excellent long-term returns. The academic research tends to confirm this assessment for several reasons: first, companies controlled by families will generally prioritise longer-term objectives over short-term earnings guidance, which leads to long-term out-performance over shorter-sighted competitors. Secondly, founder-led businesses have been found to focus more on R&D rather than near-term profit maximisation. And, thirdly, they concentrate more on building shareholder value and participate less in M&A activity, which is often value destructive.

Billionaire hedge fund manager Richard Perry writes on the subject, 'You need both great management and a great asset. Having one without the other is a bad recipe. Without proper management, the asset's value will erode over time, making what was once a bargain price look much more expensive. That's a value trap, not value investing.'

However, if the owner-operator is prioritising dividend payments versus reinvesting in the business or there is an excess cash build-up on the balance sheet, this is a red flag. The owner or founder may be entering 'wealth pres-ervation' mode and be potentially more interested in their discretionary spending ability than further growth of the business.

In general, we don't want any single person or entity to own more than 50 percent of the shares outstanding, or shares representing more than 50 percent of the voting rights. Essentially, this would mean they control the course of the business and that we are just passengers on their ship. With the right captain in charge, this may be fine; however, the best captains would have been well advised to reduce their ownership concentration to make their stock more liquid and, thus, more widely available to purchase by other investors.

It's also often a good sign if not just senior management but all manage-ment receive some form of stock-based compensation. A company with an employee discount stock-purchase programme is encouraging. When it comes to stock options, I see them as generally the 'least bad' option for structuring management compensation. The issue with stock options is that shareholders are diluted when the options are exercised, and the exercise price is usually changed if the business hits a hard patch so as not to 'discourage' management! Have you ever heard of a worse example of 'heads I win, tails you lose'? It is, therefore, important to keep an eye on the number of shares in issuance and how this changes over time. As a final note on compensation, Terry Smith put it succinctly when he said, 'Whether we are comfortable admitting it or not, material rewards are how we keep score in the business world. The best employees don't work solely for money, but nobody works without it.'

Looking out for businesses whose employees own a significant portion of the business or which are essentially owner-operated is a useful screen, but it is no guarantee of success. When most of an employee's or owner's net worth is on the line, it is easy to assume they will behave in a way that is not reckless, but that is not always the case. If we look at the financial crisis of 2007–9, the employees of both Bear Stearns and Lehman Brothers held upwards of 30 percent of their firms' shares. Yet both firms pursued perilous trading and funding strategies that ultimately led to the implosion of the net worth of those employees. Therefore, the nature of the business as well as an evaluation of the risk-taking culture at the firm are important.

Insider Buying and Selling Review

When looking at insider buying and selling, we should give more weight to insider purchases than sales, especially if the purchases are material relative to the individual's compensation or net worth. In normal situations, insider selling is not an automatic sign of trouble within a company. There are many reasons that officers might sell. They may need the money to pay their children's tuition or to buy a new house or to satisfy debt. They may be diversifying. Many sales focus around tax year end or as part of an already disclosed stock divestment plan. However, if the share price has halved and seven out of ten company directors are selling, this would clearly be abnormal and most likely a sign to sell first and ask questions later. Also, if any significant insider were to sell most of their shares unexpectedly, this would warrant investigation.

In the end, though, like all investors, there is only one reason why company insiders would buy a significant amount of stock, and that is because they think the stock is undervalued and will go up significantly. I like to see insider purchases during times of market distress or turbulence, especially if the purchases are significant. Although not a buy signal, it is a confirmation signal that I look for if I'm considering investing or adding further to a position. Clearly, the more insider buyers there are around these periods, the stronger will be the signal. Finally, it's also important to differentiate between new shares being bought and exercising options from an executive compensation plan, which would not be a confirmation signal.

Sectoral Analysis

In our evaluation of a individual company, we want to gain an understanding of where it sits within its sector. Jim Collins, author of the bestselling book *Good to Great*, showed through his research that '[a] company does not need to be in a great industry to become a great company. Each good-to-great company built a fabulous economic engine, regardless of the industry. They were able to do this because they attained profound insights into their economics.' The implications for value investors are twofold: first, just because a business is operating in an out-of-favour sector does not mean that it cannot produce substantial long-term returns. Secondly, the main driver of these returns comes from management's attitude in terms of how they run the business in light of the issues the sector is currently experiencing. In this scenario, we are looking for a management team that acknowledges the issues, is not blinkered when it comes to identifying the challenges, and devises solutions to overcome them, rather than burying their heads in the sand and hoping things will eventually get better. Even in the most competitive and out-of-favour sectors, a well-managed firm with a competitive advantage can thrive (e.g. Nucor in the American steel sector).

From a business cycle and reversion-to-the-mean perspective, it's also important to understand whether the sector is currently in favour or out of favour relative to the market and its historic valuation. If we find an attractive-looking business which compares favourably on valuation metrics to its peers, but the entire sector is trading at sky-high valuations compared to the past, then unless something has fundamentally shifted in the sector to warrant the higher valuations, our selected stock may be a poor value pick. Relative value analysis needs to be done at the firm level, sector level and market level to ensure we are not being led astray.

Media (On- and Offline) Review

Google (aside from being an exceptional business) is often a surprisingly good source of information when we want to research a business or the people running it. It's worth taking the time to look through past newspaper articles about the business, as well as what previous employees have said about it on message boards. From these sources, we can sometimes gain insight into the culture and operations of the business. Although, be aware that only those people who are either extremely happy or extremely angry tend to post anything. In some instances, you may find out something surprising, for example, the CEO is going through an acrimonious divorce, which, although personal, is important to know. We want a management team that is fully dedicated to the task at hand. Character is often defined as how you behave when you think no one is watching, so I would argue that how executives behave in their personal lives can often be mirrored in their working lives. It's important, then, that if the CEO has an Instagram account, the photos are not all of client entertainment in Macau (unless he runs a casino company).

Businesses Attributes Evaluation

Establishing the traits that will enable a business to have a long growth runway is essential. As mentioned in Chapter 2, Arie de Geus, author of *The Living Company*, found that the average life span of a business is forty to fifty years, which would indicate that by the time most businesses are accepted into the Fortune 500 list of the world's biggest companies, they are already past their peak. His research identified four common characteristics of long-lived companies:

1. Sensitivity to the environment – representing a company's ability to learn and adapt.
2. Cohesion and identity – aspects of a company's innate ability to build a community and persona or culture for itself.
3. Tolerance and its corollary, decentralization – both symptoms of a company's awareness of ecology and its ability to build constructive relationships with other entities, both within and without.
4. Conservative financing – one element in a very critical corporate attribute: the ability to effectively govern its own growth and evolution.

Point 4, as we have seen, can be quantitatively tested. But for Points 1, 2 and 3, we need to search for answers using more qualitative measures. We need to ascertain a solid understanding of both the structure and the decision-making processes within the business. In general, I find that the best returns come from organisations that are either entirely centralised in their decision-making processes or entirely decentralised. Employees at all levels must know the chain of command and how to get things done effectively within the organisation. Businesses that do not have clear decision-making processes usually present early warning signs of poor management.

When fund manager Nick Sleep was examining his own investment portfolio at Nomad, he noted two things about the successful businesses. The first was that they were most often run by their founders, which we have discussed in detail, and the second was that low operating costs were ingrained into their culture. Sleep elaborated:

> Costco Wholesale measures costs in basis points and at Amazon.com they take the light bulbs out of the vending machines to save money.

In another sphere, the Olympic Team GB Cycling coach and Sky Tour de France Chief Sir Dave Brailsford might refer to this type of behaviour as seeking 'the aggregation of marginal gains'. Just as it leads to gold medals and yellow jerseys, its effect is that AirAsia, for example, is the lowest-cost airline in the world. Good things follow when you take care of the pennies.

My takeaway from this is twofold. First, in certain businesses, lowering your operating costs is the only way to grow your moat, so this must form part of the DNA of that business. Second, success often comes through slow and incremental progress, not instantaneous and revolutionary change. In which case, it is even more important to think long term as a business owner to capitalise on this.

A final area I believe warrants thorough evaluation is whether the company's profitability is heavily dependent on the prices of inputs that lie outside the company's control. An example would be a chocolate manufacturer who is entirely reliant on the price of raw cocoa. In these situations, we want to establish what actions have been taken to insulate the business against unforeseen price rises or input shortages. These might include long-term supply contracts, hedging the risk of price increases, or, in the case of the chocolate producer, leasing or buying cocoa plantations to guarantee its supply and having adequate stored materials in case of a short-term supply issue. With the increase of just-in-time (JIT) inventory management, many companies' supply chains are more and more vulnerable to short-term supply issues – as we saw during the Covid pandemic.

Very few businesses should make it all the way through your qualitative analysis – and this is how it should be. Remember: fat, juicy salmon are rare. For any exceptional business that does make it through, it's now time for action.

Step 5: Investment Decision

When all the stars align, there is no sense tiptoeing into a position, you have to go for the jugular.

— George Soros, founder of Soros Fund Management and philanthropist

There are three different decisions we can now make: a 'buy' decision for a potential new investment for inclusion in the portfolio, or a 'hold' or 'sell' decision for a current portfolio holding. In Step 5, we focus on the 'buy' decision, as this requires the potential investment idea to successfully pass through our filtering processes in Steps 1 to 4. In my experience, both the 'hold' and 'sell' decisions for current portfolio holdings tend to be more art and less science. As such, we will explore both in greater detail in Chapter 13 (Portfolio Management).

To confirm the 'buy' decision, I always end our individual securities selection process by summarising in one paragraph my thesis on why this is a good investment. In a second paragraph, I play devil's advocate, exploring what would make this investment fail. This should take no more than one paragraph for each investment idea that is still under consideration after the quantitative and qualitative analyses have been completed. This informal word limit forces me to narrow my investment thesis down to the few salient points that are integral to the success or failure of any single business. If I cannot easily identify these points, the analysis has not been done correctly.

The description should be simple enough that a teenager could under-stand it. You should also be able to explain it to someone else in as many words as you've written down. If not, again, I would argue, the drivers of the investment thesis are not well enough understood, so more work is required.

Although not essential, an investment peer can act as a useful sounding board at this stage, especially when analysing the cogency of your two para-graphs. This helps to ensure that none of those pesky cognitive or behavioural biases have crept in.

From my experience, if you lack objectivity, this will be clear as your positive paragraph will be far more specific than your negative paragraph. I find that the negatives become generalities such as 'The market may crash, which will push the share price down.' We are looking for well-balanced arguments that use specifics. The same way that a company's success hinges on two or three factors, its failure also often hinges on just a few factors.

At Gronager Partners, we also include modelling for each new investment idea to determine the probability of a permanent loss of our capital. (Protecting our downside always comes first.) This includes estimating the risk/ reward in the purchase as well as the degree of correlation the new investment has relative to the other securities currently held in the portfolio. This circles back to portfolio construction: we want a diversity of sectors and geographies for the investments in our portfolio.

Some investors I've met have very complex buying processes when it comes to executing the 'buy order' of a company's shares once they have decided that they want to own it. They like to 'haggle' with brokers to ensure that they buy at what they perceive to be the lowest price possible. This has always struck me as ridiculous. If all your investment research has told you that this is a good business to own for the long term, whether you buy it at an average price of $10.50 or $10.52, or even $11, should make absolutely no difference to your investment thesis. If it does, the stock does not trade at a great-enough discount to its intrinsic value to consider purchasing in the first place. As Terry Smith points out, far too many investors get caught up being 'penny wise and pound foolish' – trying to buy at the 'relative lows' and then missing out as the stock moves higher while waiting for a pull-back.

Once I have found a business that I want to own, I buy at the market price. As a rule, I don't like my buying activity to be more than 20 percent of the volume traded on a given day. There is no point in pushing the price deliberately against myself as the market tries to supply the liquidity to fill my order. Hence, I am perfectly happy to buy my position over several days at 20 percent of the volume-weighted average price (VWAP). I use the same rules, but in reverse, when it comes to executing my sell decisions. The exception being if I believe there has been fraud committed, in which case, I sell as fast as possible. From a portfolio construction perspective, liquidity is very important. For example, if we find an exceptional business but we cannot buy enough stock because it is not liquid enough or the market cap is too small relative to our AUM, then it does not meet our portfolio construction criteria. Establishing the target liquidity profile for our portfolio during the portfolio construction phase saves us going through the entire individual securities selection process and then belatedly realising that the stock is not liquid enough to qualify for inclusion.

Each year, I re-examine my analysis of every portfolio holding, beginning with my two-paragraph 'for-and-against' investment summary. This is to ensure that my original investment thesis is still relevant and intact and that the potential negatives that I had foreseen have not come to pass and are no more likely to come to pass and that I have not missed any other key drivers. As the business evolves, it is possible that the salient points originally identified will change over time, but we must be careful to never fit our thesis to match the data. Over time, the data should always support our investment thesis.

Watchlists

Long ago, Ben Graham taught me that 'Price is what you pay; value is what you get.' Whether we're talking about socks or stocks, I like buying quality merchandise when it is marked down.

— Warren E. Buffett, chairman of Berkshire Hathaway

It may be that once you have done your analysis and been through your individual securities selection process, some ideas have not been dismissed but they don't end in an investment decision. When a meaningful compounder or great business is found, the stock price will often already reflect a very rosy future for the company and, thus, the discount to intrinsic value will be too small. If so, add it to your watchlist and buy a few shares, so that you can embrace the ownership mentality and, therefore, follow it more closely. On the basis that you never truly understand a business until you own it, owning some shares in your watchlist companies will generally lead to a keener understanding of each business over time. This watchlist allows you to cultivate a small group of stocks for potential inclusion as full-sized positions in the portfolio if they are caught, for example, in a general market sell-off or have an earnings hiccup. Personally, I like to keep up to 10 percent of my portfolio in the 'watchlist nursery' with individual position sizes at about 1 percent of the overall portfolio. This way, if I am correct on a stock's outlook but incorrect on how expensive it is (regret minimisation) I will still capture some of the move. A 10× on a 1 percent portfolio allocation is significantly better than not catching any of the move at all!

Given the volatility of 'Mr Market', we can often be presented with an opportunity to buy the business at a favourable price if we watch it closely over time. To do so, though, we must be aware of it in the first place, which is the purpose of the small position and the watchlist. I treat small positions in my watchlist as seriously as I treat full positions within the portfolio. If this attitude changes for any reason, they should be sold and exit the list. To recognise a business as being exceptional but at the current price already incorporating the rosiest of futures and to not buy it requires substantial discipline. In general, the higher a stock has risen, the more attractive it seems to become. Allowing myself to purchase some shares when I add it to my watchlist seems to negate this tendency to want to make it a full position at an all-time high price. It allows me to add to my position when the discount to intrinsic value widens from time to time and, thus, averages down.

When a stock has traded in a range for a long time, we tend to presume its value lies within that range. Value investors must fight this anchoring bias, because price and value are not the same thing. The only thing we should care about is if we assess the fundamentals of the business to be significantly more or less favourable than the market's current appraisal. This only should inform our buy, sell or hold decision, not whether the stock price has been range-bound for an extended period. This said, if my investment thesis is not borne out within five years, I will exit the position. Clearly, in that case, I have missed something significant. The objectivity that comes with selling the position and not allowing myself to buy it again for at least a year usually allows me to finally see the issues that I could not see before.

Summary

If we at Gronager Partners are in doubt regarding our investment process, we defer to Buffett's 1994 Letter to Berkshire Shareholders:

> There are no bonus points for complicated investments. Our investments continue to be few in number and simple in concept. The truly big investment ideas can usually be explained in a short paragraph. We like a business with enduring competitive advantages that is run by able and owner-oriented people. When these attributes exist, and when we can make purchases at sensible prices, it is hard to go wrong (a challenge we periodically manage to overcome).

The quantitative analysis (i.e. the valuation part of the investment process) often generates the most concrete results when compared to the qualitative analysis. I would argue, however, that more time should be spent on the qualitative aspects of a business, as these are more open to interpretation which can give an investor an edge. As fund manager Mohnish Pabrai advises, 'Do not weight too highly the valuation part of the security analysis process. The question that needs to be answered for long-term success is: Is the business getting better or worse?'

Some investors believe that the more information they have and the more they evaluate it, model it and examine it, the better off they will be. But I don't agree. There are only ever a few key factors that will fundamentally affect the trajectory of any business. In my opinion, the art of investing is being able to distil your investment down to encompass only those salient points. It is always important to distinguish between information and knowledge. We live in a world of abundant information on almost any topic imaginable, and accessible immediately. This, however, is entirely different from knowledge, which is accumulated slowly. Investment ideas usually come to us gradually as we assimilate and distil what we believe to be relevant information and allow ourselves the time to reflect, revise and refine our interpretation. It is not an instantaneous process. The abundance of information available to us on any investment idea likely masks the few important facts that we really do *need to know* about the business. As fund manager Nassim Taleb quips, 'Almost all data is noise.'

And as hedge fund manager Ray Dalio advises, 'The best choices are the ones that have more pros than cons, not those that don't have any cons at all.

Watch out for people who argue against something whenever they can find something – anything – wrong with it, without properly weighting all the pluses and minuses. Such people tend to be poor decision makers.'

You must recognise that there is never 100 percent certainty regarding an investment. No matter how much data you've been given, there's still risk. The decision to take that risk or not comes down to your own instinct as an investor, developed and honed through experience.

If we look back in time, we can easily identify different periods of both euphoria and fear within market cycles during which different investment approaches would have prevailed. For example, there are periods during which future earnings and growth projections for businesses are more important to current market valuations than near-term cash flows (usually during times of optimism) and times when the reverse is true (usually times of pessimism). I would argue that no successful investor can be pigeonholed into a single investment style for the entirety of their career. As we have said many times, in markets, all knowledge is cumulative, and it is natural that every investor's distinct style evolves over time as a product of both their successes and failures. In my view, the very best of investors have a style more akin to that of an investing Swiss Army knife, evolving a series of specific investment styles during their careers. Their skill lies in knowing which one to use to evaluate each unique investment opportunity.

CHAPTER 12: MANAGEMENT

I try to buy stock in businesses that are so wonderful that an idiot can run them. Because sooner or later, one will.

— Warren E. Buffett, chairman of Berkshire Hathaway

Despite the hundreds of analytical models constructed to describe various business scenarios or the thousands of pages devoted to dissecting and interpreting financial statements, such analyses overlook one of the most essential aspects of any business: the management team. Although we touched on management in the last chapter on qualitative analysis, it's worth examining the topic of management in greater detail, as it's a hugely important determinant of any business's long-term success or failure.

On one hand, you have investors like Buffett who point out that the best businesses are great regardless of the quality of their management. Buffett's view is that '[w]hen a management with a reputation for brilliance tackles a business with a reputation for bad economics, it is the reputation of the business that remains intact.'

Great management in and of itself cannot rescue a failing business, but I would argue it can often ruin a good one. This comes down to a multitude of factors, but the most important one (you guessed it!) is *incentives*. Most management teams are incentivised to do one thing and one thing only: increase EPS every year. They also know that the average tenure as a C-suite executive in a publicly listed company is about four years. As such, they will do everything in their power to achieve the short-term goal of raising EPS so they can get paid as much as possible before they leave. Regardless of the often-negative long-term impact this focus on achieving short-term goals can have on the business.

On the other hand, according to business professor Robert Hagstrom, the primary reason an investor should take the time to evaluate management is that it provides positive (or negative) early-warning signals of eventual financial performance. If you look closely at the words and actions of a management team, you will find clues for measuring the value of their work long before it shows up in the company's financial statements. This is why I recommend reading and listening to all management transcripts and calls by a company you are invested in or are considering investing in.

There are, hopefully, many years of 'footprints in the snow' that we can use to cross-check with actual results the things management said they would do and the results they said they would achieve. In general, I am more interested in how management speaks in terms of quality and candour than the actual words they say. We are trying to ascertain how investor- friendly they are, how honest and open their communication style is, and in whose best interests they are running the company. This can be apparent from the structure of a management call itself:

1. Does the CEO speak or is most of the communication shouldered by the CFO?
2. Who answers the questions in the Q&A and how detailed are the answers?
3. Often more importantly, are their answers obfuscating or enlightening?
4. Do I get a positive feeling that these are people that I want to partner with?

When it comes to written communications from management, it will very quickly become apparent to you where that communication was authored. For example, is the CEO and/or Chairman's letter to shareholders written by those people themselves or has it been drafted by a team of lawyers in conjunction with the PR department? Both (lawyers and PR) are red flags. Lawyers because they often seek to obfuscate or limit legal exposure and PR departments because they tend to be overly optimistic and effusive. We are looking for honesty. If mistakes are made, are they readily acknowledged or glossed over? Are failures owned or is an external party or event always to blame for underperformance? In my experience, highly promotional management teams almost always over-promise and under-deliver, whereas conservative but candid management teams tend to humbly acknowledge and share the credit for outperformance around their organisation and shoulder individually more than their fair share of the blame when things go wrong. They also tend to prefer to let their results speak for themselves.

When we examine the academic research on what makes great business leaders and great businesses, 'culture' is often cited. In his book *The Living Company*, Arie de Geus found that successful businesses generally had several characteristics in common, and that such characteristics were usually instilled in the company culture by senior management. The first was that the management team saw themselves as 'in business' rather than managing a business; they lived and breathed the company and were always looking for opportunities for incremental improvement. Another was that management liked to push decision-making control as far down the chain of command as possible, thus giving those closest to the coalface the opportunity to control their own destiny and think like entrepreneurs. Going against the grain or thinking outside the box in terms of implementing change and risk-taking was also seen as positive, not negative. Finally, de Geus identified that management promoting a conservative financing policy was perhaps the single biggest contributor to whether a company would exist for an extended period or not. As he summarised:

> A business person's life is full of irresistible temptations, and the most irresistible of all is probably impatience. We often get into positions in which we have the power to foster quick growth, with impressive short-term results – at the expense of the long-term health of the enterprise. If there are negative consequences to this growth, the consequences won't be felt for months or years. So, instead of evolution, we go for revolution. Instead of building an enterprise, we set out on a quick adventure. We take a gamble. But good business people are not gamblers. They should be the opposite; they are stewards and custodians of the company they manage. Conservatism in financing helps them avoid the temptation of gambling.

Capital Allocation & Resisting the Institutional Imperative

Beware bureaucracy! It is a construction by which management is conveniently separated from the consequences of its own actions.

– Nassim Nicholas Taleb, Lebanese-American risk analyst, trader and author of *Skin in the Game*

Nick Sleep of Nomad Capital identified three questions that he sought to answer while evaluating a business:

1. What are the returns on incremental capital and the longevity of those returns?
2. Are management correctly incentivised to allocate capital appropriately?
3. What is discounted by the current stock price?

Of the three, it is management's ongoing attitude to capital allocation and value creation that is most important for ensuring excellent returns over the long term. In terms of raising capital, as we have seen, management can either issue debt, issue additional equity, or use excess free cash flow. Buffett described what he called the tendency for management to veer from the course on sensible capital allocation as the 'institutional imperative' (i.e. the necessity to be seen to be doing something):

> Rationality frequently wilts when the institutional imperative comes into play. For example: (1) As if governed by Newton's First Law of Motion, an institution will resist any change in its current direction; (2) just as work expands to fill available time, corporate projects or acquisitions will materialize to soak up available funds; (3) any business craving of the leader, however foolish, will be quickly supported by detailed rate-of-return and strategic studies prepared by his troops; and (4) the behaviour of peer companies, whether they are expanding, acquiring, setting executive compensation or whatever, will be mindlessly imitated.

The only businesses I have found that tend to have a strong natural tendency to resist the institutional imperative are founder-operated or -controlled businesses. The stability of this setup affords them the ability to focus on long-term decision-making and, in turn, on the most important thing for shareholders: profits and how profits are used to their maximum benefit. Charles Koch, billionaire chairman and CEO of Koch Industries, one of the largest privately owned companies in the world, is famous for saying that he did not care about sales or costs; he cared about profits. He wanted to know the ROI of any investment proposition to ensure it was the very best use of his money. We want our management teams to treat our capital just the same.

One of the worst uses of capital, as I have alluded to throughout this book, is mergers and acquisitions. Academic evidence demonstrates that if management wants to destroy shareholder value, M&A is the fastest way to do it. Management professor Michael Porter analysed 2,700 mergers and acquisitions by twenty-two major US companies over a thirty-six-year period (1950–1986). His report, published in 1987, found failure rates between 50 and 75 percent ('failure' meaning disposal of the acquired business). A more recent Dutch study found failure rates of up to 60 percent. Beware growth through M&A and doubly beware if M&A is a key part of the business's strategy. As we have seen, there is no easier way to obfuscate the financial statements of a business than through M&A.

In his book *How the Mighty Fall*, business analyst James Collins explores the five stages of business decline. [FIG. 28]

I found one of his findings particularly interesting as it tied back to Buffett's point of searching out companies that resist the institutional imperative. Collins found that leading companies stumble and fail more through overreaching than complacency or lack of innovation. He found that success often led to hubris, which led to management overpromising in terms of results. Then when the promises became too great, rather than under-deliver, management would take greater and greater risks to try to meet the unrealistic expectations they had set.

We must also be wary of a management team who focus only on beating next quarter's analyst earnings targets and emphasise these in both their

28 The Five Stages of the Business Lifecycle

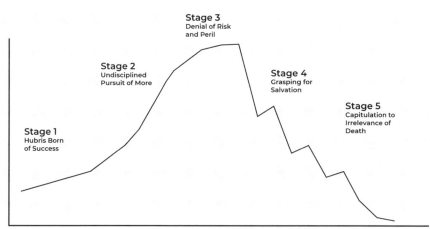

SOURCE: Collins, J. (2009). How the mighty fall: and why some companies never give in. New York: Harper Collins Publishers

presentations and Q&A. We are looking for business leaders with a long-term vision for the business and a strategic path for how they will get there, not near-term earnings management for the benefit of short-term speculators.

Of course, achieving the long-term vision and following the strategic path is often harder to do in public corporations because of constant reporting requirements and business targets. Operating a public corporation comes with an enormous amount of external pressure compared to that experienced in operating a private company. Wall Street analysts will clamour for meetings with management to guess at the following quarter's results, so they can tweak their financial models and issue a new stock price target.

Wall Street is essentially a giant marketing machine, and any management team that devotes serious time to meet with them has, in my view, taken their eyes off their job, which is to run and grow the business. Wall Street targets and internal targets can be double-edged swords. When studying management behaviour, Professor Michael C. Jensen of Harvard Business School found that two things generally happened when a manager is told they will receive a bonus if they hit a particular target. The first is they will talk down business prospects to set the target as low as possible. The second is they will then do everything they can to reach it, including accounting shenanigans that boost near-term results at the expense of larger future returns.

Summary

Humility is essential for successful investing. I would argue that it is also an essential characteristic of the very best managers. The best managers build a world-class executive team, hiring the best people for each role without bias. They look to hire people better than themselves and recognise that they must set the culture and tone for the organisation through leading by example. Tyrannical and supposedly superstar CEOs who worship at the cult of personality can indeed produce spectacular results during their tenure. However, companies run by these kinds of people often suffer over the long term. They either make their name through deep cost cuts that impact the long-term operational efficiency of the business, or they deliberately prevent the development of a deep bench of talent able to replace them. Either way, the business's fall after they leave is often as spectacular as its rise while they were there – something the celebrity CEO revels in, despite being the reason for both the success and the failure.

As we learned from fund manager Peter Lynch, mistakes and failures are an inevitability of investing. As a professional investor, he writes, 'You get a lot of A's and B's in school. In the stock market, you get a lot of F's. And if you're right six or seven times out of ten, you're very good.' Failure is also a necessary part of success in business. The inner drive to keep trying and not be discouraged by failure, but to learn from it and adapt, is the hallmark of both a successful investor and businessman. As the old saying goes, most people stop digging when they are a foot from gold. Lakshmi Mittal, the billionaire CEO of Arcelor Mittal Steel, said that most of his success in life could be attributed to turning up. He had an inner drive and hunger that none of his competitors had; he wanted success more and was willing to work harder to achieve it.

In my experience, asking people about their experiences of failure reveals far more than asking about their successes. We seek to invest in businesses where the senior team have clearly spent significant time examining their past mistakes. In other words, they can identify them, explain them, and, most importantly, say what they learnt from them. We are taught from a very early age that being wrong and making mistakes is bad, but success in anything is impossible without failure. What is bad is glossing over mistakes or brushing them under the carpet. This simply leaves the management team open to repeating them.

Academic research has shown there is a strong link between employee satisfaction or morale and business performance. Professor Edmans of the London Business School examined *Fortune Magazine*'s list of the best companies to work for as voted by employees versus share price performance. The highest-rated companies outperformed their peers by an average 3.5 percent increase in share price annualised over the five-year period following receiving their ratings. This finding is important for long-term investors. First, it shows a link between high levels of satisfaction amongst employees and their companies outperforming their peers. Secondly, over the long term, the beneficial effects of having happy employees begin to materialise in the form of superior performance.

It is also worth reiterating that when it comes to the financial statements of any business, management can 'adjust' them to show what they want. Especially if they have a willing auditor who receives a large fee for signing off the audit and whose firm also supplies lucrative management consulting services to the business. The latter situation represents a clear conflict of interest and is something that I believe should be banned. This is why the integrity of management is so important. As Buffett said when asked what he looked for in hiring managers, 'You want someone who is intelligent, energetic and moral. But if they don't have the last one, you don't want them having the first two.'

When it comes to the management and the board of directors, you want to ensure they have adequate skin in the game. Not only should they all have substantial stock holdings in the company relative to their annual compensation or net worth, but the pay for management should be tied closely to performance. Their performance should be measurable against hard-to-manipulate metrics that ensure their compensation is tied firmly to the long-term returns of their shareholders.

For the board, I like to see that they have enough independence to challenge the CEO. In other words, they are not all 'Yes' men handpicked by the CEO. As Buffett quipped on the subject, 'When seeking directors, CEOs don't look for pit bulls. It's the cocker spaniel that gets taken home.' Directors should all be successful enough to not have to worry about their job security and, therefore, not feel they have to give the CEO an easy ride to ensure they can continue clipping their salary coupon.

When I look at our portfolio of companies at Gronager Partners, most of them are firms run by the original founder or the first-generation children of the founder. On average, they own about 40 percent of the business, and in most cases, the company is either buying back shares or has meaningful insider buying. When looking for business leaders, I am looking for low ego, honest and highly capable individuals who are passionate about what they do. Leaders who are obsessed with their business and are always curious. Relentlessly looking for ways to make their business better and their competitive moat wider and deeper. I want them to be risk-takers. As Jeff Bezos wrote in his first Amazon annual letter to shareholders in 1997, 'Given a 10 percent chance of a hundred times pay-out, you should take that bet every time.' I want management to spend as little time as possible predicting the future and zero time trying to impress investment analysts and short-term speculators. Lastly, I want them to have a long-term ownership orientation. For example, despite being well into his eighties, billionaire CEO of Koch Industries Charles Koch is still working on incredibly long timelines. After fifty years of running the business and adding hundreds of billions of dollars of market value, his plans for the business are, as he puts it, 'still in the early stages'.

CHAPTER 13: PORTFOLIO MANAGEMENT

Establishing and maintaining an unconventional investment profile requires acceptance of uncomfortably idiosyncratic portfolios, which frequently appear downright imprudent in the eyes of conventional wisdom.

— David Swensen, CIO of the Yale University Endowment and author of *Pioneering Portfolio Management*

Once you have found and vetted your prospective investment ideas and assembled them in your portfolio, there will be an ongoing portfolio management process to consider. At Gronager Partners, this includes:

- Portfolio turnover
- Hold and sell decisions
- Liquidity management
- Portfolio rebalancing
- Currency hedging

Portfolio Turnover

Treat your portfolio as if you were the chief executive officer of a holding company. A parent company that owns a subsidiary with superb long-term economics will not sell the company's crown jewel. Yet the same CEO will impulsively sell stocks in his own personal portfolio with little more logic than 'you can't go broke taking a profit.' In our view, what makes sense in business also makes sense in stocks: An investor should ordinarily hold a small piece of an outstanding business with the same tenacity that an owner would exhibit if he owned all of that business.

— Warren E. Buffett, chairman of Berkshire Hathaway

When we look at the returns of any investor, one thing that may not be immediately clear is the costs associated with their portfolio turnover. For those companies that disclose it publicly, the costs are often very low, as they recognise that the lower the costs and charges are, the higher the reported returns to investors will be. This low turnover strategy has an added kicker for taxable investors, as it reduces both the amount and frequency of capital gains tax. The combined effect of these two results can turbocharge investors' returns, especially over the long term. Let's take a closer look at both.

Transaction costs are often unseen, but they prove to be an increasingly punitive cost on any actively managed portfolio. The costs involved are not just the headline cost of execution, which may be a few dollars per trade, but also the costs of crossing the bid–offer spread. The bid is the price someone else will pay (or bid) and, hence, the price that you can sell at. The offer is the price at which someone will sell (or offer) the security; thus, it is the price that you can buy at. In general, the smaller or less liquid the security, the wider the spread. The range can be large, but we typically see anything from about 0.1 percent to about 5 percent. With any sort of active trading strategy, the transaction costs quickly add up to several percent a year. This cost is deducted directly from the assets of the portfolio. As our asset base gets larger, we also fall prey to 'slippage', where the price of the stock moves against us in response to our buying and selling. These are some of the 'hidden costs' of high turnover portfolios, illustrating that inactivity on the part of a portfolio manager can be accretive to investor returns.

On the subject of taxes, Robert Jeffrey and Robert Arnott researched the effect of portfolio turnover on individual investors' after-tax returns. They published a paper in the *Journal of Portfolio Management* titled 'Is Your Alpha Big Enough to Cover Its Taxes?' The purpose of the paper was to establish the point at which portfolio turnover began to have a detrimental effect on investor returns. Their results were surprising and completely counterintuitive. They found that the greatest 'tax damage' to a portfolio occurs at the outset of turnover and that tax damage decreases as turnover increases. 'Conventional wisdom thinks of any turnover in the range of 1 percent – 25 percent as categorically low and inconsequential, and of anything greater than 50 percent as being high and presumably of considerable consequence; the reality is just the opposite.'

They found that the average tax drag on an actively managed portfolio is between 1 percent and 3 percent per year. At a 25 percent portfolio turnover ratio, the investor incurs 80 percent of the taxes that would be generated if the portfolio turnover were 100 percent. They concluded by recommending that we be aware of each incremental increase in portfolio turnover from a very low level, and they found that the optimal range would be around 5 percent in terms of enabling investors to achieve the highest after-tax returns. The table below is based on their study and shows the additional return the average portfolio manager would need to earn for their investors to achieve the highest after-tax returns, based on their portfolio turnover and the rate of return of the market (i.e. the excess return or 'alpha' they need to generate). [FIG. 29]

Now, none of this is to say that we cannot adjust our portfolio relative to the state of the surrounding investment environment because of these frictional costs, but for a value investor this process will occur naturally. If stocks become wildly overpriced relative to their fundamentals, it makes sense to potentially sell your holdings that are caught up in the euphoria. But in such a market it is also unlikely there will be many attractive investment opportunities into which to reinvest the proceeds. This will lead to the portfolio becoming more defensively positioned as we sit on more cash or cash-equivalent securities (short-term government bonds). Naturally, the reverse will be true when there are more opportunities than you have funds available. Your portfolio cash holding will be very small, which will naturally make your portfolio

29 Additional Annual Pre-Tax Growth Required To Offset Taxes

Market Growth	4%	6%	8%	10%	12%
Turnover 5%	0.51	0.70	0.85	0.99	1.11
10%	0.89	1.22	1.51	1.77	1.99
25%	1.51	2.15	2.73	3.26	3.76
50%	1.90	2.78	3.63	4.44	5.23
75%	2.06	3.07	4.06	5.03	5.99
100%	2.15	3.23	4.31	5.38	6.46

SOURCE: FactSet, J.P Morgan Asset Management

more aggressively positioned for future growth. Being fearful when others are greedy and greedy when others are fearful is a natural part of portfolio management for value investors.

Hold and Sell Decisions

One of the most hazardous remarks to your financial health is to believe the adage that no-one ever went broke taking a profit.

– Warren E. Buffett, chairman of Berkshire Hathaway

Everyone buys a stock for the same reason: because they believe it is going up. However, when it comes to holding or selling stocks, investors continue to hold or sell for many different reasons. The arts of holding and selling are perhaps the hardest and least concrete of all the components that make up the practical side of successful investing. Each situation and each investment must be evaluated on its own merits. In this section, we will look at the requirements for continuing to hold a position, some of the motivations for selling, how to sell correctly, and typical mistakes.

Up to this point in Part Two, the focus has been on how to find, evaluate and select businesses for inclusion in your portfolio (the 'buy' criteria). What we buy is far more important for returns than timing or when we buy. One of my favourite examples of this comes from Warren Buffett, who described the outcome that came from purchasing one share of Coca-Cola stock at its IPO price and holding through to today:

Coca-Cola went public in 1919 at $40 per share; the following year, it was selling at $19 per share. At the time, people said this was because of an increase in the price of sugar and bottling plants going on strike. Years later, you had the Great Depression, World War Two, sugar rationing. In summary, there is always an excuse not to make a purchase, but the absolute fact is if you had bought at the IPO price of $40 and held it to today while re-investing the dividends in more Coca-Cola stock, it would be worth over $10 million [in 2024]. The sheer earnings power if you invest in a good business will far outweigh any and all extraneous factors over time.

However, despite all the work and effort that has gone into the buy decision, the real work has only just begun. I find that most investors, myself included, only truly begin to understand a business once they have invested in it – once there is real money on the line. Your 'buy' criteria are not necessarily the same as your 'hold' criteria. Successful investing is not meant to be easy, which is one of the reasons why it seems paradoxical that the conditions a stock needs to fulfil to be included in a portfolio versus the conditions needed to continue to hold that stock in your portfolio are not the same.

I certainly don't agree with the statement that 'you buy your portfolio every day' or, indeed, every time you look at it. Although you must ensure that the reasons why you bought the stock are still true today, this assessment is an annual process, not a daily one. Anyone who has run a business will tell you that change in business takes time. Like an ocean liner, the larger the business, the longer it takes to change course. The financial metrics of a business fluctuate during the year, but these fluctuations should not colour your long-term mindset. Unless something significant happens that negatively impacts the business fundamentals and, therefore, changes your investment thesis. The very best businesses can outperform the market more than you could possibly have imagined when you initially purchased them. They are always looking for fresh opportunities to expand their compounding engines. To cut your position because you think the stock now looks 'too expensive to add here' can be one of the biggest mistakes any investor can make.

When I am monitoring my portfolio businesses, the last thing I want to look at is the stock price. Instead, I evaluate any new data about a business as impartially as possible. This allows me to form my own view as to whether this information should be positive or negative for the business, *before* checking how the share price has reacted. I find by doing my research in this order, I am not guided by the stock price performance (and, therefore, not prone to anchoring bias). If I believe the news or data are positive and the share price has underperformed, I have either made a mistake in my analysis or 'Mr Market' may be offering me a nice opportunity to add to my position. Either way, I can have the courage of my convictions only if I am confident in my research and the conclusions formed. We are looking for a fundamental improvement in the business over time which will drive the stock price higher. Not a rising share price with signs of a static or sinking business – which is, of course, a firm 'sell' signal.

The 'hold' time frame to allow for an investment thesis to come to fruition will vary from investor to investor. Some will want to see progress every year, while others such as Ben Graham have suggested allowing four years before throwing in the towel. Buffett suggests using five-year moving averages. Investors and businesses are often far too focused on individual twelve-month periods of returns instead of focusing on returns over continuous periods. Personally, I evaluate all new data on my portfolio as it arrives, but I do my best to look at performance – both individual and collective – as infrequently as possible. Remember, patience is a virtue.

At Gronager Partners, we have only three reasons for selling a position in our portfolio:

1. If an event has occurred or information has come to light that disproves our investment thesis to the downside (i.e. if we were wrong).
2. If the investment performs as we had expected or, hopefully, better than expected, and, despite our continuously revising our estimate of intrinsic value to the upside, the business is now egregiously over-priced on every measure.
3. We have found a new business that is superior to the existing holding in every way.

Humility is a topic we keep coming back to. The ability to admit that we are wrong is such an integral part of the investing process, yet it often surprises me how frequently it becomes a stumbling block for investors. There is ego in each of us and a desire to be right – not to mention original – in every-thing we do. Thus, when we begin to question our investment thesis, it is important to treat any loss or gain with equanimity. As we saw in Chapter 8, our cognitive and behavioural biases make us unwilling to sell a position at a small loss, even if our thesis is clearly wrong. This leads inevitably to large losses, which become very expensive. Capital deployed has an opportunity cost, so waiting for a small loss to recover or to become a small gain still has a cost attached to it, as that capital could be reinvested elsewhere. As the saying goes, 'You don't need to make the money back the same way you lost it.'

Our first reason, 'being wrong', is in many ways the easiest reason to sell. It is often obvious and logical. But ego makes it tough. I agree with fund manager Nick Sleep, who writes that

Most mistakes are analytical mistakes. In most cases we had a static view of the firm formed at the time of purchase, which failed to evolve as the facts changed (this can lead us to sell both too early or too late!). This error was reinforced by misjudgments such as denial (the facts had changed) and ego (we can't be wrong). There was also an over-reliance on price to value ratio-type analysis.

Sleep's point regarding holding a 'static view' links neatly into our second reason to sell. The temptation may be to sell and capitalise on a real or perceived overpricing. You may think that you will get back in when the stock corrects, but this is a dangerous tactic, especially if the price keeps going up and you realise that you were, in fact, wrong about the overpricing. The most important reason to monitor your portfolio is not to monitor the change in share price but to reassess your thesis and your estimate of intrinsic value as new information comes to light. As Phil Fisher pointed out, if you have a very large gain in a stock but other than 'looking expensive' it still meets all your investment criteria, you are better to hold it. There will be short-term price declines, some significant, but if the fundamentals of the business remain the same or improve, you must continue to hold. The best companies can, over the long term, far exceed all rational expectations for them; this is what makes them and the returns they generate for those who hold them exceptional.

Our third reason to sell is, I believe, the most complex. In a concentrated portfolio, there is space for only a limited number of positions. To sell a current position in exchange for a new one requires a significant burden of proof that the new investment is significantly better than one or more of our current holdings. In theory, it is always possible to sell a good stock and buy a better one. What is often overlooked, however, is how much better the new purchase needs to be to be able to make the switch advantageous. Say you bought a stock for $100 that is now worth $1,000, and you have found what you consider to be a superior investment to switch to. With an assumed 40 percent marginal tax rate applied on the sale, this would leave you with $640. If your current holding doubles again, it will now be worth $2,000, However, your new after-tax ($640) investment must go up by over 300 percent to match that gain! Clearly, the maths is not on your side. Hence we should only replace a current investment with a new one when the current position rep-resents a *significantly* higher opportunity cost than the new one.

Reinvestment risk is a serious risk because there will always be new investment ideas. Brokers will be pushing for action. How else are they going to make commissions? However, we are focused solely on delivering long-term exceptional performance, and that comes through patience. The ability to tune out all the pressures and noise and sit on your hands is often incredibly hard, especially when everyone around you is in action mode. But as Sleep wrote to his investors,

> Our inclination, whilst the businesses would appear to have so much ahead of them, is to leave them well alone. It would be tempting for Zak and I to do high fives, claim victory, sell our winners and move on to new investments, but we think that course of action would be fraught with reinvestment risk. Be prepared, therefore, for portfolio turnover to be particularly low.

As long-term investors, our main advantage comes from the benefit of time – in allowing great businesses to become even better. If we are fortunate enough in our analysis to have incorporated a 100-bagger into our portfolio, the worst thing we can do is *not* allow the returns to run. Great companies can exceed all expectations. Suffice it to say that unless our thesis is dramatically disproved, the best course of action is to do nothing. Charlie Munger argues that even when a stock in his portfolio becomes 'expensive' on various metrics, he is very reluctant to sell. His reasoning is that if it is a great business, history tells him that, over time, it will likely grow into its apparently high valuation and often exceed it. Great businesses are exceedingly rare, and they should be treated as such. As Phil Fisher wrote, 'The risk of making a mistake and switching [or selling] stocks … is probably considerably greater for the average investor than the temporary risk of staying with a thoroughly sound but currently overvalued situation until genuine value catches up with current prices.'

American financier Bernard Baruch wrote extensively about the psychological difficulty of selling winners or losers:

> Many a novice will sell something he has a profit in to protect something in which he has a loss. Since the position has usually gone down the least, or may even show a profit, it is psychologically easy to let it go. With a bad stock, the loss is likely to be heavy, and the impulse is to hold on to it in order to recover what has been lost.

Concentrated value investors need to embrace this psychological difficulty, especially when it comes to averaging down on losing positions. When your investment thesis is fully intact and yet price performance has been poor, it makes perfect sense to a concentrated value investor to buy more of the stock. It is now even more of a bargain and has an even wider margin of safety than when it was initially purchased. If we are not comfortable with this course of action, then, clearly, our original investment thesis was wrong and we should sell.

To understand the concept of managing your portfolio and the 'hold' versus 'sell' decisions within it, I think it is helpful to remind yourself that you are a business owner. Your portfolio is your business and each stock in that business is an operating division. At any point in time, some will be performing well, some averagely, and some worse than expected. If you spend a great deal of time evaluating each of the operating divisions before adding them into your business, does it not make sense to allow them time to perform or improve, rather than throwing them out at the first sign of trouble? Similarly, with an excellently performing division, should you sell it and be left with currently poor and averagely performing divisions? Imagine if a business in which you own a substantial volume of stock has several subsidiaries with average performance and one exceptional performer. What would you say if the CEO told you he was thinking of selling the crown jewels but keeping the rest? You would be horrified, and rightly so!

At Gronager Partners, we do not sell investments because they have gone up, as this is not a reason to sell in and of itself. It is a sell signal for us only if the underlying fundamentals of the business have changed to the downside. Similarly, selling an exceptional performer because it is taking up more of an allocation in our portfolio than originally envisioned due to superior performance is also not a reason for us to sell. Think about the maths again. If you have made a 10× return and it doubles again, you will have made a 20×, and if it doubles one more time it would be a 40×. If you had sold at any of the intervals before the next double, you would have left more returns on the table than you originally made when you patted yourself on the back for doing a great job and making a 10× or 20×! Selling too early can be incredibly expensive. Even the legendary investors have difficulty with selling. Sir John Templeton didn't trust himself to objectively sell a stock to replace it with a new one, so he automated the decision. He made a rule that unless the proposed new stock was at least 50 percent cheaper than the current holding, it could not be sold. Beware change for change's sake. The grass is not always greener on the other side. So long as the companies' earnings are increasing over time, stick with them.

Liquidity Management

Liquidity is a coward, it runs at the first sign of trouble.

Barton Biggs, fund manager and global investment strategist

I define liquidity as the ability to enter or exit a position within a reasonable time frame with minimum market impact. It is important to think about the maximum stake you would be willing to hold in any one company. Often, as a fund manager, you will need to adjust your position size over time due to investor subscriptions and redemptions. What you do not want to be doing is cutting a position to meet redemptions, when the act of rebalancing or exiting the position, entirely because of the position's size/liquidity, pushes the price significantly against you (slippage), resulting in large losses.

During normal market periods, you can often buy and sell a security easily, but during periods of market stress, liquidity may dry up very quickly and bid–offer spreads widen dramatically, pushing up your transaction costs. When measuring liquidity, we need to look at it over a long-enough time frame, preferably including the last period of market stress, to ensure that even during tough times we would be able to safely exit our position within a reasonable period. The question I ask is, if we were to be 20 percent of daily market volume, how long would it take to exit the position using the lowest daily market-volume number? Anything over five days would likely raise a red flag and require additional due diligence.

A Word on Stop-Losses

Show me a portfolio with 10% stops and I'll show you a portfolio that's destined to lose exactly that amount. When you put in a stop, you're admitting that you are going to sell a stock for less than it is worth today.

— Peter Lynch, American investor and fund manager of the
Fidelity Magellan Fund

On paper, stop-losses seem like an intelligent portfolio tool for loss mitigation, but in real life, they are essentially loss guarantees. When we buy a stock, we are saying that the market is mispricing the security. And if we had the available funds, we would be happy to buy the entire business at the current purchase price. Why, then, does putting a stop-loss 10 percent or 20 percent below your initial purchase price make any logical sense? If you want to sell after a 20 percent fall, that tells me two things: first, that your original purchase price did not incorporate an adequate margin of safety, and, secondly, you believe 'Mr Market' is your master and knows how to value the business better than you do. A drop in the share price should be a trigger for you to buy more, not sell. Stop-losses have no place in a value investor's toolkit.

Rebalancing

Supremely rational investors take the further step of acting against the consensus, rebalancing to long-term portfolio targets by buying the out-of-favour and selling the in-vogue.

— David Swensen, CIO of the Yale University Endowment and
author of *Pioneering Portfolio Management*

Rebalancing is a particularly thorny topic among portfolio managers, who often have very strong views either in favour or against. Many managers are forced to rebalance their portfolios due to only being allowed a maximum allocation to a particular security or asset class. They may only be allowed to grow a position to a certain size before it must be cut or are only allowed to deviate from their benchmark by a certain amount. These are all examples of poor rebalancing; it's arbitrary and serves no concrete purpose other than ensuring the portfolio manager abides by the rules set by a 'risk manager', who almost certainly knows less about how to run a successful portfolio than the fund manager – at least, we hope that's the case!

When I talk about rebalancing, I am not suggesting we borrow fund manager Peter Lynch's term and 'pull out the flowers to water the weeds.' As he rightly points out, selling your winners to hold on to your losers is a poor strategy. It fails for the same reason that using stop-losses is not a good strategy for a long-term investor; they are both investment decisions based purely on the stock price and have no correlation or link to what we believe to be the company's intrinsic value. As Lynch summarises, 'The current stock price tells us absolutely nothing about the future prospects of a company, and it occasionally moves in the opposite direction of the fundamentals for extended periods of time.'

What I am talking about with regards to rebalancing is the allocation within your portfolio between equities and cash or cash-like securities (short-term government bonds). As mentioned previously, it is essential for robust portfolio construction that a portfolio manager has a portion of the portfolio in cash to take advantage of unforeseen investing opportunities and for liquidity purposes such as meeting investor redemptions. The cash or fixed income portion of your portfolio is there to act as ballast during any seen or unforeseen storms.

To outperform the markets, you have to deviate from them; you need to be a contrarian investor. Allocation-based rebalancing rules allow you to sell when markets are roaring and buy when they are panicking, regardless of the fundamentals. As the Yale Endowment CIO, David Swensen, wrote, 'The articulation of portfolio targets constitutes the most powerful determinant of investment outcomes. Casual allocation decisions, honoured in the breach and casually reversed, hold the potential to cause great harm to investor port-folios. Thoughtful policy targets, carefully implemented and steadfastly main-tained, create the foundation of investment success.'

It makes perfect sense to 'sell what's hot and buy what's not', as Swensen put it, but the discipline required to rebalance during periods of extreme market volatility can be particularly hard in the face of all the cognitive biases the market price action triggers. This is why at Gronager Partners we automate the process within our portfolio management framework. We are not consensus investors, we are contrarian investors and doing things that are counter to the crowd will at times be uncomfortable, often for extended periods. Best get used to it!

Currency Hedging

Even though much ink spills and many trees fall as market prognosticators fill reams of pages in attempts to divine the future of foreign exchange rates, no one really knows where currencies will go. Sensible investors avoid speculating in currencies. Top-down bets on currencies fail to generate a reliable source of excess returns, because the factors influencing economic conditions in general, and interest rates, in particular, prove far too complex to predict consistently.

– David Swensen, CIO of the Yale University Endowment and
author of *Pioneering Portfolio Management*

Like portfolio rebalancing, whether to currency hedge or not can spark the fiercest of debates amongst investors. As with many things in finance, what appears to be a simple question can be fiendishly complex to answer. Many investors who buy securities in foreign markets using foreign currencies fear that their returns will be cut by the movement of their domestic currency versus the foreign currency, between the time they make their investment and the time they redeem it. It is true that currencies can fluctuate quite dramatically over time. The investor may argue that they want the risk of the foreign country's equity market, but not the risk of the currency as well, so what should they do?

Our value-investing cohort at Tweedy, Browne have conducted a lot of research on the returns of currency hedging on investor portfolios. Their conclusion was that investors should either hedge 100 percent of the time or not at all. Any middle ground opens us up to trying to time the market, which is guaranteed to lead to significant underperformance. They also found that over the short term, the difference in returns between currency (FX) hedging or not was minimal. But as the time horizon lengthens to the medium or long term, which we care most about as value investors, any potential positive contribution to returns from currency hedging is outweighed by the costs involved. They also noted that, over the long term, stock prices and the foreign currency tended to correlate inversely, meaning that a weakening currency would often be offset by a higher stock price.

Concentrated value investors look for significantly outsized returns over the long term. I use the rule that if a 50 percent movement of the foreign currency against me would make the investment unattractive, it is not a good enough investment in the first place. However, it is also important to look at the foreign exchange rates at a company level to ensure that there is not a large mismatch between the currency in which any borrowing is conducted and the currency in which business is conducted (i.e. from which repayments will be made). The same applies at the country level, as a mismatch between your funding currency and the currency in which your liabilities are denominated can indicate serious trouble for both a company and a country – extremely quickly. For history lessons on this problem, have a look at Mexico's Tequila Crisis of 1994 and the Asian financial crisis of 1997.

Keep it Simple

There are no bonus points for complicated investments.

– Warren E. Buffett, chairman of Berkshire Hathaway

Finance and investing can be as impenetrable and complex as you wish to make them. Einstein said, 'The definition of genius is taking the complex and making it simple.' To claim any sort of mastery or expertise in the world of finance and investing demands the ability to simplify complex ideas and theories down to easy-to-understand and implementable advice. As Buffett wrote in his 1994 Chairman's Letter to Shareholders, 'If you are right about a business, the whole value is largely dependent on a single key factor that is both easy to understand and enduring, the payoff is the same as if you had correctly analysed an investment alternative characterized by many constantly shifting and complex variables.'

People have a strange tendency to act in ways that suggest they believe they know better than others. In finance, it is easy to find people who employ a form of intellectual snobbery by speaking in jargon ('options gamma', 'delta hedging' and 'bond convexity', to name a few examples) or using unnecessary complexity to make themselves appear smarter than perhaps they are. When I look at any portfolio allocation decision, I am always careful to ensure that I am not incorporating undue complexity into my investing process. As we have seen, complexity in the form of, say, FX hedging is likely to be an impediment to our long-term investing success, even if it makes us feel smart and sophisticated while doing it. Humility, not hubris, is at the core of successful investing.

We need only get a few decisions right to enjoy a superb track record. As the mutual fund pioneer Walter Morgan wrote, 'You don't need to be great to thrive as an investor.' Forget about putting a little bit of money into everything or believing that you can pick the 'outperformers of the outperformers' within your portfolio. As Bill Ruane, one of the super investors of Buffett's Graham and Doddsville, said, 'I don't know anybody who can really do a good job investing in a lot of stocks except Peter Lynch.' Instead, look for investments that you understand. When you find them, buy a decent amount of them.

In my opinion, a concentrated portfolio should have no less than ten positions in it and no more than thirty. Gronager Partners keeps things simple. We equal-weight our full positions (~5 percent each) and allocate 1 percent each to our watchlist positions. We waste no energy trying to guess what our best idea is. Every holding in our portfolio has the potential to be our best idea; otherwise, it wouldn't be in there. Over time, we want to let our winners run and compound to become a larger portion of the portfolio. Our expectation is that over a ten-year period, our top three positions will grow to be about 50 percent of the portfolio. The key to achieving this goal, and the exceptional returns that will accompany it, is having adequate patience to hold on to the great businesses in our portfolio for the long term.

Summary

The basic building blocks of a concentrated value portfolio come from buying great businesses at fair prices. The prices paid for these businesses incorporate a significant margin of safety relative to the size of their economic or competitive moat. Once chosen, they must be allowed time to compound and, hopefully, grow to become a larger portion of your portfolio. Again, managing winning positions is more art than science. How much volatility an investor is ready to embrace should be determined by their own personal circumstances as well as their temperament. That said, the biggest errors we can make as value investors are often errors of omission, not errors of *commission* that can fall to zero. The stock that doubled which we then cut; the stock we didn't buy because we thought it was too expensive; and both go on to become 100-baggers.

Our portfolio construction methodology as well as investment selection and portfolio management strategies must incorporate what history tells us is the most likely route to success. They must also be adaptable to the vagaries of both the market and our temperament. Constant humility and objective self-evaluation of our behaviours and emotions is required for consistent success. As we will see in Chapter 14 (Investment Mistakes and Warnings), the more emotionally provoking a situation – such as a 50 percent fall in the value of our portfolio – the more important it is that we have an automatic system in place that will stop us panicking or being paralysed by indecision. During times of crisis, the worst thing we can do is panic; but for contrarian investors looking to succeed over the long term, doing nothing at all is a close second.

CHAPTER 14: INVESTMENT MISTAKES AND WARNINGS

To be wise one must study both good and bad thoughts and acts, but one should study the bad first. You should first know what is not clever, what is not just, and what is not necessary to do.

— Leo Tolstoy, Russian writer and author of *War and Peace*

In this chapter we are going to explore the root causes of many investing mistakes, as well as examine the red flags or warnings that most commonly occur during our individual securities selection process. Where possible, I have provided worked examples so you can see for yourself how easily we can be led astray.

We are conditioned from a very early age to avoid mistakes. Instead of working to the adage 'If at first you don't succeed, try, try again,' most of us instead act as if we subscribe to its adaptation: 'If at first you don't succeed, remove all evidence that you ever tried in the first place.'

However, as we have seen throughout this book, success in any walk of life is impossible without failure. This is nowhere truer than in the field of investing. Acknowledging and examining our own failures and those of others to further ourselves as both human beings and investors is a guaranteed way to accelerate our progress and achieve success. Humility, as we have explored, is a key part of the investment process; it is also a core personality trait of the most successful investors we've met in this book. The ability to admit you're wrong, identify how the error occurred, and incorporate that knowledge into mental models for better future decision-making is what sets apart the successful. Phil Fisher remarked that '[s]tudying possible mistakes can be even more rewarding than reviewing past successes.' As human beings and investors, we can learn far more from our mistakes than from our successes. If we really want to accelerate our personal development, we should keenly examine the mistakes of others to develop rules to add to the ones we already have in place that have been learnt from our own mistakes. Charlie Munger pointed out that not only does this help us to learn at a faster rate but '[l]earning from other people's mistakes is also much more pleasant.'

Like so many investors, I eagerly anticipate the release of Berkshire Hathaway's Annual Report and Buffett's Chairman's Letter to Shareholders. Buffett himself has been described by Munger as a 'learning machine', someone who is intellectually honest, rational and always curious. This honesty and humility is evident in every one of Buffett's letters. Since taking the helm at Berkshire, Buffett has used the word 'mistake' in his letters well over 200 times. As a long-term market participant, Buffett is no stranger to failures or mistakes. However, the attitude that he adopts is one that we would all be wise to clone. We don't need to do it in public like Buffett, but by candidly examining our decision-making track record, we can remind ourselves that it is human to err. There is much to learn from mistakes if we have the courage to bring them out into the open for examination and learning rather than sweeping them under the rug.

Even the very smartest people have had their fair share of mistakes, all of which we can learn from. Take Sir Isaac Newton as an example. With an estimated IQ of 190, he is widely regarded as one of the smartest people to have ever lived. Newton made good money investing in the stock market during the initial stages of what became known as the South Sea Bubble in the 1720s. However, he sold once the market had risen substantially. In contrast, the public's appetite for the stock market continued to grow, to such an extent that Newton couldn't stand watching people he knew get richer as he sat on the sidelines. He eventually succumbed to his emotions and bought twice the amount of stock he had sold, using margin, just as the market peaked. He lost a substantial part of his life savings. Writing about the event afterwards, he lamented, 'I can calculate the motions of the heavenly bodies, but not the madness of people.'

Nearer to the present day was John Meriweather, who, along with several other notable academics and Nobel Prize-winners founded the hedge fund LTCM that we discussed in Chapter 1. Their initial success and unquestioned faith in their models made them believe they were invincible, and they took on more and more leverage before their fund's capital was vaporised in a matter of days. According to their models, the event that killed them was so unlikely that it would have happened only once between the beginning and end of the universe! These examples suggest that intelligence and overconfidence is a dangerous combination when it comes to investing. Unfortunately, Meriweather didn't learn his lesson. He went on to found and blow up two more hedge funds!

Even in the value-investing space, there are significant lessons to learn from the great figures of the past. Take Benjamin Graham, the father of value investing, as an example. He only came to discover the founding principles of value investing after sidestepping the excesses of the 1929 stock market bubble. He then leveraged himself, trying to pick the bottom as the market fell, and lost 70 percent of his capital between 1929 and 1932. Despite being a phenomenal stock-picker when it came to buying a dollar bill for 50 cents, upon his death, most of his net worth, surprisingly, came from the single 'growth stock' in his portfolio: the insurance company GEICO that he had held for over twenty-five years. Thus, he had stumbled upon a method superior to his own, a method which Buffett would make famous: buying great businesses at fair prices.

In today's world, with the ease of access to financial markets, leverage, and speculative products (CFDs, spread betting, options, futures, forwards) on everything from cattle to exotic currency crosses such as JPY/TRY, it is more important than ever that we have a solid grasp of history. Remember the words of philosopher George Santayana: 'Those who cannot remember the past are condemned to repeat it.' We need this knowledge because it helps us to reinforce our circle of competence.

Most of the biggest investing mistakes from the past could have been avoided if the investors in question had stayed within their circles of competence and embraced contrarianism. This is easy to say but incredibly hard to do in practice. Just think of Buffett, who refused to buy tech stocks during the late 1990s tech boom because, as he readily admitted, he did not understand them. People condemned him for being a dinosaur. They said he was past his peak. During this time, the pressure on him must have been immense. Berkshire Hathaway's stock halved. Despite this, he refused to engage in markets or with securities that were outside his circle of competence. He was ultimately vindicated; the tech boom turned into a spectacular crash in the year 2000, and Berkshire stock more than doubled.

Identifying Fraud

When the words 'fraud' and 'mismanagement' are used regarding an investment you own, the usual best course of action is to sell first and investigate later.

— Phil Fisher, investor and pioneer in the field of growth investing

Some accountants will tell you that if the management of a company are fraudulent and deliberately go out of their way to falsify documentation and results, there is no way to identify the fraud before everything falls apart – which it inevitably always does. I agree. Identifying sophisticated frauds can be very difficult, especially when the companies have veneers of respectability and public market adoration prior to their collapse – remember Enron and Wirecard? However, if those companies had been examined closely enough, as they should have been to be included in an investment portfolio, I believe there were enough red flags that should have stopped people from investing.

To be clear, fraud executed by publicly traded companies in developed markets is extremely rare. The primary reason is that because they are public companies and, therefore, relatively large, there is often more than one person in senior management calling the shots. Therefore, the first red flag occurs when the CEO and CFO roles appear to overlap, and when the executives have risen up the ranks together along with most of the senior management team.

In general, the larger the firm, the harder it will be to perpetrate a fraud from the top down, as more people would need to collude to pull it off. Often, frauds are perpetrated by businesses that are seen as the 'golden child' or as exceptions in terms of outperformance within relatively poor-return industries. A management fixation on the share price and on beating earnings expectations would be another red flag. These signs are easy to spot in the management Q&A along with how overly friendly management are towards analysts asking questions, addressing them by first names, for example, and greeting them like old friends.

Interestingly, research outlined in *The Dictator's Handbook: Why Bad Behaviour is Almost Always Good Politics* shows that one of the best early warning indicators of corporate fraud is that senior management is paid less than one would expect given the firm's reported performance. Fraudulent management are often the smoothest of salesmen; they supposedly spend every waking hour working for the company; and everything they do is for the benefit of its shareholders. Yet they insist on taking lower compensation for reported better performance.

Rapidly increasing corporate debt is another red flag. Once they are committed to it, management will do anything they can to perpetuate the fraud. This often involves borrowing large amounts of money to manufacture the results they have tricked the market into believing they are producing. The better the reported results of a company and the faster those results appear, the more sceptical you should be. As we have mentioned, quarterly earnings are not worth the paper they are printed on from a company valuation perspective. They are also not audited by an accounting firm, which makes them even more dubious. Only the year-end results are audited, which makes them slightly less open to manipulation. Just another reason (if you still needed one) to adopt a long-term mindset and focus only on results annually, and, even then, in the context of a minimum five-year investment time horizon.

It's important to understand that frauds can continue for a very long time. Investors, analysts and the regulatory bodies can all be hoodwinked. Ironically, the longer a fraud is perpetuated, the seemingly less likely it is to be detected – because no one can believe a fraud could continue for that long. Ultimately, though, all frauds end the same way: not necessarily with management going to jail, but with shareholders being robbed. Interestingly, some companies are known within the market for using aggressive accounting practices: for example, AOL during the dot-com bubble. AOL was even investigated by the SEC for these practices and had to publicly announce the investigation. This acted like an anchor on their stock price, preventing it from rising. Once the investigation was over, AOL had to restate years of financial results and pay a fine. Most investors believed the bad news was 'behind' AOL; thus, the shares rallied significantly – before crashing spectacularly when the dot-com bubble finally burst. As it turns out, it's very hard for a leopard to change its spots, and AOL was a victim of its own aggressive accounting policies when the bubble burst. Be doubly cautious of buying stocks after they have been given the all clear by regulators after suspected wrongdoing. Especially if the management or culture has not changed. It's likely the same issues will arise again.

Remember, as with almost everything in life, when something seems too good to be true, it often is. When in doubt, do not invest.

Red Flags

I can't afford the operation, but would you accept a small payment to touch up the X-rays?

— Warren E. Buffett, chairman of Berkshire Hathaway

When assessing companies for potential investment or reassessing the companies in your existing portfolio, it's important to be aware of various red flags that should demand your attention for further investigation. At Gronager Partners we use a surprisingly simple method, our Side-by-Side Test, to identify them. I'll show an example with LVMH below.

As long-term value investors, we are much more concerned with the quality of earnings than their consistency. Anyone who has worked in or started their own business will know that nothing about running a business is consistent. It is always subject to peaks and troughs, and that is entirely normal for any business. To check the quality of earnings, I like to look at several years of income statements side by side and calculate the percentage change in each line item over time to determine the trend. My next step is to compare what management said they were going to do versus what they actually did,

30 Side-by-Side Analysis
LVMH Moët Hennessy Louis Vuitton – Financials

USD (Millions)	2019	YoY %△	2020	YoY %△	2021	YoY %△	2022	YoY %△	2023	5 Year CAGR %
Market Cap	234,000	34	314,000	(13)	416,000	(13)	362,000	12	405,000	15
Cash & Equivalents	7,000	257	25,000	(63)	12,000	(63)	4,500	167	12,000	14
Preferred & Other	2,000	1,750	37,000	13	38,000	13	43,000	19	51,000	125
Total Debt	64,500	32	85,000	(5)	86,500	(5)	82,500	7	88,500	8
Enterprise Value	257,500	31	337,500	(12)	446,000	(12)	390,500	12	437,500	14
Revenue	59,500	(8)	54,500	23	72,500	23	89,000	6	94,000	12
Gross Profit	39,500	(11)	35,000	16	49,500	16	57,500	12	64,500	13
EBITDA	18,000	(6)	17,000	8	26,500	8	28,500	14	32,500	16
Net Income	8,000	(25)	6,000	11	13,500	11	15,000	10	16,500	20
EPS (Diluted)	316	(28)	2.27	10	5.40	10	5.94	11	6.62	20
Shares Outstanding	2,500	0	2,500	0	2,500	0	2,500	0	2,500	0
Cash From Operations	13,000	(4)	13,500	(10)	21,000	(10)	19,000	5	20,000	11
CAPEX	(3,500)	(14)	(3,000)	57	(3,500)	57	(5,500)	55	(8,500)	25
Free Cash Flow	9,000	17	10,500	(23)	17,500	(23)	13,500	(15)	11,500	6

SOURCE: FactSet, J.P Morgan Asset Management

along with the results. I find our side-by-side test and subsequent analysis is the simplest way to identify potential red flags in a company's financial statements over time. [FIG. 30]

At Gronager Partners we also have a list of what we have identified as the most common 'red flag' areas within any potential investment. These fall into two broad categories: financial statement-related and business practices-related. These red flags tend to be identified in Step 3 of our individual securities selection process (Quantitative Analysis), but some can also be identified in Step 4 as part of the qualitative analysis of the business. We will explore both, as each identified area requires additional scrutiny in a pre-investment checklist:

- Earnings smoothing
- Depreciation charges
- Inventory management
- One-off charges and write-downs
- GAAP vs. non-GAAP or adjusted earnings
- Accrual vs. cash-based accounting
- Mergers & Acquisitions (M&A)
- Derivatives
- Capital structure
- Capital raises
- High dividend yields
- Business risk management
- Going public
- Management integrity

Earnings Smoothing

As we have seen, management compensation is generally skewed towards ensuring that the share price rises over the short term of their tenure. (The typical S&P 500 CEO lasts only four years!) To help achieve this, they want to keep Wall Street analysts happy, because they are the people who write (positive) research reports about the stock. The only thing Wall Street analysts want to see is steadily increasing earnings, with no surprises. Consistency is a key factor for their earnings forecasts for the business, and they rely heavily on management guidance for their evaluation.

Management often get themselves into a bind by trying to smooth out their company's earnings from quarter to quarter and year to year and trying to show consistent growth marginally above Wall Street's and, therefore, investors' expectations. If they can do this, they will be applauded as industry leaders. As soon as they don't, their ability to run the business will be questioned, earnings forecasts will be downgraded, and the stock price will often crater. It's the classic case of always overpromising and somehow underdelivering. Jack Welch, the former CEO of General Electric (GE) was lauded for his ability, over many years, to 'manage' quarterly earnings so that they consistently beat analysts' estimates. However, as we learnt from *Power Failure*, the excellent book by William Cohen on the history of the now-defunct conglomerate, Welch employed every trick in the book to smooth earnings. The culture of short-termism that he fostered in his managers was at least partly to blame for the company's ultimate fall.

Once they have begun, accounting manipulations are very hard to reverse. And they tend to grow over time, until they become too large and management is often fired as earnings are restated and the share price gets hammered. The accounting fraud uncovered at the supermarket Tesco in December 2015 is an almost textbook example of this. Google it.

One of the biggest red flags for me when it comes to earnings is when I hear management boasting about their long streak of beating Wall Street expectations for quarterly earnings or some other metric. This is a surefire sign of a management that is focused on making sure the numbers please Wall Street rather than focusing on enhancing the intrinsic value of the underlying business. To identify the smoothing of earnings from quarter to quarter, I generally look for three things:

1. Recording of revenue too early or including entirely fictionalised revenues (double counting).
2. Moving current expenses or income to a later period or future expenses or income to the current period.
3. A catch-all description usually including 'one-time gains or losses' or anything that looks like a method of hiding expenses or losses.

The main issue for me with earnings smoothing or any similar strategy is that it shows management are not singularly focused on improving the business. Therefore, because management has taken their eye off the ball, the company may be vulnerable to competition and at risk of a decreasing or entirely evaporating economic moat over time.

Depreciation Charges

A company's depreciation schedule can have a large impact on its reported profits, despite this being a non-cash charge. For example, I have seen a majority family-owned business which hated to declare substantial profits, as they disliked paying the taxes on them. They had an incredibly aggressive three-year depreciation schedule for factory assets that would actually last for well over twenty years, thus giving an unfair representation of the business's true economics.

This practice is relatively unusual for public companies, where management is incentivised to show as large a profit as possible. Therefore, we should be particularly aware of the inverse situation where a company changes its depreciation policy by lengthening it. This has the effect of increasing gross margins and making the company look more profitable than it is. Any change in a company's depreciation policy should be a red flag, as it can indicate a form of earnings manipulation. However, because management cannot extend the depreciable life of assets forever, the bad news will eventually come out.

Inventory Management

When a company reports an increasing inventory build-up, this is often a telltale sign of a more significant issue. Management will usually defend the build-up as necessary for projected increased future demand or for seasonally adjusted demand (e.g. overstocking for Christmas). One way to determine if this justification is warranted is to check its veracity by comparing the growth in the absolute level of inventory with the company's expected revenue growth or the growth in inventory from a comparable previous reporting period (e.g. last Christmas).

If the inventory growth exceeds the expected sales growth or the growth over the prior comparable period, the increase in inventory is probably unnecessary and should raise further questions. In terms of the inventory itself, if the products the company is storing have a certain shelf life (e.g. perishable goods for supermarkets), additional care should be taken to ensure the value of inventory is being consistently written down as time passes.

One-Off Charges and Write-Downs

Charges and write-downs are par for the course in a business. They should, however, be taken as soon as possible and not stored up to release in one go at an opportune time for management (e.g. during a general market downturn). Management should shoulder responsibility for bad decisions, not place the blame opportunistically on 'external factors'.

Care must also be taken to ensure that charges and write-downs are not being taken on productive assets to establish fictitious reserves that can then be released opportunistically by management to pad or smooth earnings. The best way I have found to identify this is if reserves are 'released' more than once per year (i.e. to smooth quarterly earnings). Anything of this nature is a mark against the integrity of management and should raise a serious red flag.

GAAP vs. Non-GAAP or Adjusted Earnings

Generally accepted accounting principles (GAAP) reporting is required by most regulators; however, management can also report Non-GAAP or Adjusted Earnings if they believe these methods of reporting better represent the company's true performance.

Management should not be switching from one reporting method to another; therefore, consistency is key. Management often prefer using Non-GAAP figures for closely watched business metrics such as EBITDA, as the Non-GAAP methodology allows more room for massaging the figures. What I like to check, therefore, is that the change or percentage change in the GAAP versus Non-GAAP figures is consistent year over year. If there is a wide discrepancy, you need to find out why. It may indicate sleight of hand. If the outright GAAP numbers materially lag the Non-GAAP ones this can also be a cause for concern.

Accrual vs. Cash-Based Accounting

Accounting rules require a company to report its earnings performance using the accrual basis. This means that they report revenue when it is earned (rather than when the actual cash is received) and charge expenses when the benefit has been received (rather than when the actual payment is made or cash leaves the business). In other words, the income statement, although useful, often does not help us to understand the actual cash position of the company, which is essential to know. As the saying goes, 'Many "profitable" businesses go bankrupt because they run out of cash.'

Cash is king, and the increasing number of frauds uncovered from companies recording revenues too soon or hiding expenses to flatter the income statement has made some investors question the value of the income statement. Instead, they prefer to rely on the statement of cash flows (SCF). The SCF shows how a company's cash balance has changed during the period. It presents all inflows and outflows of cash, reconciling the beginning balance to the ending balance. This then gives investors a more accurate view of the actual cash position of the business – or at least it should!

Companies are required to produce the SCF highlighting inflows and outflows from three main sources: operating, investing and financing activities. [FIG. 31]

Many investors, me included, weight the operating activities section of the SCF as the most important, as this represents the cash generated by the actual operations of the business. Thus, it is the purest expression of the performance of the business. It is possible to manipulate this section of the accounts, but as it represents actual cash movements, it is harder to do. It's always important to

31 The Statement of Cash Flows is Organised into Three Sections: Operating, Investing and Financing Activities

	Operating Activities	Investing Activities	Financing Activities
Inflows	Customer collections Interest collections Dividend collections	Investing sales Plant/equipment sales Business disposal	Bank borrowings Other borrowings Stock issuance
Outflows	Vendor payments Employee salaries Tax payments Interest payments	Capital expenditures Investment purchases Property purchases Business acquisitions	Loan repayments Stock repurchases Dividend payments

SOURCE: Gronager Partners

EBITDA

Earnings before interest, depreciation and amortisation (EBITDA) is an alternative measure of profitability to net income. By excluding depreciation and amortisation as well as taxes and debt payment costs, EBITDA attempts to represent the cash profit generated by the company's operations. But it's not a metric recognised under GAAP.

confirm that the SCF coincides with what you understand from the income statement (i.e. if one is showing strong results, it's important that this is also reflected by the other). Large discrepancies between the two are often a cause for concern.

Mergers & Acquisitions (M&A)

Any company that is transacting a merger or acquisition must be regarded through a lens of scepticism, for two reasons. The first reason is that, as NYU finance professor Aswath Damodaran puts it, 'More value is destroyed by acquisitions than any other single action taken by companies.' The second is that the intricacies of acquisition or merger accounting are so complex and so reliant on management to decide how to report them that, in my view, they are the easiest way to achieve deception in a company's accounts. Enron was a classic example of this. Over the years, they made hundreds of acquisitions designed to increase reported revenues, which was what analysts focused on. A simple side-by-side comparison of the numbers as suggested in the chapter introduction would have helped investors spot the red flags. Reported revenues rose by a factor of ten, but net income (harder to manipulate) only doubled. Investors should have asked why. [FIG. 32]

As president and founder of Kynikos Associates Jim Chanos wrote, 'Growth by acquisition is the last bastion of legalized accounting fraud in America.'

Therefore, when we come across a company that is a serial acquirer of other businesses, we value investors must be doubly cautious. The accounts are no longer intelligible using our simple side-by-side test, and significant work is required to reconstruct an apples-to-apples comparison. Take cash flow from operations (CFFO), which is my preferred way of comparing the performance of the underlying business over time. Each acquisition will likely give a boost to CFFO, thus making performance look better than it really is.

32 Enron's Revenue and Net Income 1995 to 2000

($millions)	1995	1996	1997	1998	1999	2000
Revenue	9,189	13,289	20,273	31,260	40,112	100,789
Net income	520	584	105	703	893	979

SOURCE: Schilit, H.M., Perler, J., & Engelhart, Y. (2018). Financial Shenanigans: How to Detect Accounting Gimmicks and Fraud in Financial Reports (4th Edition).

We must, therefore, be careful to adjust CFFO for the cost of the acquisition and capital expenditures, to get back to figures that are comparable over time.

Of course, not all serial acquirers are frauds. In fact, some, such as Teledyne, operated by Henry Singleton, were exceptional. Indeed, Buffett himself has said, 'Dr Henry Singleton of Teledyne has the best operating and capital deployment record in American business.' That said, serial acquiring businesses usually go into my own 'too hard' pile, as the accounts are just too complex for me to differentiate between fraud and genius. But that's okay! As we saw in Chapter 11 (Investment Selection), there are always new and potentially better avenues to explore.

Derivatives

The excessive use of derivatives by any company (financial institutions included) is a red flag. The only exception might be if their use is specifically required as part of a business operating strategy (e.g. FX hedging foreign income). I am not a fan of companies that engage in interest rate swaps (IRS) on their debt. Unless they are a market-maker at a bank, what possible edge could they have over the market in knowing where interest rates will be in the future? Notes to financial statements for financial institutions are notoriously long, and no area is given more pages than derivatives. In my mind, if it takes more than a couple of pages to explain what the derivatives are, along with a clear explanation of why they are required for the business, then the business goes – you guessed it – into my 'too hard' pile. If the people writing the statements cannot present their case concisely, this tells me everything I need to know about their level of understanding, or lack thereof.

In a similar vein, for the individual investor, derivatives are almost always a recipe for disaster. As fund manager Peter Lynch explained, 'I know that the large potential return is attractive to many small investors who are dissatisfied with getting rich slow. Instead, they opt for getting poor quick.' Munger has also spoken of derivatives as 'often representing a giant transfer payment from the wary to the unwary.' As Lynch said, individual investors are often attracted by the potential large gains, but these only come about by our double-edged friend, leverage. Leverage is to be avoided. And, therefore, derivatives – with their implicit or gross leverage – are *definitely* to be avoided.

Capital Structure

As we discussed in Chapter 11, debt used by businesses in limited quantities, at attractive fixed rates, and for long periods of time can be accretive to shareholder value. Any other quantity, format or time frame is probably a red flag.

In my experience, you will almost never come across frauds at companies with little or no debt. If an unscrupulous person is going to try to steal money, they will logically want to steal as much as possible. Typically, that means they will have as much debt on the company's books as possible to perpetuate the fraud. Companies with complex capital structures are inherently more 'fragile' than those without. In the game of investing, we want our portfolio businesses to be the equivalent of the last man standing. Staying away from companies with excessive leverage cures a lot of problems.

Capital Raises

Skin in the game for management is an essential part of minimising the principal–agent problem we covered in Chapter 6. When management has a significant amount of their own money on the line in terms of their net worth invested in the stock, if the firm gets into trouble, they will probably look at every possible option to protect their position first. And, in the process, they will also be protecting their fellow shareholders.

This self-interest is important, as far too many companies execute dilutive capital raises or secondary share offerings when there are far more sensible ways of raising the capital required that are less detrimental to long-term shareholder value. If an equity raise does become unavoidable, a large equity–holding management will often opt for a rights offering, allowing all investors to participate in the raise and, thus, avoid dilution. As opposed to a third-party capital injection, which is essentially a forced dilution of current shareholders.

However a capital raise is executed, it should raise red flags about the quality of both management and the underlying business.

High Dividend Yields

High dividend yield stocks are some of the most widely misunderstood in terms of both their positive and negative attributes.

We have seen that, in terms of stock-price outperformance, we are looking for two types of companies that generate a large amount of free cash flow. The first type, such as Amazon, has huge opportunities to redeploy this money back into the compounding engines of their business and grow their moat. The second is a company like the homebuilder NVR, where excess capital is consistently returned to shareholders through stock buybacks when they believe the current share price undervalues the underlying business.

High dividend yield stocks neither redeploy their money nor conduct stock buybacks. Companies that are either distressed or working in unfavourable sectors will often institute a policy of unusually high dividends to entice investors.

To be clear, a high dividend yield does not mean that the company is producing large excess FCF that it is funnelling to investors. Many companies borrow money in the debt markets or liquidate assets over time to pay a consistently high dividend to shareholders. In general, companies that pay a 6 percent-plus dividend yield when the industry norm is around 1 to 2 percent are clearly not high-growth companies; they may, in fact, be 'value traps'. Value investors must always carefully evaluate why the shares (which are often trading at a low multiple of earnings) trade where they do. When I look at high dividend yield stocks, I like to spend additional time going through the capital structure of the company and comparing the yields on the often-multiple tranches of debt that the company has. Often, the debt also trades at a yield premium to other companies and not far off the dividend yield on the stock that can be changed at any time. Thus, it often provides a wider margin of safety to invest in the debt of the business versus the equity.

Dividend considerations, then, should be given the least – not the most – weight by those looking to select outstanding stocks. Perhaps the most counterintuitive aspect of this much-discussed topic comes from Phil Fisher's findings from over fifty years ago. He found that those giving dividends the least amount of consideration and focusing on the business's capacity for reinvestment and growth usually ended up getting a significantly higher cash return than those who focused on the current payers of the largest dividend. This is because those companies that focused least on dividends usually grew their cash flow significantly over time and, thus, increased their dividends and their share price. An unusually high dividend yield should be seen as a potential investment red flag and not as a sure sign of a bargain purchase.

Business Risk Management

When it comes to assessing businesses or evaluating the performances of the businesses in your portfolio over time, it makes sense from a risk management perspective to spend more time on those segments of the business that are growing the fastest and/or represent the largest fraction of revenues and profits, rather than those that are growing slower or declining.

In a similar vein, the way management responds to underperforming businesses can be quite telling. Letting loss-making divisions continue to operate or subsidising them from other parts of the business long-term is not good business. As investors we need to scrutinise the company's investment strategy to understand the true long-term potential. It is often the things that management fails to worry about through overly optimistic forecasts or assuming they pose no risk that prove the most harmful to the intrinsic value of the business.

Going Public

The method by which a firm becomes publicly listed is very important. If management are keen to avoid scrutiny from the listing authority (e.g. the SEC in the US), they will often try to sidestep the process entirely. They can do this by merging with an already listed company. Big. Red. Flag!

This is especially true if the company they are merging with is essentially a shell company, if the process is a reverse merger, or if the company is going public through a Special Purpose Acquisition Company (Trump's Truth Social went public via an SPAC). The issue with this 'backdoor' process is that the companies that do this avoid the typically detailed review that is part of the normal IPO process, which is there for the safety of investors to help prevent fraud and poor accounting practices.

Management Integrity

Senior management changes, especially if they are unscheduled or poorly communicated, are frequently a sign that you need to take a closer look at the business. Every company should have a clearly defined succession plan and a deep bench of talent pre-identified to fill any vacancy at the senior management level. That said, if a company is already under pressure and senior management quit, this can be a very big red flag. Think Jeffrey Skilling when he quit as the CEO of Enron. I would also be wary of the CFO becoming the CEO of a company, which is becoming a more and more common practice today. CFOs generally know better than anyone else how to manipulate earnings, so it's vital that they be people of integrity. Something that Enron's CFO Andrew Fastow was not.

When an incumbent management gets into trouble and begins arguing with their auditors over their results, usually because their filings are late or an extension is requested, this should also give you pause. You need to dig deeper to ensure that the management team are people you want to be in business with (i.e. you will want to confirm that the extension or delay is for easily identifiable and legitimate reasons).

When it comes to owning up to errors during normal market times, incumbent management generally prefer to drip feed this information to investors. They do this by issuing relatively small but frequent earnings restatements or corrections and try to pass them off as nothing to do with the future trajectory of the business – which is almost never true. When this happens, it is a warning sign, as the initial revisions are often far too small. Many times, investors would be much better off waiting until the smoke has fully cleared before getting involved with such companies, if at all. Evaluating the company's true performance becomes very difficult, as does working out its intrinsic value and the margin of safety for a purchaser. Which is, of course, the whole point.

During periods of market volatility and, therefore, significant earnings revisions either for the whole market or a particular sector, pay particular attention to earnings. During such periods, incumbent management often try to 'clean shop' in one go by releasing all the accumulated revisions and impairments that they had not wished to declare publicly before. To be clear, the issue with this behaviour for us as long-term business owners is not that errors occur and need to be reflected accurately in the accounts; it is the lack of honesty from management in recognising and admitting problems quickly and learning from them. If they attempt to hide their problems, they are not the right partners for any business-minded investor.

Another example on this theme is when a new CEO is hired to run the business. The temptation for the new CEO will be to show what a great job they are doing relative to their predecessor. One of the fastest ways to do this is to take significant impairment charges and write-offs a few weeks after taking up the reins, as part of a 'strategic review'. The larger the write-downs, the better. Investors often do not discount these charges by hammering the share price, as they see it as the new CEO 'reinvigorating the business' and 'putting it on a new trajectory to greater success'. The CEO has now significantly lowered the bar against which their future performance will be judged and can revalue assets and record one-off revaluation gains as and when required to boost the quarterly numbers from the artificially low levels to which they were revised.

Although this is a widely used tactic, the issue for us as business-minded investors relates, again, to the honesty and integrity of management. Especially if the write-offs were not really warranted and were only initiated to provide 'head room' for the new CEO. There may therefore be a misalignment between the CEO's behaviour and how we expect the leaders of our businesses to act.

Learning From Our Mistakes

As we have seen, there are certain things that value investors need to stay away from. However, when we do make a mistake, the first step is to address it and correct it as quickly as possible. The second is to carefully examine why it occurred and what may need to change in our investment process to ensure it doesn't happen again. Being honest about and learning from our mistakes is key to our long-term development as successful individuals and investors.

As I mentioned in the introduction, when I was a novice investor at university, I tried a lot of different approaches. I experimented with day trading foreign exchange and commodities. In one single trade, I lost half of the money I had saved over many years. The European Sovereign Debt Crisis was reaching its climax, and markets were vacillating violently each day as people worried about the breakup of the Eurozone. I discovered that you could trade derivatives on the volatility index, the VIX – better known as the 'Wall Street Fear Gauge'. My macro view was that the situation would get worse before it got better, so I bought derivatives betting that the VIX would continue rising. I doubled my money in a week and got greedy, adding to my position with margin, believing that I could not be wrong. I even began looking for confirmatory evidence in the daily newspapers that things were getting worse, not better. (If only I had listened to Munger on biases!) Over the next two weeks, I lost all the money that I had made, as well as 50 percent of my capital (a little over $100,000!).

I also tried shorting, believing that the contagion from Greece potentially defaulting and crashing out of the Eurozone would cause a cascade of defaults, slowing global growth and, therefore, causing the oil price to fall. I bought CFDs (contracts for difference, which are leveraged derivatives) betting on the oil price falling. I checked the market obsessively, even waking up during the night to make sure the position was not going against me. I had used margin and knew the maths – that the most I could make could well be significant, but also that the amount I could lose was theoretically unlimited, a very poor bet! Needless to say, after a few sleepless days and nights, I closed the position at a loss. After these and many other trials by fire, I came to conclude that nothing worked as well as buying great businesses when they were trading below their intrinsic values. This new approach did wonders for my blood pressure and sleep.

If you want to learn from my most expensive lessons, I recommend you never engage in trend-following on charts or momentum; have a 'trading' mentality; use margin or derivatives; short stocks; try to time the market; or have a short-term investment time horizon. We are going to explore the last three in more detail as I believe they are the easiest mistakes to make.

Shorting Stocks

Look at the Forbes 400 list, or any top rich list. How many of them are short-sellers? I'll tell you, not a single one. The vast majority are long only and concentrated. With that knowledge, what investment strategy do you want to follow?

— Ardal Gronager, fund manager

Shorting stocks should come with the same health warnings that tobacco and firearms carry: that they can seriously damage your health – albeit your financial health. On the face of it, shorting individual stocks seems to make sense. You see a company; you do your analysis and believe its stock price is too high, and it's overvalued. So, you decide to short it and take a profit when the share price falls as the rest of the market belatedly realises that your analysis is correct. However, this is all completely wrong – and if you don't believe me, you should listen to one of the world's most successful hedge fund managers, billionaire Steve Cohen of Point72:

> Just because a stock price goes up and up and seems incredibly high is not a reason to short it. If that's the extent of your analysis, that the price seems high, you have no business in this market. If you shorted loss-making Amazon in June 1998, just because the share price had rallied 100s of % to a new high in the space of less than a year since its IPO, in seven months you would have lost 12× your money.

Even if the stock you selected is overvalued, shorting it may still be a bad idea for two reasons. The first is timing. Remember what Keynes said: 'The market can stay irrational longer than you can stay solvent.' You have absolutely no way of accurately predicting when or even if the stock price may fall. Even the greats like Buffett and Munger have said they have always been right in the long term about companies they believed would make good short candidates, but they have also always been wrong on the timing. Add to this the additional hurdle that over the last more than one hundred years, the stock market has returned 8 percent per year on average, and the wind is clearly blowing against you from the start.

The second reason is the risk/reward of the trade. Value investors look for asymmetric bets where the downside is limited but the upside is unlimited.

When we buy a stock, the most we can lose to the downside is 100 percent of what we invested. But there is no limit to how high a stock price can go. So, you are looking at a capped downside and unlimited upside when you buy stocks. These are the investment ideas that we want in our portfolio. Shorting stocks flips this risk/reward; our maximum upside is 100 percent if the stock falls to zero from where we shorted it, and the maximum downside as the stock rises is theoretically unlimited. Think of it in terms of Russian roulette. Would you ever play with a loaded gun where the upside was a doubling of your net worth, but the downside was certain death?

As a final argument against shorting, proponents of the strategy throw out the example of Jim Chanos and his fund Kynikos Associates ('kynikos' is Greek for 'cynic') as an example of a successful short seller. But it is telling that Chanos is the only person anyone can think of who has been consistently successful at short selling. He is, without doubt, an industry legend and has forged a career as a short-only fund manager. Among other achievements, Chanos was at least partly responsible for uncovering the massive fraud at Enron, and he became a billionaire by building a reputation from successfully shorting the stock.

However, if we cast our own cynical eye over Kynikos, the question becomes, have their returns been as wealth-enhancing for their investors as they have been for Chanos himself? Chanos acknowledges that being a short-only investor makes it almost impossible to consistently earn a positive return. His fee structure reflected this: he got paid if he 'outperformed' the S&P 500 by losing less than the amount the market rose by (e.g. if the S&P was up 20 percent and he lost 12 percent, he had, therefore, generated 'positive alpha' of 8 percent, and his clients paid him a fee for losing only 12 percent of their money). In my view, the only person that can end up rich from this structure is the manager. As an epitaph, Chano retired and closed his fund in 2023 after years of client redemptions and poor performance from shorting Tesla.

Shorting stocks has no place in a value investor's toolkit.

Trying to Time the Market

If we get out, our mentality being what it is, we shall never get back in again until much too late and will assuredly be left behind when the recovery does come. If the recovery never comes, nothing matters.

— John Maynard Keynes, English economist, philosopher and fund
manager

Time in the market, not timing the market, is what matters for investor performance. We have acknowledged that the future is uncertain, and the further into the future we look, the more uncertain it becomes. Therefore, being able to consistently pick the peaks and troughs of the market and trading accordingly is impossible. Despite knowing these facts, you may still believe that you and you alone have the capacity to clearly see the future and invest accordingly. As Terry Smith said astutely, 'When it comes to so-called market timing there are only two sorts of people: those who can't do it, and those who know they can't do it. It's safer and more profitable to be in the latter camp.'

The biggest risk with exiting the market or not deploying your cash into it is that most of the biggest up days follow the biggest down days. Thus, if we sit out the fall, we will very likely sit out the rise, too. The more the market rallies, the more we will try to convince ourselves that it's a bear market rally and will soon drop again. Only, it doesn't happen, and we eventually buy back in at a higher price than when we exited.

Take one of the most volatile decades of recent times: 2009 to 2018. We had both the Global Financial Crisis (GFC) and the European Sovereign Debt Crisis to contend with, along with escalating wars in the Middle East, to name just a few issues. Yet as the chart below shows, if you had invested $1,000 in the S&P 500 and hadn't touched it through the full period, it would have grown to $2,775, an average annual return of 10.75 percent (excluding dividends). But if you missed just thirty of the biggest up days – 1.1 percent of the total trading days in the ten-year period – you would have lost 8.18 percent of your $1,000 investment and ended the ten years with $918. It is time in the market, not timing the market, that counts. [FIG. 33]

The market, as we know, is a second-order system, meaning that to predict where the market is going, we not only have to be able to predict future events – inflation, wars, pandemics – but we also have to know what part

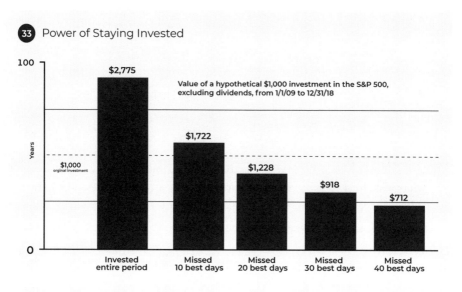

SOURCE: Thompson Reuters and S&P 500 Index

of the impact (if any) of these events is already priced into the markets and, therefore, what its reaction (if any) will be should they come to pass. This is in addition to getting our timing right regarding when these events will happen! My advice is not to waste even a nanosecond of time trying.

Short Investment Time Horizons

As we know, the psychological pain of experiencing losses in the market can negatively impact our emotions and lead us to make poor decisions. We know this intuitively, which is why, as we have seen throughout this book, we often try to engage in loss-mitigation techniques that prevent us having to feel the pain of loss. Investing in the markets is risky, and over the last ninety-one years, the S&P 500 has generated a negative return in 27 percent of years. However, as we lengthen our holding periods or investment time horizon, the chance of us experiencing a loss falls away significantly if we remain invested. [FIG. 34]

If we extend our investment time horizon from one year to three, our chances of experiencing a loss over that period almost halve to 17 percent. Since inception, 94 percent of any ten-year rolling period of investing in the S&P 500 has been positive. This circles back not only to how important it is to

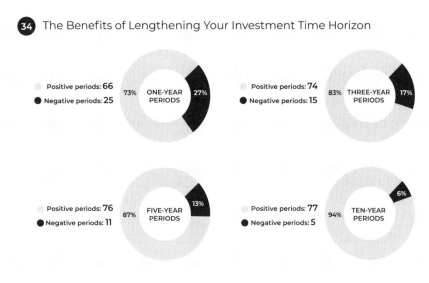

34 The Benefits of Lengthening Your Investment Time Horizon

Positive periods: **66**
Negative periods: **25**
73% ONE-YEAR PERIODS 27%

Positive periods: **74**
Negative periods: **15**
83% THREE-YEAR PERIODS 17%

Positive periods: **76**
Negative periods: **11**
87% FIVE-YEAR PERIODS 13%

Positive periods: **77**
Negative periods: **5**
94% TEN-YEAR PERIODS 6%

SOURCE: Thompson Reuters and S&P 500 Index

have a long investment time horizon but also to how often you should check your portfolio to ensure you don't trigger a panicked response to a short-term loss. The maths is simple: the probability of an up day is 53 percent for the S&P 500 on a daily basis, a little better than a coin flip. The odds increase as we increase our investment time horizon from daily to weekly (57 percent), to monthly (63 percent), to yearly, which has a 73 percent chance of a positive return. The takeaway from this is just as simple: check your portfolio as infrequently as possible. It will dramatically improve your financial health!

As an aside, be careful with averages. 'Stocks make between 8 and 10 percent per year on average' is a line commonly repeated by market commentators, but the last time the S&P 500 returned between 8 and 10 percent was 1962. Averages can be very misleading.

Summary

Investing is complex. There are an infinite number of mistakes that can be made, and what we have explored here is just the tip of the iceberg. However, many of the potential mistakes fall into just a few broad categories. Therefore, having this knowledge and the ability to identify potential mistakes will allow you to avoid those red flag businesses, so you don't make the mistake in the first place. Knowledge is more than half the battle.

Asked how to describe a complex process such as nuclear fission, Einstein reportedly replied, 'Everything should be made as simple as possible, but not simpler.' Having a pre-investment checklist that forces us to investigate potential risk areas is one of the simplest ways to ensure we don't fall prey to them.

To successfully navigate the ever-changing investment landscape, investors should take heed of the philosophical concept known as Occam's Razor. It is the problem-solving principle that recommends searching for explanations constructed with the smallest possible set of elements. Applying this to investing, it says that if we can condense our investment theses, both positive and negative, down to the few salient points, there is less room for error. When making mistakes – and you will make them – the key is to have the humility to examine them openly, honestly, and to learn from them. It's worth repeating that the ability to admit you are wrong, identify how the error occurred, and incorporate this knowledge into your mental models for better future decision-making is what separates the successful from the rest.

CHAPTER 15: PATIENCE IN INVESTING

The truly brilliant investors weren't investors; they were entrepreneurs that didn't sell.

— Nick Sleep, co-founder of the Nomad Investment Partnership

If all success in investing ultimately comes down to having the correct temperament, which aspect of it is the most important to master, I hear you ask? Patience, in my experience, is not only the single most important aspect to master but also the least understood. Therefore, it is the most frequently overlooked aspect of many investors' investment processes – and why I am dedicating an entire chapter to its exploration.

In life, progress is too often associated with action. Nowhere is that truer than in investing. Yet, ironically, there are few impediments to performance as large as the constant call for action. I think this disconnect between action and results is best exemplified by an excerpt from BBC Radio 4's *Desert Island Discs*, that I stumbled across in the writings of fund manager Nick Sleep. The castaway episode featured the naturalist Sir David Attenborough. The host, Kirsty Young, introduced Sir David as follows:

> He has seen more of the world than any person who has ever lived. The depth of his knowledge and breadth of his enthusiasm have had a fundamental effect on how we view our planet. From sitting hugger-mugger with the mountain gorillas of Rwanda, to describing the fragilities of the flightless kakapo; the wonders of the natural world are his stock-in-trade. His passion can be traced right back to his days as a lad when he cycled his bike through the Leicestershire countryside trawling for fossils. He says he knows of no deeper pleasure than the contemplation of the natural world. David Attenborough, you have visited the North and South Poles; you witnessed all of life in between from the canopies of the tropical rainforest to giant earthworms in Australia. It must be true, must it not – and it is quite a staggering thought – that you have seen more of the world than anybody else who has ever lived?

Attenborough replies, 'Well … I suppose so … but, on the other hand, it is fairly salutary to remember that perhaps the greatest naturalist that ever lived and had more effect on our thinking than anybody, Charles Darwin, only spent four years travelling and the rest of the time thinking.'

I found the humility of Attenborough's response staggering. His achievements are endless, and yet here is a man so comfortable in his own abilities and contributions to the world that he immediately brushes off the acclaim and points out that others have contributed far more with far less running around. The ability to stop and really think doesn't come naturally to most of us. Most people require constant interaction and dislike being alone with their own thoughts for too long. We are, after all, social animals. That said, the ability to carefully examine and consider our own thoughts with regards to our investments is a vital skill in the contrarian investor's toolkit … patience.

Patience in the Securities Selection Process

All of humanity's problems stem from man's inability to sit quietly in a room alone.
— Blaise Pascal, mathematician and philosopher

According to Mohnish Pabrai, the term 'investment team' is an oxymoron. One of the best examples of why comes from Lee Freeman-Shor, fund manager at Quilter Asset Management. Freeman-Shor oversaw a stable of market-beating fund managers and noticed that, in general, most of them made money on only about half of their investments. Their gains were skewed heavily by a few big wins. According to the fund managers themselves, these few big winners were always destined to be big winners. So Freeman-Shor set up a new fund which would cherry-pick the best investment idea as suggested by each of his market-beating fund managers and combine them into one new 'Best Ideas Portfolio'. The results were terrible. The portfolio underperformed dramatically and was closed within a few years.

The main reason for its failure, as identified by Freeman-Shor, was that no one can really know in advance which of their investments will perform the best. Often it's the ideas in which we have the least conviction that go on to outperform those we thought were 'dead certs'. Another reason was that once an idea was selected as that fund manager's 'best idea', they would continue holding it, even when it became clear their original investment thesis was wrong – those pesky cognitive and behavioural biases gone haywire again!

I also believe that successful investing is a minority sport. It is not a business where groupthink and making decisions by consensus are the right ways to do things. Often-outperforming fund managers themselves have no clue as to which of their ideas is the best, so how could a group of less-qualified people know which of the managers' ideas are the best? Despite what they might say, most institutional investors and fund managers are run by committee. Seeking broad consensus requires considerable compromise to incorporate each person's perspective. The result is decision by the lowest common denominator: a choice that everyone can live with but no one is really happy about. This plays right into the hands of the value investor, as we know that we can only outperform by thinking like a contrarian and having a differentiated investment process. The moment you start hiring stock analysts to 'help' fund managers, you should throw in the towel. Successful investing is a solo sport.

Peter Lynch summarised it thus: 'If no great book or symphony was ever written by committee, no great portfolio has ever been selected by one, either.' When it comes to successful investing, there is no such thing as the wisdom of crowds. James Surowiecki, who wrote the modern classic *The Wisdom of Crowds*, contends that 'If you put together a big enough and diverse enough group of people and ask them to make a decision affecting matters of general interest, that group's decisions will, over time, be intellectually superior to the isolated individual, no matter how smart or well informed he is.' But it just doesn't work in financial markets. As renowned fund manager Walter Morgan stated, 'The crowd is always wrong.' The collective intelligence of the group is always less than the sum of its parts. The more people involved, the less precise the decision-making, and the slower it becomes. German philosopher Friedrich Nietzsche concluded as much when he wrote, 'Madness is the exception in individuals and the rule in crowds.'

Successful investing is, therefore, a solitary activity. The best way for a fund manager to manage money is to manage it as if it were their own money, making all decisions based on what is best for the portfolio, not what is best for their business.

Your business should be set up before the portfolio is even constructed to ensure it is solid enough to withstand the external pressures that come with managing money. At Gronager Partners, we set up our business in a way that it also ticked the investment criteria that we use for our own portfolio businesses. We think like business owners. We have a highly experienced management team with significant 'skin in the game' that prompts us to take a longer-term perspective. We keep our business anti-fragile by not using debt, and we cultivate growth by carefully selecting whom we wish to partner with. Finally, we have an unassailable moat around the business through our differentiated fee structure that has been borrowed from the original Buffett Partnerships. We don't charge a traditional management fee. Our personal returns mirror those of our Investor Partners and are entirely driven by our fund's performance, on which we are entirely focused.

As the fund manager with my name above the door, I know that my Investor Partners expect me to manage their money. It would be irresponsible for me to outsource any aspect of our investment process or to be susceptible to distraction. As such, I take firm ownership of the entire investment process from start to finish. I am fully responsible for the success or failure of our investment decisions. As the Managing Partner, the buck stops with me.

The best practical way that I have found to amplify the positive effects of patience in my investing is to build it into every aspect of my everyday life. For example, I do my absolute best to remove distractions from my working life. I keep my diary as empty as possible. I only do investor meetings at certain times and on certain days. I am paid for my investment results and, therefore, monitoring the current portfolio and searching for and evaluating new investments must be my top priority. I want as few demands on my time as possible so I can dedicate as much time as possible to evolving my investment process. I truly love this process. As the saying goes, 'Life is about the journey, not the destination', and the same goes for investment management. The security selection process is the part of the process that I find most exciting and the part where I, as the fund manager, add the most value. Therefore, I do everything I can to minimise interruptions to the process so I can have the focus and objectivity required to make good investment decisions.

I recommend giving yourself a minimum five-year investment time horizon on each of the holdings in your portfolio, like we do at Gronager Partners. This will immediately separate your portfolio management from the crowd. By doing so, you will give yourself a large advantage over other less-patient investors. From our experience, this is also the minimum time required to evaluate changes in a company, whatever the volatile movements in the stock price may otherwise suggest. As fund manager Anthony Bolton said of short-term versus long-term investing, 'Often, there is so much analysis of the branch or even the leaves on the branch; there are fewer people taking a view on the tree, let alone a view of the forest. There is an opportunity for those willing to take the wider perspective.'

As you already know, we should assign almost no value to quarterly reports. How can any business change so dramatically in just sixty-seven working days (a business quarter) that it would make you want to buy or sell the business? Business, as every entrepreneur knows, is a messy, complex endeavour, and it's not run from a spreadsheet. There will always be an enormous amount of noise in the quarterly numbers, which will not be the case if we look at the business over several years.

Underperforming the market for small or even significant periods of time is par for the course if you are seeking to outperform the market by doing something different. We can see this from the performance of every fund manager that we've met throughout this book. To highlight a few:

- John Maynard Keynes, who managed the Chest Fund for eighteen years, underperformed the market for one-third of the time. Indeed, he underperformed the market the first three years he managed the fund, which put him behind the market by 18 percent. Over the entire period, he compounded at 15 percent, almost double the market.
- Sir John Templeton underperformed the market 40 percent of the time, yet he compounded at a net annualised rate of 14 percent for thirty-eight years, smashing any index.
- The Sequoia Fund run by Bill Ruane underperformed the market 37 percent of the time, including its first four years in operation. Over the forty years he ran the fund, it achieved an annualised net return of 14.65 percent, versus 10.93 percent for the S&P 500.
- Over fourteen years, Charlie Munger underperformed 36 percent of the time. His worst relative performance put him behind the S&P 500 by 37 percent. Over the entire period, he annualised a gross rate of return of 19.8 percent, versus 5 percent for the Dow Jones.
- If we look at any of the value investors whose track records are referenced in Buffett's famous Graham and Doddsville speech, they all

underperformed the index 30 to 40 percent of the time (except for Buffett himself), and all trounced the index over time.

For contrarian investors like me, the key takeaway from these results must be that when it comes to investing, patience is measured in decades. All concentrated portfolios can be expected to underperform for a prolonged period: four, five, even six years out of ten. However, the periods of underperformance are generally when the indexes made even greater advances and the concentrated manager's periods of underperformance were either led or followed by large outperformance.

There are two additional things that I think are important to remember. The first is that fixation on any benchmark, and one's performance relative to it, is the wrong way for a value investor to invest. The second is that the greatest returns come to those who add at the bottom, the lowest from those who quit.

Patience in Portfolio Management

The big money is not in the buying and selling... but in the waiting.

– Jesse Livermore, legendary American stock 'operator' and investor

Some years ago, a widely cited article, purportedly written by Fidelity, one of the world's largest asset managers, said that they had conducted an anonymised study of the performance of the individual investors who held accounts with them. The conclusions were intriguing. There was a direct negative correlation between investor engagement (i.e. how actively they looked at and traded the positions in their portfolios) and performance. In fact, the best performing accounts were in the names of people who were deceased or had forgotten entirely that they had the accounts. Fidelity denied the article came from them but did acknowledge that the findings discussed would be consistent with their broad expectations.

Regardless of who wrote the article, it makes intuitive sense that those who had employed a set-and-forget strategy enjoyed the best performance versus those who had watched CNBC all day long and were constantly buying and selling. However, even when we insist that we will 'set it and forget it', the inevitable urge to constantly monitor performance and change our minds regarding our portfolio's composition can lead to a second category of underperformance.

What separates those who successfully invest for the long term from the rest is the patience to be the masters of their own emotions as well as their investment processes. This allows them to ignore the fluctuations in both the market and their portfolio's value. As John Maynard Keynes wrote,

> The spectacle of modern investment markets has sometimes moved me towards the conclusion that to make the purchase of an investment permanent and indissoluble, like marriage, except by reason of death or other grave cause, might be a useful remedy for our contemporary evils. For this would force the investor to direct his mind to the long-term prospects and to those only.

When we look at the stocks that have made outsized gains over time – the 100-baggers and more – clearly, the biggest mistake one could have made with any of them was to sell. We explored the investment case for Amazon in the Introduction. It's worth revisiting, as it's one of the most successful businesses of our time. Its products and services have changed the way we live and at the same time generated tremendous returns for investors. The question is, why are there not more Amazon millionaires and billionaires?

Amazon is up an incredible 38,600 percent since its 1997 IPO, compounding at 35.5 percent annually. This would have grown a $1,000 investment into $387,000 in 2024. But the degree of difficulty of turning that $1,000 into $387,000 twenty-seven years later cannot be overstated. Amazon lost over 50 percent of its market value on three separate occasions during this period. On one of those occasions, from December 1999 through October 2001, it lost 95 percent of its value! Over that time, our hypothetical $1,000 investment would have shrunk from a high of $54,433 down to $3,045 – a $51,388 loss. To have been able to sit through all the peaks and troughs in Amazon's share price; to have asked ourselves only the simple question, 'Is the business getting better?'; and to have based all of our portfolio management decisions on that answer – that is what long-term investing is all about.

As long-only investors, our downside is capped at 100 percent, but our performance downside through errors of omission or what we didn't own is infinite. When one of our stocks is performing badly, it can have a very detrimental effect on our decision-making regarding the other investments in our portfolio. We must remember to be patient and remember that the effect on our ultimate performance of selling a single 100-bagger too soon, versus riding one of our holdings into bankruptcy, is an outcome many times worse. It's always a good idea to keep track of the performance of companies after you have sold them, as we need to incorporate into our evolving investment process the lessons from errors such as selling too soon.

As concentrated value investors, patience is built into our investment and portfolio management process. Having a few positions in the portfolio, as opposed to hundreds, and being focused on their long-term trajectory and growth means we need to make relatively few decisions per year. This allows us to be far more disciplined and methodical in our securities selection process compared to the manager who must monitor whether his investment thesis is correct or not for more than a hundred positions. Concentrated value investors look for 'single' or 'one decision' stocks. The only decision that needs to be made is to buy the shares of a great business at a reasonable price and let the business grow. This is the opposite of the activity or action which is craved by Wall Street to justify their high fees.

In his investor letters, fund manager Nick Sleep wrote, 'Our portfolio inaction continues, and we are delighted to report that purchase and sale transactions have all but ground to a halt. Our expectation is that this is a considerable source of value added!' This 'value added' comes in many forms: reduced transaction costs, reduced taxes, reduced overheads from not having teams of staff and all the office space and systems that goes with it.

Once they have taken the time to create their investment process, and the additional time and energy to select a portfolio of businesses, it seems strange that most investors then fall at the final hurdle: they don't have the patience to allow time to deliver the expected returns. Often, stocks will not move at all or move in a tight range for years at a time before re-rating. There is nothing to say that your portfolio won't fall in the short-to-medium term. You need to have enough conviction in your methodology to persevere through these periods of underperformance. This is clearly easier said than done, but it is why it is so important to ensure that if you are a fund manager, your investors are aligned with you in terms of investment time frame.

There is a saying in markets that you should never marry your holdings. I fundamentally disagree and believe that what Nick Sleep wrote on the subject is true: 'We think it is absolutely critical to fall in love with, or have a deep, deep commitment, both intellectual commitment, and if you like, emotional commitment to the ideas that you build into an investment portfolio. How else are you going to stick with them through thick and thin … in order to capture the full potential of an investment?' As business owners, we need to have a profound and long-term commitment to each of our holdings.

Look at the Walton family, who are estimated to be the richest family on earth. How did they become so rich? To me, the answer is simple. They have almost never sold a share of Walmart stock other than to meet tax and philanthropic obligations or to keep their combined ownership of the company below 50 percent. By allowing Walmart, which operates a great business with a strong moat, to compound over the years, the family's net worth has continued to increase. They see themselves as owners of the business in the truest sense of the word, and it would be anathema for them to voluntarily sell shares, especially if the business was underperforming. This is why the business owner's mindset is so important to successful long-term investing.

Of course, this doesn't mean that we don't monitor our portfolio on an ongoing basis and spend significant time re-examining our assumptions about the businesses and what we may have missed in our original thesis. But one quarter, one year, or even several years of poor stock price performance due to the irrationalities of 'Mr Market' doesn't mean the underlying business is not improving. When your actions are dictated by the price rather than the business fundamentals, you are engaging in speculating, not investing.

We value investors require clear evidence that our original investment thesis is wrong before altering our holdings. Unfortunately, it usually takes a long time for this evidence to appear, and the stock price has usually suffered in the interim. On the flip side, this reluctance to sell will allow us to capture the 100-bagger stocks because we will continue to hold them even during periods when their prices get cut in half, as sometimes happens in markets. In the words of Charlie Munger,

> If you're not willing to react with equanimity to a market price decline
> of 50 percent or more two or three times a century, you're not fit to
> be a common shareholder and you deserve the mediocre result you're
> going to get compared to the people who do have the temperament,
> who can be more philosophical about these market fluctuations.

Patience in Business

Time is the friend of the wonderful business, the enemy of the mediocre.

— Warren E. Buffett, chairman of Berkshire Hathaway

Patience is not just important for our own investing process, it is also an important attribute to look for in potential businesses worthy of inclusion in our portfolio. One of the best expressions of this mentality, I think, is expressed by the title of a section heading in Jeff Bezos's first letter to Amazon shareholders, written in 1997: 'It's All About The Long Term'. In an interview in 2011 in which he referred back to that letter, Bezos said,

> If everything you do needs to work on a three-year time horizon, then you're competing against a lot of people. But if you are willing to invest on a seven-year time horizon, you're now competing against a fraction of those people, because very few companies are willing to do that. Just by lengthening the time horizon, you can engage in endeavors that you could never otherwise pursue. At Amazon we like things to work in five to seven years. We're willing to plant seeds, let them grow – and we're very stubborn. We say we are stubborn on the vision and flexible on details.

What Bezos said perfectly encapsulates what we are looking for in the management of a business. Entrepreneurs who are true business owners have no issue with passing on opportunities for short-term gain if they would come at the expense of greater long-term success. Bezos also recognised that the time frame over which businesses are measured (quarterly) makes no sense at all, as it focuses management actions on the short term. This is the antithesis of what long-term investors want.

Phil Fisher wrote, 'Time keeps working on the side of the unusually well-run company. The endless resources of human ingenuity ... creates a background of steady improvement in the fundamentals of such a company. Recognition of such improvement comes in irregular leaps, but it does come, bringing with it corresponding gains in the market value of the shares involved.' Slow change in the underlying business, coupled with great execution, can lead to outsized returns over time.

Summary

In the conclusion to his book *Thinking, Fast and Slow*, behavioural psychologist Daniel Kahneman wrote that when given the choice between 'fast' or 'slow' decision-making on complex subjects (such as investing), slower is always better. The reason is that decision-making on complex subjects requires computation and evaluation of far more factors than the 'fast' decision side of our brains can cope with. In fact, our brains are often so overwhelmed by complexity that we deliberately opt for the 'fast' process as a way to eliminate the mental effort required to make a decision slowly. Patience, then, is a requirement for complex decision-making and should be incorporated into all aspects of our investment process.

Investing is the most complex of intellectual pursuits, as it incorporates all worldly knowledge on all subjects. Therefore, 'slow' thinking is an essential aspect of success in investing. We need to guard ourselves and the decisions we make from all the things that can impact our judgement. These include things such as loss aversion, which may make us feel like we should be more active on days when the market or our portfolio is up, in contrast to the days when it is down. Remember, years with positive returns in the market are three times more likely than negative ones. In my experience, having a pre-investment checklist as part of your investment process forces you to think 'slow' and not fall prey to the tendency for 'fast' decision-making shortcuts that result in poor outcomes.

Value investing is about mastering the art of patience and incorporating it into all aspects of your investment process. From portfolio construction to individual securities selection to portfolio management. But, most importantly, in how you conduct yourself in all aspects of your life. If you succeed at this, then the art of value investing will likely make you richer, and happier as well!

CHAPTER 16: BECOMING A SUCCESSFUL VALUE INVESTOR

It is not the critic who counts: not the man who points out how the strong man stumbles or where the doer of deeds could have done better. The credit belongs to the man who is actually in the arena, whose face is marred by dust and sweat and blood, who strives valiantly, who errs and comes up short again and again, because there is no effort without error or shortcoming, but who knows the great enthusiasms, the great devotions, who spends himself for a worthy cause; who, at the best, knows, in the end, the triumph of high achievement, and who, at the worst, if he fails, at least he fails while daring greatly, so that his place shall never be with those cold and timid souls who knew neither victory nor defeat.

— Theodore Roosevelt, US President 1901–1909

Throughout this book we have referenced hundreds of different authors along with many great investors, businessmen and entrepreneurs. What strikes me is that no two paths to success were the same. We can certainly study and learn from the most successful investors of the past and present and look for mental models, investment strategies and worldly wisdom that we can apply to our own investment process. But clearly, each investor must find his or her own path to success. What is most important is that our investment process be fundamentally *our own*, that we understand its construction from the ground up and, therefore, the results that it produces. As we have said throughout this book, all knowledge is cumulative. Limitless intellectual curiosity ensures that our investment process will constantly evolve and improve, to achieve long-term investing success.

No one is born a successful investor; in fact, no one is born exceptional at anything. We are each born with a broad set of abilities that are either nurtured or extinguished during the early stages of our cognitive and behavioural development. Roger Federer, widely regarded as one of the greatest tennis players of all time, said of his exceptional success,

Talent has a broad definition. Most of the time, it's not about having a gift. It's about having grit. In tennis, a great forehand with sick racket head speed can be called a talent. But in tennis, like in life, discipline is also a talent. And so is patience. Trusting yourself is a talent. Embracing the process, loving the process is a talent. Managing your life, managing yourself. These can be talents, too. Some people are born with them. Everybody has to work at them.

Learning gets harder, not easier as we get older. Always keep moving forward.

Becoming a successful investor is not guaranteed. As American financier Bernard Baruch famously put it,

> If you are ready to give up on everything else and study the whole history and background of the market and all principal companies whose stocks are on the board as carefully as a medical student studies anatomy – if you can do all that and in addition you have the cool nerves of a gambler, the sixth sense of a clairvoyant and the courage of a lion, you have a ghost of a chance.

To me, investing is much more of an art than a science. Intelligence, experience, diligence, a knowledge of history, an open mind, and an obsessive nature are all important ingredients for success. As are intuition, imagination, flexibility, and luck!

Phil Knight, the billionaire founder and CEO of Nike, when asked about the cause of his success, said, 'Luck plays a big role. Yes, I'd like to publicly acknowledge the power of luck. Hard work is critical, a good team is essential, brains and determination are invaluable, but luck may decide the outcome. The harder you work, the better your luck.' No one succeeds at anything in life without luck. You can call it 'chance' or 'serendipity', but, ultimately, luck plays a significant role in all our lives. I believe that 'chance favours the prepared mind' and 'the harder you work, the luckier you get.' We investors will experience the highs and lows laid down by Lady Luck more viscerally than almost anyone else. When things can't get any worse, they always will, and when they can't get any better, they always will. It's just part of the game.

For this reason, although we might lionise great investors like Buffett and can learn an incredible amount from them, we should not seek to 'be them'. There will only ever be one Warren Buffett, no matter how hard we might try to replicate his character. Buffett's hero was Ben Graham, but his ultimate success was in purchasing companies with entirely different characteristics from those suggested by Graham. There is no school that can teach you to be a great investor. If there were, its tuition fees would be too high for almost anyone to afford. Success lies in forging your own path, in managing money your own way and investing by your own carefully crafted set of investment rules that suit your own temperament.

To do this, we first have to understand ourselves and objectively assess our own strengths, weaknesses and biases. We must adapt our strategy to our own nature and talents and operate within our own circle of competence. All of this points to an important conclusion that applies to both investing and life: resounding victories tend to be the result of small, incremental advances and improvements sustained over long periods.

To truly know yourself, you must understand your temperament and be able to develop a system for controlling your emotions. All human beings are, at times, irrational and emotional. As we have seen in this book, we can be risk-averse and yet risk-seeking at the same time, depending on the framing of the question. We are easily led astray by anchoring and any number of other cognitive biases and behavioural tendencies. We all experience failure. The truly great investors examine these failures to try to establish the root causes, so as to not allow past mistakes to interfere with future decisions.

Fund manager Michael Steinhardt said, 'Losing money early in your investment career is a good thing, as you will have less of it to lose.' Every investor pays a price for their education in the market, and it can often be substantial. But by doing so, we can develop our own expertise which, ultimately, results in superior performance. No matter how much money you have to start with, it's important to invest using real money and not spend too long 'paper trading'. Paper trading, although initially useful, is not the same as having real money on the line, which always brings emotions into play. As the boxer Mike Tyson famously once said, 'Everyone has a plan until they get punched in the face.'

If you cannot accept failure and remain optimistic, then becoming a concentrated value investor may not be for you. There are few fields that are quite as humbling, regardless of your skills and intelligence. Almost everyone I speak to says that as they get older the greatest lessons come from their failures, not their successes. To be successful in any activity in life, we need to be able to acknowledge and learn from our mistakes. That is the gift of failure. As fund manager Howard Marks puts it, 'Experience is only a name we give to our failures.'

Experience is clearly very important for an investor. When processed fully, it can result in investment wisdom. Confucius explained it thus: 'By three methods may we learn wisdom: First, by reflection, which is noblest; second, by imitation, which is easiest; and third is by experience, which is the bitterest.' Therefore, it makes a great deal of sense to learn as much as we can about the history of markets, successful investors and investments, but also, paradoxically, about the most unsuccessful investors and the worst investments. We want to take the best of what we believe was responsible for success and combine applying those things with avoiding the elements that we believe led to ruin. The Irish playwright George Bernard Shaw put it best when he wrote, 'Men are wise not in proportion to their experience, but to their capacity for experience.' It is not the direct experience that is important; what we learn from it and what we learn from others results in wisdom. This is why intellectual curiosity and a love of business and markets bordering on an obsession is so essential for long-term investing success.

On 23 June 1989, *Outstanding Investor Digest* published a piece about the discipline of Warren Buffett, which after reading it more than twenty years ago, I've never forgotten. It went like this:

> Buffett was playing golf at Pebble Beach with Charlie Munger and two other people. One of them proposed 'Warren, if you shoot a hole-in-one on any hole on this 18-hole course, we'll give you $10,000. If you don't shoot a single hole-in-one, you'll owe us $10.' Warren thought about it and said, 'I'm not taking that bet.' The others said, 'Why don't you? The most you can lose is $10. You can make $10,000.' Warren replied, 'If you are not disciplined in the little things, you won't be disciplined in the big things.'

What stood out to me was that Buffett applied his investing mindset not just to multi-billion-dollar acquisitions but also to small-change side-bets proposed by friends. Clearly, it would have made no difference to him financially to lose $10 or win $10,000. But the very act of making a bet when he knew the odds were worse than a thousand to one for him to win would have been irrational and gone against what makes him a great investor. All investors can learn something from this story. For me, the main takeaway is that Buffett's investment style and his personality are perfectly in sync, which is something we must all strive for.

One of the things that I love best about being an investor is the solitude. The ability to express my personal thoughts about business and the world through my portfolio, where everything that happens is because of my own judgement. I believe that success in this industry is more the result of inaction than action and that, therefore, successful investing is a solo pursuit, not a team sport. As Munger said, 'I don't trust in groups reaching decision by majority or consensus as it usually reduces the decision-making process to the lowest common denominator.' Being a lone wolf removes the social pressures of having to conform. Bubbles and panics are situations where calm detachment from the crowd comes into its own. These irrational market phenomena are due to human nature and will always reappear. Bubbles, from the human desire to get rich with minimum effort; and panics, as the same crowd attempts to flee the bursting bubble.

Keep your own counsel. I truly believe that, in most cases, 'Those who say don't know, and those who know don't say.' Buffett's 'inner scorecard' is particularly useful here. When he speaks of living by an inner scorecard, he is saying that he doesn't care about the opinions of others. He has his own clearly defined set of beliefs and principles by which he conducts himself, lives his life and against which he measures himself. Too many of us float through life with no fixed views or principles about anything. It is this indifference or lack of awareness that so often leads to character issues and errors of judgement. How can we know how to act or whether our actions are appropriate if we have never taken the time to establish our own inner scorecard? Our inner scorecard forces us to lead by example.

The greatest freedom that financial independence can give you is the ability to decide with whom you will spend your time. Surround yourself with people who add something to your life, who care for you, who cherish your successes and offer a helping hand through difficult times.

Don't allow yourself to be fooled by your own 'genius' during periods of good returns, or by your 'failure' during periods of poor performance. The direction of the market is outside anyone's control. Value investors are almost guaranteed to underperform when markets reach bubble territory, and it is usually during periods of market turbulence or bear markets that we set the stage for our future outperformance. We don't try to pick tops or bottoms of markets. As Buffett likes to say, investors who do this are 'dancing in a room like Cinderella at the ball staring up at the clock waiting for its hands to strike midnight. The issue is they are dancing in a room where the clock has no hands.'

Vince Lombardi, the famous American football coach said this about winning: 'Winning is not a sometime thing; it's an all-the-time thing. You don't win once in a while; you don't do things right once in a while; you do them right all the time. Winning is a habit. Unfortunately, so is losing.' Forming the right habits early in life and early in your investing journey is crucial. This begins by having the right role models, crafting your own set of values that you wish to live your life by – your inner scorecard, which will also be applied to all your investing decisions. Clearly, you need to want to win; you have to want to beat the game; but you can only do this by playing the game your own way.

Robert Kuok, the billionaire entrepreneur and philanthropist, wrote in his memoirs, 'I realized that strong physical and mental health are vital for a long and successful business career and critical for the ability to bounce back from the inevitable adversities along the way.' To be successful over the long term, I believe it is also wise to be in peak physical shape. 'Mens sana in corpore sano' is Latin for 'a healthy mind in a healthy body'. Pay attention to how you feel, the amount of sleep you get, what you eat, how often you exercise, and your general mental and physical condition. We want to be in peak physical and mental condition to ensure we are in the best possible state to be making investment decisions. If we make decisions when we are feeling unwell, hungover or in any sort of physical pain, it is unlikely they will be the best objective decisions.

Taking good care of yourself physically, mentally, and emotionally, will have a multiplier effect on your life both as an individual and as an investor. Eat well, sleep well, exercise often, remove as many external demands and stresses from your life as possible, and the worst that will happen is you will live a much happier life.

I found that clearing my diary as much as possible and limiting intrusions – whether phone calls, emails, or meetings during my peak working hours – allows me to operate with complete focus on investing. Finding a routine that works for you is an often-overlooked aspect of operating at peak performance. I wake up and go to sleep at the same time each day, I work out first thing in the morning and have my breakfast. I eat lunch and dinner at approximately the same time each day. This structure allows me the freedom to not only be in the best physical and mental shape but also to spend my time focusing on whatever aspect of the investment process is most important to me. This routine and discipline is entirely in sync with who I am as a person and what I most enjoy spending my time doing. I wake up each morning fully energised for the day ahead, and I spend the absolute minimum amount of time dealing with things that I don't enjoy. Life is too short to operate in any other way.

I was recently reminded of how even the best businesspeople can be driven to irrational decision-making by a friend of mine who had sold his business and invested the proceeds into the stock market. He was relatively risk-averse, so he had essentially indexed everything. I saw him a month or so later and asked him how he was enjoying his new life. To my surprise, he told me that he hated it. He was having trouble sleeping. Every time he looked at his portfolio, he was either up $50,000 or down $100,000, and the volatility was driving him crazy. His solution was to sell everything and go to cash. He fundamentally understood that nothing had changed about the businesses he held from one day to the next, but it didn't help. I asked him how often he used to look at the financial reports for his old business. He laughed and said, 'Almost never,' as he knew that if sales were going up that would feed through to a stronger bottom line. I told him he should do the same thing with the businesses in his portfolio, that he should look at them only once a year and delete the trading app from his phone.

If ordinarily rational decision-makers and successful businesspeople like my friend can let their emotions get the better of them, what hope does the average person have? Many people describe investing as 'gambling'. Most of the time, they have no idea what they are talking about and use their own money-losing experiences as justification for their point of view. But have you ever met anyone who was even remotely successful at anything without having put in a huge amount of effort? It just doesn't happen. However, a fool and his money are soon parted. In financial markets, the speed of the separation can be truly shocking. The wisest advice for most people who wish to invest in the stock market is to simply buy a broad index of securities through a low-cost provider and never look at it again. If you genuinely want to beat the market, you are going to have to dedicate a lot of time and effort, with no guarantee of success. This is why you need to be an entrepreneur with a burning passion for business. If you are only driven by money, you will never succeed.

As you have read this book, I hope you have been able to find some ideas that resonate with you and are worthy of incorporating into your own evolving investment process. The barriers to entry in terms of finding good investments are as low as they have ever been in history with the amount of data now freely available and easily accessible over the internet. As Buffett reminds us, 'Everyone can read what I read.' The playing field has never been more level.

Investing is the broadest of intellectual pursuits, a field within which all knowledge is cumulative and there is no end, no plateau to reach, just a continuous series of ever-higher peaks to climb. Billionaire fund manager Steve Cohen described his passion for investing as like 'running a race with no finish line.' Markets are an intellectual challenge that can never be won, which is why competitive people continue to want to play. For the intellectually curious, there is nothing more exciting than waking up in the morning with the objective of going to bed that night a little wiser. Real success comes from gradual and incremental improvement applied over time.

Treat each day as a new opportunity to take a step further on your own path to becoming a successful value investor. As the legendary fund manager Paul Tudor Jones told a reporter when asked about his success, 'Anything is possible with persistence and hard work. It can be done, and your own determination to succeed is the most important element.'

Never give up!

APPENDIX A: BIBLIOGRAPHY

ACADEMIC & RESEARCH PAPERS

Arnott, R.D., & Hsu, J.C. and Hsu, J.C., & Moore, P. (2005). Fundamental Indexation. *Financial Analysts Journal*, *61*(2), 83–99. Available at SSRN: https://ssrn.com/abstract=604842 or http://dx.doi.org/10.2139/ssrn.604842

Arnott, R.D., & Jeffrey, R.H. (1993). Is Your Alpha Big Enough To Cover Its Taxes? *The Journal of Portfolio Management*, *19*(3), 15–25.

Bessembinder, H. (2018). Do Stocks Outperform Treasury Bills? *Journal of Financial Economics*, *129*, 440–457.

Bishop, K., Sonnenfield, J., & Ward, A. (1999). Pyrrhic Victories: The Cost to the Board of Ousting the CEO. *Journal of Organisational Behaviour*, *20*, 767–781.

Buffet, W.E. (1984). The Superinvestors of Graham & Doddsville. *Hermes*, Columbia Business School.

Buffet, W.E. (1999). *An Owner's Manual* [White paper]. Berkshire Hathaway Inc.

Callahan, D.J., Majd, D., & Mauboussin, M.J. (2016). *Measuring the Moat: Assessing the Magnitude and Sustainability of Value Creation* [White paper]. Credit Suisse.

Cembalest, M. (2014). *The Agony & The Ecstasy: The risks and rewards of a concentrated stock position* [White paper]. J.P. Morgan Asset Management.

Chew, J. (ed.). *Teledyne and Dr. Henry Singleton, Case Study in Capital Allocation* [White paper]. Credit Suisse. http://csinvesting.org/wp-content/uploads/2015/05/Dr.-Singleton-and-Teledyne-A-Study-of-an-Excellent-Capital-Allocator.pdf

Cooley, P., Hubbard, C., & Walz, D. (1994). *Sustainable withdrawal rates from your retirement portfolio*. Bierwirth. 10.

Gorton, G.B., & Rouwenhorst, K.G. (2005). Facts and Fantasies About Commodity Futures, Yale School of Management.

Gruber, M.J., & Melton, E.J. (1977). Risk Reduction and Portfolio Size: An Analytic Solution. *Journal of Business*, *50*, 415–437.

Harris, R.S., Jenkinson, T., & Kaplan, S.N. (2016). How Do Private Equity Investments Perform Compared to Public Equity? *Journal of Investment Management*, *14*(3), 14–37.

Jordà, Ò., Knoll, K., Kuvshinov, D., Schularick, M., & Taylor, A.M. National Bureau of Economic Research Working Paper Series 24112. Published as: (2019) The Rate of Return on Everything, 1870–2015. *The Quarterly Journal of Economics*, *134*(3), 1225–1298. https://doi.org/10.1093/qje/qjz012

J.P. Morgan. (2017). *Guide to the Markets* [White paper]. J.P. Morgan.

Locke, E.A. (1968). Toward a theory of task motivation and incentives. *Organizational Behaviour and Human Performance*, *3*(2), 157–189. https://doi.org/10.1016/0030-5073(68)90004-4

Lyons, D. (1979, July 9). The Singular Henry Singleton. *Forbes*, 45–50.

Martin, G.S., & Puthenpurackal, J. (2008). Imitation is the Sincerest Form of Flattery: Warren Buffett and Berkshire Hathaway. SSRN Electronic Journal. 10.2139/ssrn.806246.

de Mesquita, B.B., & Smith, A. (2004). The Political Economy of Corporate Fraud: A Theory and Empirical Tests. NYU Working Paper No. CLB-06-001, NYU Stern School of Business. Available at SSRN: https://ssrn.com/abstract=1291024

O'Shaughnessy, P. (2014, November). How Concentrated Should You Make Your Value Portfolio? *The Investor's Field Guide.*

Pabrai, M. (2002, December 12). *The Danger in Buying the Biggest.* The Street.com.

Sleep, N., & Zakarias, Q. (2021). Nomad Investment Partnership Letters to Partners 2001–2014. https://igyfoundation.org.uk/wp-content/uploads/2021/03/Full_Collection_Nomad_Letters_.pdf

Statman, M. (1987). How Many Stocks Make a Diversified Portfolio? *Journal of Financial and Quantitative Analysis*, 22: 353–363, doi:10.2307/2330969

Tweedy, Browne Company LLC. (2009). *What has worked in Investing – Studies of Investment Approaches and Characteristics Associated with exceptional returns* [White paper]. Tweedy, Browne Company LLC.

Tweedy, Browne Fund Inc. (2018). *How Hedging Can Substantially Reduce Foreign Stock Currency Risk* [White paper]. Tweedy, Browne Fund Inc.

Tweedy, Browne Company LLC. (2020). *The Dichotomy Between U.S. and non-U.S. Returns* [White paper]. Tweedy, Browne Company LLC.

SPEECHES

Li L. (2015, October 28). *The Prospects for Value Investing in China* [Speech transcript]. Speech at Peking University Guanghua School of Management. (Translated by Graham F. Rhodes, CFA.)

Li L. (2019, November 29). *The Practice of Value Investing* [Speech transcript]. Speech at Peking University Guanghua School of Management.

ARTICLES

Edelman, R. (2016, January 15). Why so many lottery winners go broke. *Fortune.*

BOOKS

Abell, S. (2018). *How Britain Really Works: Understand the Ideas and Institutions of a Nation.*

Acharya, V.V., Richardson, M., Van Nieuwerburgh, S., & White, L.J. (2011). *Guaranteed To Fail: Fannie Mae, Freddie Mac and the Debacle of Mortgage Finance.*

Adler, M.J., & Van Doren, C. (2014). *How To Read A Book: The Classic Guide To Intelligent Reading.*

Ahuja, M. (2012). *The Alpha Masters: Unlocking the Genius of the World's Top Hedge Funds.*

Aikman, J.S. (2010). *When Prime Brokers Fail: The Unheeded Risk to Hedge Funds, Banks, and the Financial Industry.*

Ammann, D. (2009). *The King of Oil: The Secret Lives of Marc Rich.*

Babin, L., & Willink, J. (2017). *Extreme Ownership: How U.S. Navy Seals Lead and Win.*

Barry, P. (2002). *Rich Kids: How the Murdochs and Packers lost $950 million in One. Tel.*

Baruch, B.M. (1965). *Baruch: My Own Story.*

Batnick, M. (2018). *Big Mistakes, The Best Investors and Their Worst Investments.*

Beard, P. (2007). *Blue Blood & Mutiny: The Fight for the Soul of Morgan Stanley.*

Belfort, J. (2008). *The Wolf Of Wall Street.*

Belton, T.M., Burghardt, G.D., Lane, M., & Papa, J. (1994). *The Treasury Bond Basis: An In-Depth Analysis For Hedgers, Speculators and Arbitrageurs* (Revised Edition).

Benello, A.C., Van Biema, M., & Carlisle, T.E. (2016). *Concentrated Investing: Strategies of the world's greatest concentrated value investors.*

Bernstein, P.L. (1998). *Against The Gods: The Remarkable Story of Risk.*

Bernstein, W.J. (2010). *The Investor's Manifesto: Preparing for Prosperity, Armageddon, and Everything in Between.*

Bhide, A.V. (2000). *The Origin and Evolution of New Businesses.*

Bhimani, A., Horngren, C.T., Datar, S.M., & Foster, G. (2008). *Management And Cost Accounting* (Fourth Edition).

Biggs, B. (2006). *Hedge Hogging.*

Biggs, B. (2008). *Wealth, War & Wisdom.*

Biggs, B. (2011). *A Hedge Fund Tale of Reach and Grasp: Or What's a Heaven for?*

Bishop, M. (2009). *Economics: An A-Z Guide.*

Blanchard, O., Amighini, A., & Giavazzi, F. (2010). *Macroeconomics: A European Perspective.*

Blas, J., & Farchy, J. (2021). *The World For Sale: Money, Power and the Traders who Barter the Earth's Resources.*

Blenko, M.W., Mankins, M.C., & Rogers, P. (2010). *Decide & Deliver: 5 Steps to Breakthrough Performance in Your Organisation.*

Blink, J., & Dorton, I. (2007). *Economics: Course Companion.*

Bloomberg, M.R. (2019). *Bloomberg by Bloomberg.*

Bolton, A. (2009). *Investing Against The Tide: Lessons From a Life Running Money.*

Bouquet, T., & Ousey, B. (2008). *Cold Steel: Lakshmi Mittal and the multi-billion-dollar battle for a global empire.*

Bower, T. (2009). *The Squeeze: Oil, Money & Greed in the 21ˢᵗ Century.*

Bower, T. (2011). *No Angel: The Secret Life of Bernie Ecclestone.*

Bower, T. (2014). *Branson: Behind The Mask.*

Braun, N. (2018). *Company Tax.*

Braun, N. (2019). *Salary Versus Dividends.*

Brealey, R.A., Myers, S.C., & Allen, F. (2008). *Principles of Corporate Finance* (Ninth Edition).

Broad, E. (2012). *The Art of Being Unreasonable: Lessons in Unconventional Thinking.*

Brown, A. (2006). *The Poker Face of Wall Street.*

Brown, J., & Portnoy, B. (2020). *How I Invest My Money: Finance Experts Reveal How They Save, Spend, And Invest.*

Bruck, C. (1989). *The Predator's Ball: The Inside Story of Drexel Burnham and the Rise of the Junk Bond Raiders.*

Bryant, A. (2018). *The Complete Guide to Property Strategies.*

Bullough, O. (2019). *Money Land: Why Thieves & Crooks Now Rule the World & How to Take it Back*.

Burrough, B., & Helyar, J. (2004). *Barbarians At The Gate: The Fall of RJR Nabisco*.

Burton, K. (2007). *Hedge Hunters: Hedge Fund Masters on the Rewards, the Risk, and the Reckoning*.

Carey, D., & Morris, J.E. (2012). *King of Capital: The Remarkable Rise, Fall, and Rise Again of Steve Schwarzman and Blackstone*.

Carlisle, T.E. (2017). *The Acquirer's Multiple: How the Billionaire Contrarians of Deep Value Beat the Market*.

Carnegie, D. (2006). *How to Win Friends and Influence People*.

Carter, S., & Jones-Evans, D. (2006). *Enterprise and Small Business: Principles, Practice and Policy* (Second Edition).

Chan, A.B. (1996). *Li-Ka-Shing: Hong Kong's Elusive Billionaire*.

Chomsky, N. (2016). *Who Rules The World?*

Choudhry, M. (2010). *An Introduction To Bond Markets* (Fourth Edition).

Cialdini, R.B. (2007). *Influence: The Psychology of Persuasion*.

Clark, D. (2016). *Alibaba: The House that Jack Ma Built*.

Clydebank. (2016). *Taxes for Small Businesses*.

Coffey, A. (2019). *The Private Equity Playbook: Management's Guide to Working with Private Equity*.

Cohan, W.D. (2008). *The Last Tycoons: the Secret History of Lazard Freres & Co.*

Cohan, W.D. (2009). *House of Cards: How Wall Street's Gamblers Broke Capitalism*.

Cohan, W.D. (2011). *Money & Power: How Goldman Sachs Came to Rule the World*.

Coll, S. (2012). *Private Empire: ExxonMobil and American Power*.

Collins, J. (2001). *Good to Great: Why Some Companies Make the Leap...and Others Don't*.

Collins, J., & Porras, J. (2005). *Built To Last: Successful Habits of Visionary Companies*.

Collins, J. (2009). *How the mighty fall: and why some companies never give in*.

Collins, J.L. (2016). *The Simple Path to Wealth: Your Road Map to Financial Independence and a Rich, Free Life*.

Connolly, K.B. (2004). *Buying and Selling Volatility*.

Cooper, G. (2008). *The Origin of Financial Crises: Central Banks, Credit Bubbles and the Efficient Market Fallacy*.

Copeland, T.E., Weston, J.K., & Shastri, K. (2005). *Financial Theory and Corporate Policy* (Fourth Edition).

Crabtree, J. (2018). *The Billionaire Raj: A Journey Through India's New Gilded Age*.

Craig, A. (2020). *Live On Less Invest The Rest: A Plain English investment workbook. Sorting your finances out once and for all*.

Cunningham, L.A. (2002). *The Essays of Warren Buffett: Lessons for Investors and Managers*.

Cuthbertson, K., & Nitzche, D. (2001). *Financial Engineering, Derivatives and Risk Management*.

Cutler, A., & McShane, R. (1960). *The Trachtenberg Speed System of Basic Mathematics*.

Dalio, R. (2017). *Principles, Life & Work*.

Damodaran, A. (2011). *The Little Book of Valuation: How to Value a Company, Pick a Stock, and Profit.*

Darnell, A. (2010). *Quantitative Methods For Finance* (Third Edition).

Das, S. (2006). *Traders, Guns & Money: Knowns and Unknowns in the Dazzling World of Derivatives.*

Das, S. (2011). *Extreme Money: The Masters of the Universe and the Cult of Risk.*

Davidson, B., & Davidson, M. (2018). *To Trust or Not to Trust – Love's Labour's Lost. A Sad Family Story.*

Day, A.L. (2005). *Mastering Financial Mathematics: A Practical Guide for Business Calculations.*

Deibel, W. (2018). *Buy Then Build: How Acquisition Entrepreneurs Outsmart the Start-up Game.*

Dennis, F. (2007). *How To Get Rich: The Distilled Wisdom of one of Britain's Wealthiest Self-Made Entrepreneurs.*

Diamond, J. (2017). *Guns, Germs & Steel: A short history of everybody for the last 13,000 years.*

Dix, R. (2019). *The Complete Guide to Property Investment: How to Survive & Thrive in the New World of Buy-to-Let.*

Drever, M., Stanton, P., & McGowan, S. (2007). *Contemporary Issues In Accounting.*

Drobny, S. (2006). *Inside The House Of Money: Top Hedge Fund Traders on Profiting in the Global Markets.*

Drobny, S. (2011). *The invisible Hands: Top Hedge Fund Traders on Bubbles, Crashes, and Real Money.*

The Economist. (2009). *Investment: An A-Z Guide.*

Eichengreen, B. (2011). *Exorbitant Privilege: The Rise and Fall of the Dollar.*

Einhorn, D. (2007). *Fooling Some Of The People All Of The Time: A Long Short Story.*

Elliott, B., & Elliott, J. (2011). *Financial Accounting and Reporting* (Fourteenth Edition).

Ellis, C.D. (2009). *The Partnership: The Making of Goldman Sachs.*

Endlich, L. (1999). *Goldman Sachs: The Culture of Success.*

Fabozzi, F.J. (2012). *The Handbook of Fixed Income Securities* (Eighth Edition).

Fallon, I. (1991). *Billionaire: The Life and Times of Sir James Goldsmith.*

Ferguson, N. (2008). *The Ascent of Money: A Financial History of the World.*

Ferguson, N. (2011). *Civilization: The West and the Rest.*

Ferguson, N. (2012). *The Great Degeneration: How Institutions Decay and Economies Die.*

Fisher, P.A. (1975). *Conservative Investors Sleep Well.*

Fisher, P.A. (2003). *Common Stocks and Uncommon Profits.*

Fisher, R., & Ury, W. (2012). *Getting to Yes: Negotiating an Agreement Without Giving In.*

Frank, R. (2007). *Richistan: A journey through the 21st Century Wealth Boom and the Lives of the New Rich.*

Frank, R. (2011). *The High-Beta Rich, How the Manic Wealthy Will Take Us to the Next Boom, Bubble and Bust.*

Frank, T. (2012). *Pity The Billionaire: The Hard-Times Swindle and the Unlikely Comeback of the Right.*

Freedman, S. (2009). *Binge Trading.*

Freeland, C. (2012). *Plutocrats.*

Freeman-Shor, L. (2015). *The Art of Execution: How the world's best investors get it wrong and still make millions.*

Fukuyama, F. (1992). *The End Of History And The Last Man.*

Galbraith, J.K. (1992). *The Great Crash 1929.*

Galloway, S. (2017). *The Four, The Hidden DNA of Amazon, Apple, Facebook and Google.*

George, R. (2013). *Ninety Percent of Everything: Inside Shipping, The Invisible Industry that puts Clothes on Your Back, Gas in Your Car, And Food on Your Plate.*

de Geus, A. (2002). *The Living Company: Habits for Survival in a Turbulent Business Environment.*

Giridharadas, A. (2018). *Winners Take All: The Elite Charade of Changing the World.*

Gladwell, M. (2000). *The Tipping Point: How little things can make a big difference.*

Gladwell, M. (2008). *Outliers: The Story of Success.*

Gladwell, M. (2009). *What the Dog Saw, and other adventures.*

Gladwell, M. (2013). *David & Goliath: Underdogs, Misfits and the Art of Battling Giants.*

Glanville, A. (2003). *Economics from a global perspective* (Second Edition).

Goodhart, C., & Pradhan, M. (2020). *The Great Demographic Reversal: Ageing Societies, Waning Inequality, and an Inflation Revival.*

Gow, I.D., & Kells, S. (2018). *The Big Four: The Curious Past and Perilous Future of the Global Accounting Monopoly.*

Graham, B. (2006). *The Intelligent Investor: The Definitive Book on Value Investing.*

Graham, B., & Dodd, D.L. (2009). *Security Analysis* (Sixth Edition).

Gramm, J. (2016). *Dear Chairman: Boardroom Battles and the Rise of Shareholder Activism.*

Green, W. (2021). *Richer, Wiser, Happier: How the World's Greatest Investors Win in Markets and Life.*

Greenblatt, J. (1997). *You Can be A Stock Market Genius: Uncover the Secret Hiding Places of Stock Market Profits.*

Greenblatt, J. (2010). *The Little Book That Still Beats the Market.*

Greenblatt, J. (2011). *The Big Secret for the Small Investor: A New Route to Long-Term Investment Success.*

Griffin, T. (2015). *Charlie Munger The Complete Investor.*

Gross, D. (1996). *Forbes Greatest Business Stories Of All Time: 20 inspiring tales of entrepreneurs who changed the way we live and do business.*

Gross, M. (2014). *House of Outrageous Fortune.*

Grylls, B. (2012). *A Survival Guide For Life: How to achieve your goals, thrive in adversity and grow in character.*

Hadnum, L. (2010). *Selling Your Business: A UK Tax Planning Guide.*

Hagstrom, R.G. (1999). *The Warren Buffett Portfolio: Mastering the Power of the Focus Investment Strategy.*

Hagstrom, R.G. (2000). *Latticework: The New Investing.*

Hagstrom, R.G. (2014). *The Warren Buffett Way* (Third Edition).

Hannam, J. (2017). *What Everyone Needs to know About Tax.*

Harding, T. (2019). *Legacy: One Family, a Cup of Tea and the Company that Took on the World.*

Hawkins, D.R. (2012). *Power Vs. Force: The Hidden Determinants of Human Behaviour.*

Heath, U. & Ratcliffe, J. (2018). *The Alchemists: The INEOS Story, An Industrial Giant Comes of Age.*

Heilbroner, R. (2000). *The Worldly Philosophers: The Lives, Times and Ideas of the Great Economic Thinkers.*

Helmer, H. (2016). *7 Powers: The Foundations of Business Strategy.*

Herman, A. (2001). *How The Scots Invented the Modern World: The True Story of How Western Europe's Poorest Nation Created Our World & Everything in It.*

Hill, N. (2009). *Think and Grow Rich.*

Hollingsworth, M., & Lansley, S. (2010). *Londongrad: From Russia With Cash.*

Hope, B., & Wright, T. (2018) *Billion Dollar Whale: The Inside Story of Jho Low and the 1MDB Scandal.*

Hull, J.C. (2012). *Options, Futures, And Other Derivatives* (Eighth Edition).

Iger, R. (2019). *The Ride of a Lifetime: Lessons in Creative Leadership.*

Isaacson, W. (2011). *Steve Jobs.*

Iverson, K. (1998). *Plain Talk: Lessons from a business maverick.*

Jay, J. (2019). *Business Buying Strategies: The Solution to Your Business Growth Problem.*

Kahneman, D. (2011). *Thinking, fast and slow.*

Kampfner, J. (2014). *The Rich: From Slaves to Super Yachts: a 2000-Year History.*

Kelly, J. (2012). *The New Tycoons, Inside the Trillion Dollar Private Equity Industry That Owns Everything.*

Kelly, K. (2014). *The Secret Club That Runs The World: Inside the Fraternity of Commodity Traders.*

Keown, A.J., Martin, J.D., Petty, J.W., & Scott, D.F. (2008). *Foundations of Finance: The Logic and Practice of Financial Management* (Sixth Edition).

Klare, M. (2005). *Blood And Oil.*

Klarman, S.A. (1991). *Margin of Safety: Risk-Averse Value Investing Strategies or the Thoughtful Investor.*

Knight, P. (2016). *Shoe Dog.*

Koch, C.G. (2015). *Good Profit: How Creating Value for Others Built One of the World's Most Successful Companies.*

Koo, R.C. (2018). *The Other Half of Macroeconomics and the Fate of Globalization.*

Kotter, J.P. (1997). *Matsushita Leadership: Lessons From the 20th Century's Most Remarkable Entrepreneur.*

Kroijer, L. (2010). *Money Mavericks: Confessions of a Hedge Fund Manager.*

Kuok, R. (2017). *Robert Kuok: A Memoir, with Andrew Tanzer.*

Lack, S. (2012). *The Hedge Fund Mirage.*

Lauder, L. (2020). *The Company I Keep: My Life in Beauty.*

Lefevre, E. (2005). *Reminiscences of a Stock Operator.*

Leonard, C. (2019). *Kochland, The Secret history of Koch Industries and Corporate Power in America.*

Levinson, M. (2016). *The Box: How the Shipping Container Made the World Smaller and the World Economy Bigger* (Second Edition).

Lewis, M. (1989). *Liar's Poker: The Book that Revealed the Truth about London and Wall Street.*

Lewis, M. (2007). *The Real Price of Everything: Rediscovering The Six Classics of Economics.*

Lewis, M. (2010). *The Big Short: Inside The Doomsday Machine.*

Lewis, M. (2011). *Boomerang: The Meltdown Tour.*

Lewis, M. (2011). *The Money Culture.*

Lewis, M. (2017). *The Undoing Project: A Friendship that Changed the World.*

Lewis, M. (2018). *The Fifth Risk: Undoing Democracy.*

Liaw, K.T. (2006). *The Business of Investment Banking.*

Livermore, J. (2001). *How To Trade in Stocks.*

Lowe, J. (2000). *Damn Right! Behind the Scenes with Berkshire Hathaway Billionaire Charlie Munger.*

Lowe, J. (2002). *The Man Who Beats the S&P: Investing With Bill Miller.*

Lowenstein, R. (1995). *Buffett: The Making of an American Capitalist.*

Lowenstein, R. (2002). *When Genius Failed: The Rise and Fall of Long-Term Capital Management.*

Lowenstein, R. (2010). *The End Of Wall Street.*

Lukeman, J. (2000). *The Market Maker's Edge.*

Lynch, P. (2000). *One Up on Wall Street: How to Use What You Already Know to Make Money in the Market.*

Mackay, C. (2006). *Extraordinary Popular Delusions and the Madness of Crowds.*

Magnus, G. (2011). *Uprising: Will Emerging Markets Shape or Shake the World Economy?*

Mahar, M. (2004). *Bull! A History of the Boom and Bust, 1982–2004: What 21st Century Investors Need to Know About Financial Cycles.*

Malkiel, B.G. (2007). *A Random Walk Down Wall Street: The Time-Tested Strategy for Successful Investing.*

Mallaby, S. (2010). *More Money Than God: Hedge Funds and the Making of a New Elite.*

Malmsten, E., Portanger, E., & Drazin, C. (2001). *Boo Hoo: A dot.com story from concept to catastrophe.*

Marcovici, P. (2016). *The Destructive Power of Family Wealth: A Guide to Succession Planning, Asset Protection, Taxation and Wealth Management.*

Marks, H. (2011). *The Most Important Thing: Uncommon Sense for the Thoughtful Investor.*

Marks, H. (2018). *Mastering The Market Cycle: Getting the Odds on Your Side.*

Marshall, P. (2020). *10 ½ Lessons From Experience: Perspectives on Fund Management.*

Mayer, C. (2015). *100 Baggers: Stocks That Return 100-To-1 and How to Find Them.*

McCleery, M, (2011). *The Shipping Man.*

McCullough, T., & Whitaker, K. (2018). *Wealth of Wisdom: The Top 50 Questions Wealthy Families Ask.*

McDonald, L. (2009). *A Colossal Failure Of Common Sense: The Incredible Inside Story of the Collapse of Lehman Brothers.*

McGee, S. (2010). *Chasing Goldman Sachs: How The Masters of the Universe Melted Wall Street Down...And why they'll Take us to the Brink Again.*

MacGregor, N. (2012). *A History Of The World In 100 Objects.*

McLean, B., & Elkind, P. (2004). *The Smartest Guys In The Room: The Amazing Rise and Scandalous Fall of Enron.*

McWilliams, D. (2005). *The Pope's Children: Ireland's New Elite.*

Mehta, N., Murphy, L., & Steinman, D. (2016). *Customer Success, How Innovative Companies are Reducing Churn and Growing Recurring Revenue.*

De Mesquita, B.B., & Smith, A. (2011). *The Dictator's Handbook, Why Bad Behaviour is Almost Always Good Politics.*

Michael, A. (2011). *Auditing & Assurance Services.*

Mihaljevic, J. (2013). *The Manual of Ideas: The Proven Framework for Finding the Best Value Investments.*

Morris, C.R. (2005). *The Tycoons: How Andrew Carnegie, John D. Rockefeller, Jay Gould, and J.P. Morgan Invented the American Supereconomy.*

Morris, I. (2010). *Why the West Rules – for Now: The patterns of history and what they reveal about the future.*

Munger, C.T. (2008). *Poor Charlie's Almanack: The Wit and Wisdom of Charles T. Munger* (Expanded Third Edition).

Natenberg, S. (1994). *Option Volatility & Pricing.*

O'Clery, C. (2007). *The Billionaire Who Wasn't: How Chuck Feeney Secretly Made and Gave Away a Fortune.*

Osorno, D. (2019). *Carlos Slim: The Power, Money and Morality of one of the World's Richest Men.*

Pabrai, M. (2004). *Mosaic: Perspectives on Investing.*

Pabrai, M. (2007). *The Dhandho Investor: The Low-Risk Value Method of High Returns.*

Parkin, M., Powell, M., & Matthews, K. (2008). *Economics* (Seventh Edition).

Parnham, S. (2017). *The Absolute Essence of Inheritance Tax Planning.*

Partnoy, F. (1997). *F.I.A.S.C.O.: Blood in the Water on Wall Street.*

Paulson Jr, H.M. (2010). *On The Brink: Inside the Race to Stop the Collapse of the Global Financial System.*

Paulson Jr, H.M. (2015). *Dealing With China: An Insider Unmasks the New Economic Superpower.*

Peretti, J. (2017). *Done: The Secret Deals that are Changing our World.*

Perkins, B. (2020). *Die With Zero: Getting All You Can from Your Money and Your Life.*

Peterson, J.B. (2018). *12 Rules for Life: An Antidote for Chaos.*

Phelps, T.W. (2014). *100 to 1 In the Stock Market.*

Phillips, T. (2009). *Extraordinary Popular Delusions And The Madness Of Crowds: A Modern-Day Interpretation of a Finance Classic.*

Pickens, T.B. (2008). *The First Billion Is The Hardest.*

Piketty, T. (2014). *Capital in the Twenty-First Century.*

Ponte, S. (2019). *Business Power & Sustainability In a World of Global Value Chains.*

Poundstone, W. (2012). *Are you smart enough to work at Google?*

Rizk, R. (2009). *Management Accounting And Financial Planning And Control: Cases And Readings*.

Rogers, J. (2010). *Hot Commodities: How Anyone Can Invest Profitably in the World's Best market*.

Roubini, N., & Mihm, S. (2010). *Crisis Economics: A Crash Course in the Future of Finance*.

Rumelt, R. (2011). *Good Strategy Bad Strategy: The Difference and Why It Matters*.

Sandel, M.J. (2013). *What Money Can't Buy: The Moral Limits of Markets*.

Schilit, H.M., Perler, J., & Engelhart, Y. (2018). *Financial Shenanigans: How to Detect Accounting Gimmicks and Fraud in Financial Reports* (Fourth Edition).

Schmidt, E., & Rosenberg, J. (2014). *How Google Works*.

Schroeder, A. (2009). *The Snowball: Warren Buffett and the Business of Life*.

Schulman, D. (2014). *Sons of Wichita: How the Koch Brothers Became America's Most Powerful and Private Family*.

Schwager, J.D. (1989). *Market Wizards: Interviews With Top Traders*.

Schwager, J.D. (2001). *Stock Market Wizards: Interviews with America's Top Stock Traders*.

Schwager, J.D. (2005). *The New Market Wizards: Conversations with America's Top Traders*.

Schwager, J.D. (2012). *Hedge Fund Market Wizards: How Winning Traders Win*.

Schwager, J.D. (2020). *Unknown Market Wizards: The best traders you've never heard of*.

Schwarzman, S.A. (2019) *What It Takes: Lessons in the Pursuit of Excellence*.

Shah, O. (2018). *Damaged Goods: The Inside Story of Sir Philip Green, the Collapse of BHS and the Death of the High Street*.

Shaxson, N. (2011). *Treasure Islands, Tax Havens and the Men that Stole the World*.

Shnayerson, M. (2019). *Boom: Mad Money, Mega Dealers, and the Rise of Contemporary Art*.

Sieren, F. (2007). *The China Code: What's Left For Us?*

Skidelsky, R., & Skidelsky, E. (2013). *How Much is Enough: Money and the Good Life*.

Slater, R. (2009). *Soros: The World's Most Influential Investor*.

Smith, A. (2008). *An Inquiry Into The Nature And Causes Of The Wealth of Nations*:

Smith, M. (2018). *Efficient Estate Planning*.

Smith, T. (2020). *Investing for Growth: How to Make Money by Only Buying the Best Companies*.

Sorkin, A.R. (2010). *Too Big To Fail: Inside The Battle to Save Wall Street*.

Soros, G. (2003). *The Alchemy of Finance*.

Soros, G. (2008). *The Credit Crisis of 2008 and What It Means*.

Spier, G. (2014). *The Education Of A Value Investor: My Transformative Quest for Wealth, Wisdom and Enlightenment*.

Staiger, R. (2018). *Foundation of Real Estate Financial Modelling* (Second Edition).

Steinhardt, M. (2001). *No Bull: My Life In and Out of Markets*.

Stelzer, I. (2018). *The Murdoch Method: Notes on Running a Media Empire*.

Stilgoe, J.R. (1998). *Outside Lies Magic*.

Stoakes, C. (2009). *All you need to know about the City*.

Sun Tzu (2006). *The Art of War*.

Surowiecki, J. (2004). *The Wisdom of Crowds: Why the Many Are Smarter Than the Few*.

Sutherland, R. (2019). *Alchemy: The Surprising Power of Ideas That Don't Make Sense.*

Swensen, D.F. (2005). *Unconventional Success: A Fundamental Approach to Personal Investment.*

Swensen, D.F. (2009). *Pioneering Portfolio Management: An Unconventional Approach to Institutional Investment.*

Talbott, J.R. (2009). *The 86 Biggest Lies on Wall Street.*

Taleb, N.N. (2004). *Fooled by Randomness: The Hidden Role of Chance in Life and in the Markets.*

Taleb, N.N.(2007). *The Black Swan: The Impact of the Highly Improbable.*

Tetlock, P.E. (2017). *Expert Political Judgement: How good is it? How can we know?*

Tett, G. (2010). *Fool's Gold.*

Thaler, R.H., & Sunstein, C.R. (2009). *Nudge: Improving decisions about health, wealth and happiness.*

Vermeulen, F. (2017). *Breaking Bad Habits, Defy Industry Norms and Reinvigorate Your Business.*

Volcker, P.A. (2018). *Keeping At It: The Quest for Sound Money and Good Government.*

Wald, E.R. (2018). *Saudi, Inc. The Arabian Kingdom's Pursuit of Profit and Power.*

Wallace, B. (2009). *The Billionaire's Vinegar.*

Watson, P. (2006). *Ideas: A History From Fire To Freud.*

Walton, S. (1992). *Made In America: My Story.*

Weetman, P. (2006). *Financial and Management Accounting* (Fourth Edition).

Weiner, E.J. (2011). *The Shadow Market: How Sovereign Wealth Funds Secretly Dominate the Global Economy.*

Weiss, S.L. (2010). *The Billion Dollar Mistake: Learning the Art of Investing Through the Missteps of Legendary investors.*

Weiss, S.L. (2012). *The Big Win: Learning from the Legends to Become a More Successful Investor.*

West, D.M. (2014). *Billionaires.*

Westall, O.M. (1992). *The Provincial Insurance Company 1903–38: Family, markets and competitive growth.*

Whitehead, J.C. (2005). *A Life in Leadership: From D-Day to Ground Zero.*

Whitfield, I. (2008). *Financial Markets and Risk Management* (Second Edition).

Williams, J.B. (1965). *The Theory of Investment Value.*

Wolfe, T. (2010). *The Bonfire of the Vanities.*

Wolff, M. (2008). *The Man Who Owns The News: Inside the Secret World of Rupert Murdoch.*

Zeckendorf, W. (2014). *Zeckendorf: The autobiography of the man who played a real-life game of Monopoly and won the largest real estate empire in history.*

Zell, S. (2017). *Am I Being Too Subtle? Straight Talk From a Business Rebel.*

Zuckerman, G. (2010). *The Greatest Trade Ever: How One Man Bet Against The Markets and Made $20 Billion.*

Zuckerman, G. (2019). *The Man Who Solved The Markets: How Jim Simons Launched the Quant Revolution.*

APPENDIX B: DIFFERENT ASSET CLASSES

When it comes to investing, there are several different asset classes:

- **Cash**: Cash provides the daily liquidity needed to invest. However, all the academic research and historical results show that holding too much cash is a very poor asset allocation decision. Cash is also the most vulnerable of all asset classes to the ravages of inflation over time.
- **Fixed income**: The term 'fixed income' has come to encompass all assets that pay a rate of return to the investor (lender/depositor) by the borrower.
- **Money market funds/Certificates of deposit (CD)/Fixed deposits (FD)**: Until the right opportunity for a particular amount of surplus capital is identified, short-term fixed income securities can be an excellent place for temporarily parking funds, particularly during times when interest rates are high.
- **Government bonds**: Government bonds are usually issued by the treasury or debt management office of a country to fund the difference between what the government raises in taxation and its expenditure.
- **Corporate bonds**: Bonds issued by businesses. They typically offer a higher yield than a comparable-maturity government bond, reflecting the fact that they have more credit risk than the government.
- **Foreign bonds**: A foreign bond, also known as an international bond or sovereign bond, is a debt security issued by a foreign entity, typically a foreign government or corporation, in a currency different from the one in which it is sold. These bonds allow governments and corporations to raise capital from investors outside their own countries.
- **Asset-backed securities (ABS)/Collateralised debt obligations (CDO)/Structured products**: The only thing you need to know about these products as an individual investor is that you absolutely do not need to know what they are or how to buy them. In general, they are highly priced, highly illiquid and poor-returning assets. Even those who make them don't truly understand the risks involved.

- **Long-term bonds**: Investing in long-term bonds, ten years and above, is mainly the domain of tax-exempt charities or institutional investors such as pension funds performing asset/liability matching.
- **Short-term bonds**: Short-term bonds essentially provide a 'cash management service' whereby an investor can park their available funds while searching for an opportunity to deploy them.
- **Equities**: Also known as stocks or shares, equities represent ownership in a company. When you buy shares of a company's stock, you become a part-owner of that company.
- **Commodities**: Commodities are raw materials or primary agricultural products that are traded on various exchanges worldwide. They are generally uniform in quality and are produced by many different suppliers. Examples of commodities include crude oil, natural gas, gold, silver, copper, wheat, corn, soybeans, coffee and sugar.
- **Derivatives**: For the individual investor, derivatives, or, as Buffett called them, 'financial weapons of mass destruction', serve no investment purpose. Derivatives 'derive' their value from an underlying asset or security; they effectively represent a wager on its price rising or declining.

INDEX